WIDOWS Volume 1

WIDOWS

VOLUME 1

The Middle East, Asia, and the Pacific

Helena Znaniecka Lopata, editor

Duke University Press   Durham 1987

© 1987 Duke University Press
All rights reserved
Printed in the United States of America
on acid-free paper ∞
Library of Congress Cataloging-in-Publication Data
Widows.
Bibliography: p. v. 1, p.
Includes index.
Contents: v. 1. The Middle East, Asia, and the
Pacific.
1. Widows.   2. Widows—Near East.   3. Widows—Asia.
I. Lopata, Helena Znaniecka, 1925–
HQ1058.W53   1987   306.8′8   87-5410
ISBN 0-8223-0680-8 (v. 1)
ISBN 0-8223-0768-5 (pbk. : v. 1)

Dedicated to all the women
in all the countries
who helped us learn of the
many paths of widowhood.

Contents

List of Tables

Preface

This book has a long and pleasant history. The theoretical background of support systems evolved in multiple conferences held in Warsaw, Dubrovnik, Washington, D.C., and Chicago. The Social Security Administration had funded me for a large study of widows in Chicago, and research teams in Poland and Yugoslavia were going to obtain counterpart funds (U.S. Public Law 480) to carry forth the same study in their countries. The original framework for these studies focused on changes in social roles following the death of the husband. As we kept meeting, it became apparent that this was too complex a model for comparative analysis. In cooperation with Dr. Adam Kurzynowski and Professor Jerzy Piotrowski of Poland, Dr. Nada Smilic Krkovic and her staff at the Institute of Social Work in Zagreb, Dr. Henry Brehm of the United States Social Security Administration, who was our project officer, and members of the Center for the Comparative Study of Social Roles at Loyola University in Chicago, we finally worked out a theoretical framework we all could use—that of support systems. We evolved four sets of support systems—economic, service, social, and emotional—with a total of sixty-five separate supports that could be used, with some modification, in all three countries.

Unfortunately the Polish and Yugoslav governments did not allow the studies to be conducted in those countries. Fortunately, however, I had been attending international gerontological and sociological congresses in Jerusalem, Tokyo, and Mexico City, and spoke with social scientists who might be interested in making this study a comparative one. Jackie Touba decided to conduct research in Iran, where she was teaching at that time (before and in the early stages of the political revolution). Dr. Brehm became acquainted with Dr. Newal Nadim, who was getting her Ph.D. in anthropology at Indiana University and then returning to Cairo. That study has not been completed in time for this volume, but we expect to see it soon. Dr. Jasoon Koo was obtaining her Ph.D. at the University of Missouri and her adviser, Professor Donald Cowgill, recommended that she get in touch with me. She has replicated the support systems study in Seoul, where she has returned and is presently teaching.

In the meantime, I placed a short announcement in *Gerontological News*, asking for chapters on the support systems of widows in different countries and locations in the United States. Professor Marsel Heisel, who was brought up in Turkey and has returned for visits, volunteered to study the situation of widows in rural small towns and in cities of that country. Ruth Katz responded from Israel, and her contribution is included in this volume. Evangelina Blust studied widows in the Philippines and also responded to my announcement, as did Denise Barnes, who has knowledge of China, and Robert L. Rubinstein, who had studied widowhood in Malo, Vanuatu (formerly the New Hebrides).

The second volume also grew out of that same announcement. When I heard of the situation of widows in different parts of the United States and Canada, it became apparent that the assumption that these are "developed countries," in which all members function in an ideal bureaucratic and rational manner to fulfill their self-defined needs, simply neglects a major segment of the population. The relation between informal and formal support networks in these countries is equally as interesting as that of support networks in developing countries. Thus, the number of North American chapters increased sufficiently to warrant a separate volume. Jessyna McDonald, Anne Neale and the team of Anabel Pelman and William Clark responded immediately.

A number of contributors, writing for both volumes, met over lunch at the meetings of the Gerontological Society of America in San Antonio to discuss our work. Linda Rosenman and Arthur Shulman have conducted studies of widows in Melbourne and in St. Louis and joined our venture. I have known Anne Martin Matthews for years and am very pleased that she could contribute a chapter on Canada. She will be replicating parts of a support-systems study in Guelph, but the funding came too late for this book, so her chapter is based on other sources. Jaya Sarma Gujral, who is from India and is obtaining her Ph.D. at the University of Chicago, originally came to see me on another matter but came away convinced to write a chapter about widows in her country. Several of us participated in a round-table discussion on widowhood in the world during the International Congress of Gerontology held in the summer of 1985 in New York. I spent some time in India in the fall of 1986 to see what else I might learn about the situation of widows there.

Each of us has been helped in this project by many people. I would like to acknowledge those who, in addition to the people mentioned above, were of special assistance to me. This includes Hank Brehm, who has been invaluable to both this study and a later one on the changing commitments of American urban women, which is summarized in *City Women: Work, Jobs, Occupations, Career* by H. Z. Lopata, D. Barnewolt, and C. A. Miller (New York: Praeger; vol. 1, 1984; vol. 2, 1985). Sister Gertrud Kim and Frank Steinhart were of great assistance in analyzing the support systems data. Throughout, members of the Center for the Comparative Study of Social Roles and former members of the Midwest Council for Social Research on Aging have offered encouragement and the opportunity to test some of the ideas presented in these chapters.

My colleagues at Loyola University of Chicago have also been of great encouragement. Of special help this time were Judith Wittner and David Fasenfest. Thanks also go to Richard Lopata, as usual.

1 Widowhood: World Perspectives on Support Systems

HELENA ZNANIECKA LOPATA

Changes in world societies during the past century or so have dramatically modified the support systems and life-styles of people in various circumstances at all stages of the life course. These changes have not been experienced evenly the world over; they are influenced by the extent and direction of social development of each society as well as by the extent and direction of social development of the community in which a person lives. Personal resources also help shape change. This chapter, as well as the others in both volumes of *Widows*, examines the resources and support systems of widows living in different social structures. The basic theme of support systems was first developed in my study of widowhood in metropolitan Chicago (Lopata, 1979). This theme has been used by the other authors in their research and/or in organizing their data.

Resources for Support Systems

Each human builds a support network of people organized in many different ways out of the resources available, with more or less personal initiative. Some segments of the network are inevitably involving, as when relationships with the husband's kin follow marriage. In other social situations the initiative is entirely the person's own, as in the creation of an entrepreneurial venture. The larger and more complex the society, and that part of it in which the person is located, the greater are the resources available if the person knows of them and has freedom of choice. Thus, there are three major sets of factors affecting the networks that supply different supports: society at large, the community, and the person's own resources. Let us examine all three.

The Society

Globally, societies vary considerably in their cultures and social structure. Cultures provide the basic ways of thinking, doing, and having for people who have been socialized into them. For example, culture provides the rituals of mourning and the prescribed ways of behaving as a widow. Of course, most societies have more than one culture, or subcultures, as evidenced by India, with its regional, class and caste, rural and urban, as well as religious variations. The life of a widow thus varies considerably by her position in the system. An upper-caste Hindu widow leads a very different life from that of a poor tribal widow.

The social structure of a society refers to the way in which people are organized, in their whole life or in segments of life such as occupation. Small, relatively homogeneous societies of the past and in some isolated areas of the present are usually organized into families. The composition of families varies considerably, depending on what is considered the basic unit. Some families are organized along male, or, much less frequently, female lines of descent. They can also be traced bilaterally, with various implications for the interrelationships. The basic family unit can be nuclear, with the husband-wife and children unit drawing primary loyalty and providing the greatest amount of support to its members. In addition to family and kin units, people obtain informal supports from those with whom they interact frequently—in the neighborhood, clubs and organizations, the work place, and in religious or recreational activities.

Although each society is highly dependent upon the informal support network of its members, the larger and more complex the society is the more it needs to evolve more formalized, bureaucratized social structures to meet its everyday, occasional, or emergency needs (Weber, 1958; 1956/1964). These organizations, many of which grow into enormous systems, supply the productive supports, formalize religious observances, insure recreational events, educate the young and the not so young in specialized aspects of the culture, make laws and insure that they are followed or punish the offenders, provide channels of communication, attempt to solve personal and group problems, and relate the society to other societies of the world.

The Community

Although the society may have a complex system that interweaves informal and formal support systems for all members, or for special categories of members, these are not necessarily available in all communities. In general, the smaller the community and the more isolated it is from the larger society, the more dependent its members are upon the informal system. This is certainly true of the widows in Malo, Vanuatu (formerly called the New Hebrides) studied by Rubinstein. However, the presence of formal resources does not guarantee their use by any single member. This depends upon personal resources.

Personal Resources

Formal resources for support systems may be avoided even when available if a person considers herself fully provided for by informal support systems or if there is a cultural stigma associated with their use, as is true of the Asian poor in California (see chapter 10 volume 2). The basic variable found among Chicago-area widows that influences the complexity of their support network and the utilization of a variety of resources—when controlled for health and adequate finances—is education (Lopata, 1973; 1979). We find references to education in other chapters of this book and in the literature on women in general, but with special references to developing nations. The modernized or more-developed segment of the world is dependent upon an educated population that is able to function in a bureaucratic, mobile, and mass-communication influenced culture. Work organized according to jobs requires literacy and often a great deal of specialized, ideationally transmitted knowledge. So does every other aspect of life. People who have not learned to solve new problems in the abstract, do not know how to prepare for new roles, or enter into new relationships are very restricted in their social life space in this type of society. A major finding of an earlier study of metropolitan Chicago widows was that the more education the woman had, and the more middle-class lifestyle she and her husband built when he was alive, the more disorganized her life and self-concept became when he died (Lopata, 1973). This is so because of the tremendous interdependence between husband and wife (if they stay together) in this segment of society. On the other hand, the more education the widow has, the more personal resources she has to draw upon in rebuilding her life and creating new support systems. Of course, middle-class life also offers more economic and health resources even in widowhood. However, it is the personality of the woman herself that influences the degree of initiative she shows in seeking new social roles and relations once the period of heavy grieving is over. America is an individualistic and voluntaristic society in which social engagement, after the early years of usually ascribed social involvement, requires the self-confidence and ability to utilize resources that do not come knocking on the door.

Support Systems

A support is any object or action that the giver and/or the receiver define as necessary or helpful in maintaining a style of life (Lopata, 1979). A support system is a set of similar supports, and a support network consists of all those persons and groups who provide these supports. Extensive discussions with other social scientists in Poland, Yugoslavia, Egypt, Iran, and the United States during the initial stages of planning the support systems studies developed a set of four support systems that are generally defined as necessary or helpful to widows. Naturally, national variations had to be delineated since some supports seemingly "natural" in Chicago were meaningless in other cultures. For example, several of the emotional supports suffered in translation and substitutions had to be identified.

Economic Support System

The first and basic support system is economic. Although widows are often able to obtain economic support through their own paid work, this is usually not the one and only resource. People can barter, exchange objects such as money or food, or perform services that result in economic supports. Thus, we asked if the widow receives or gives money in the form of gifts, payment, or partial payment for food, clothing, health, vacation-related expenses, or other bills. We then established the resources from which she obtains such supports or for whom she acts as a resource. We also asked about other sources of income.

Economic supports can come from intergenerational transfers of property, such as inheritance, from earnings, or from benefits obtained from past earnings, people responsible for such supports, or societal programs. Traditionally, family units supported all members throughout the life course, although there is anthropological evidence that some groups of people deserted or in other ways disposed of members who became economically unproductive (Fry, 1984). In many of the societies discussed in this volume, it is the son who is responsible for the economic support of elderly parents and widows.

In cases in which people were unable to support themselves economically and who also lacked families and whose communities were so large that no one felt responsible for their support, organized aid came from churches, as in the past in England and the United States (Lopata and Brehm, 1986). Other groups, such as voluntary associations, sometimes took on this task but were soon supplanted by governmental programs.

Widows can have jobs, pensions, or other benefits of having worked for pay in the past. They can also receive benefits from the work of their late husbands, directly from the employer, or from monies invested in insurance policies. Some societies provide economic support in the form of social security, to which the employer and employee contributed over time and which can include dependents. However, these benefits are often restricted to certain categories of workers, such as government employees, cause of death of the husband, such as the Israeli war widows, or to characteristics of the widow. Lopata and Brehm (1986) examined in detail the American social security system and found many problems, such as the absence of supports if a widow did not have entitled children yet was not old enough to receive old-age benefits. Finally, some societies, realizing that family, church, or community resources for the economic supports of people such as widows are no longer available, have instituted welfare programs. Some communities or larger social units, such as the state of California (see volume 2), have multiple programs aimed at preventing poverty among its members.

The widow may contribute to the economic supports of others through work, the provision of goods she buys, or the giving of monies. A widow with small children must be able to support them. If she is unable to do so, a larger group, such as the deceased husband's family, the community, or the state may take them away from her. In strong patriarchal families, the economic support of the children may be guaranteed by the male line, but each member is expected to contribute work and behavioral cooperation in return. A widow may work hard to maintain her children, expecting that they will provide her in turn with economic support when she is no longer able to maintain herself.

Service Support System

The type of services regarded as necessary or helpful in maintaining a desired life-style varies considerably according to the culture and social structure of the society and community. If a woman is not expected to leave her territory under any conditions except marriage, she will have no need for help with transportation. In trying to contain the number of service supports about which we asked, we started with a list applicable to the widows in metropolitan Chicago, modifying it for other locations when necessary. Thus, the supports upon which we focused included the inflow and outflow of help with transportation, house repairs, housekeeping, shopping, yard work, child care, car care, care during illness, decisions, and legal aid. Several of these are a direct outgrowth of life-styles in urban, highly developed American cities. Americans are very dependent upon the automobile, and it has, until recent decades, been the province of men. Married women were usually driven places by their husbands, and service of the car was organized and performed by men. Many of the Chicago-area women sold or gave away the family car when the husband died. This means that they either restricted their movement considerably, used public transportation, or were dependent upon others. This explains the inclusion of transportation and help with shopping in the service support system. The division of labor in the home usually involves household repairs being performed by men. Thus, the absence of a husband can lead to a need for services involving car and house care. In fact, both the Chicago and the Columbus, Ohio, widows specified help in these areas from male relatives or neighbors (see volume 2). Help with yard work, or in other locations, such as where farming is important, again was specified because of the traditional division of labor as well as its magnitude. Legal aid is associated with highly developed or rapidly developing societies, but it is not usually used by widows in a formal way. They often depend on their informal network, which may be as ignorant of the law and governmental policy as is the older, little-educated widow herself. Interestingly enough, communist China provides such services to many of its members.

Universal is the need for help with child care, care during illness, and with decisions. Housekeeping services depend upon the composition of the household and its complexity. Here the major differences in the needs and services received by widows are between those who live alone and those who live with other members of the household who must be served, who provide the major portion of the work, or with whom there is an exchange of services. Young children require a lot of care, older ones can provide it to the mother. We have found that if the work is part of the normal flow of life, it is not labeled by the widow as *help*. Help is identified as coming from outside the home or as organized by special arrangement. Thus, some women state that the children "help" with housekeeping; others state they receive no help, even as the interviewer sees a daughter preparing a meal. The widow may be expected to care for her grandchildren in return for economic supports. In fact, many of the Chicago-area widows prefer to live alone—and are able to do so with the help of social security —rather than moving to the homes of their grown children simply because they do not want to take care of the children and help with housework. They did all that at another stage of life and now do not wish to provide such services except in emergencies. Widows in other societies frequently must exchange their services for economic and other support by family members since they are not able to maintain themselves independently. In these situations, the widow may wish to do so because of cultural definitions of worth and the impossibility of imagining herself not involved in such networks and not working until she can no longer do so physically.

Service supports can be supplied to widows informally through an exchange system with people other than members of the household. Relatives, especially grown children, can supply assistance if they are available and willing to do so. Such is the case of Filipino widows with available daughters. Neighbors are an obvious source of service supports, although some neighborhoods are organized without such activities (Lopata, 1971). The amount of service support received by a particular widow may depend on her contributions to an exchange network, if not currently, then at least in the past. Voluntary organizations can provide services, such as bringing in food during funeral and official mourning periods. Some urban centers offer transportation to their elderly living in public housing or connected with special groups.

Some communities and even state governments in America have developed complex and multiple services to selected members. A perfect example is the state of California (see chapter 10, volume 2). Services include transportation, housekeeping, shopping—all the services included in our interview. The combination of formal and informal service supports can meet the needs of many people. However, some subcultures maintain negative judgments toward people who accept formal supports, not only economic but also in the form of services; thus, many people are simply not reached although they would accept supports. A gap can exist between the way people are socialized, and thus define what is acceptable, and the way the formal, bureaucratic system is organized to provide services.

Social Support System

Again, the social support system of the base interview grew mainly out of the Chicago study. There is obviously a wide range of activities people can engage in during their nonwork time, depending on the resources of the community and their own wishes and resources. In Korea, the major social events are excursions and birthday celebrations (see chapter 4, this volume). In urban America, when women "socialize" they go to public places and/or to church, visit, entertain, share a lunch, travel out of town, play games, and celebrate holidays. We (Lopata, 1979) first asked respondents if they engaged in these social activities, then asked with whom they shared them. Public places were illustrated by movie theaters and restaurants—but half of the Chicago-area women claim never to go to such places. Some, of course, never ventured to such establishments even when the husband was alive, but many do not like to go alone, and some are even embarrassed to go with other women without a male escort. That is part of the traditional female stance that developed in middle-class America since the Victorian era and has been absorbed by upwardly mobile members of lower classes. It is interesting to note that groups of women of two different types can be seen in public places in America without male escorts: the traditional ethnic woman and the "modern" woman influenced by feminist ideology.

Some formal structures are often created to insure that people do not become, or remain, isolated from each other. Social events are planned both in public housing in America and communes in China.

Many American cities have nutritional programs that include other activities. Day-care centers for the elderly also exist. Churches and other organized religious groups, as well as voluntary associations with a variety of purposes, provide contact and activity. Eating together is a major social situation for many people and social groups are aware of this. Trips may be planned by travel clubs or even local fraternal organizations. One of the most loneliness-producing situations is the lack of anyone with whom to celebrate important holidays, and there are formal attempts to prevent this from happening to those living alone without available families. This problem does not arise in joint families, except that traditionally the widow in many regions of India was not allowed to participate in social events (see chapter 3).

Emotional Support Systems

The emotional support systems available to any human being are very complex, and it is difficult to pull them apart into separate supports. One way we did this during the exploratory phase of our research was to ask widows about the various forms and components of loneliness. We found many, and from these responses as well as from questions about sources of pleasure and of positive self-images we obtained our list of supports. These include six relational and seven self-image sentiments. We asked each woman which persons of those we identified as resources she feels closest to, most enjoys being with, tells her problems to, comfort her, make her angry, and to whom she turns in times of crisis. We then asked who makes her feel important, respected, useful, independent, accepted, self-sufficient, and secure.

Emotional supports are usually provided by people in primary, significant relationships to a person, although sentiments such as anger can be directed toward formal structures such as the church or government. We found great variation in the people involved in the different sentiments. A woman may most enjoy a grandchild, feel closest to a daughter, tell problems to a confidant who is usually a same-age friend, is comforted by a daughter, and turns to a son or brother when in a crisis. A son or daughter usually provides the self-image sentiments in American society. As we will find throughout this volume, the traditional patriarchal dependence of a widow upon the son, who becomes the closest person to her, has been substituted in more-developed societies that stress the nuclear family by the daughter. In metropolitan Chicago daughters appear in the support systems of widows much more often than do sons (Lopata, 1979). The woman will often list herself as the provider of the sentiments of self-sufficiency and security, although there are many women who report not being able to do so.

Formal social systems can provide some forms of emotional support. For example, performance at work and relations on the job or in the activities of voluntary associations can provide the sentiments of being respected, useful, independent, accepted, self-sufficient, and secure. These resources appeared in our study, but most of the other research-ers found widows depending mainly on relatives, friends, and some-times neighbors or members of the commune. There are women in each society who do not receive the supports they need. Exceptions exist, however; for example, Filipino widows report receiving more supports than they expected, especially from daughters. These Chris-tian women are the only ones in the developing countries studied by our authors who do not traditionally depend fully upon the son.

Resources and Supports

One of the subjects of sociological and societal interest is the relation-ship between the social structure and the individual member of that society. Sociological textbooks abound with theories explaining the connection. We are going to be dealing with one set of these theories only, or at least with our interpretation of it, which helps in the under-standing of the support systems of widows. Briefly stated, theories of modernization or social development attempt to explain the processes by which the connecting links between societal members and social structures are dramatically modified by changes in the society and how these changes affect the lives and support systems of different types of members.

The processes are complicated and I will deal with them at greater length in chapter 11, after we have examined the support systems of widows. The rapidity of social development, the creation of a world economic system, industrialization, bureaucratiza-tion, urbanization, and all the economic changes have often removed —but not evenly or systematically—the traditional support systems of people and modified the ways in which they can relate to each other and to larger social units. There are, as we shall see, two prob-lems with these changes: new support networks and support systems have not replaced the old ones, and people have not changed at the same rate or in tune with organizational and societal changes (Inkeles, 1983; Inkeles and Smith, 1974). The more secluded they are in their own world the less likely are people to experience these changes directly. Thus, rural people, those in the lower classes who barely have enough energy to sustain themselves in the traditional ways, women, the elderly, and other relatively isolated segments of societies are the least likely to change their ways of life even when traditional connecting links are removed. For example, older rural widows may be affected by the changes in their societies only indirectly, as when the sons who are supposed to provide the majority of their supports move to towns and even to other countries. Informal, unorganized forms of work that provide economic supports decrease as commercialization and modernization of the economy increases, thus leading to poverty (National Committee on the Status of Women, 1975).

Thus, the situation the world over is changing rapidly, at uneven rates between and within societies. The women studied for these volumes have been going through varied amounts of disorganization produced by the death of their husbands and problems of reorganization as a result of either their changed status to widows or as a result of the absence of traditional supports for living—whether they be economic, service, social, or emotional. Let us now examine resources, the support systems, and life-styles, summarized in the last chapter as life frameworks of widows in other countries in volume 1 and in Canada and various locations in the United States in volume 2. The chapters are generally organized by the degree to which the informal resources for the support systems of widows are supplemented by formal ones developed purposely by the society. We thus start with Malo, Vanuatu in the South Pacific Ocean and end with the communist Chinese system.

Widowhood: Other Countries

Malo, Vanuatu

Robert L. Rubinstein presents us with an anthropological view of a small-scale and traditionally based society, with some reference to its internal divisions. Many of its members are related, all have "grown up and lived their lives with one another on a relatively small island." He writes of an "historically ongoing, densely packed bundle of human relations and strategies for maintaining, displaying, and portraying the nuances of these relations." A self-conscious form of tradition is the basis of everyday life and one source of judging behavior. Public life is the domain of men, who inherit the land, manage it together with their brothers, and pass it on to their sons. Women can form a segregated and close unit of support. Marriage is not the basic social relationship and is not imbued with all the emotional tones of the modern American marriage. Husbands and wives are not strongly interdependent, each having a wider network of interdependent relations. Remarriage is encouraged with specified alternatives of mates, preference being for the brother-in-law. Women are seen as "belonging" to the land, which is the same as belonging to the late husband's land group. Having children, especially sons and later daughters-in-law is extremely important for older widows, their absence putting a woman at a tremendous disadvantage as far as support and status are concerned.

Women's work is a major part of the family subsistence. Although widows do not seem to be much worse off than wives, their inability to own land makes both heavily dependent upon others. The society and other groups are not responsible for the widow, but the family definitely is! There is no money economy and the widow traditionally could not enter social roles outside of the family. Rubinstein indicates, however, that changing times are broadening the choices available to widows, making it possible for them to lead more independent lives.

This is thus a very different social system than the one in which Chicago-area widows are living. There is a continuous support network over the generations and an absence of social roles outside of the family from which a widow could draw supports. Geographical and social mobility are rare. Personal negotiation is important in maintaining a flow of supports. Although Rubinstein indicates that changing times are broadening the choices available to widows and making it possible for them to live more independently, the choices are narrow and the personal resources for creating new life-styles very limited.

India

The positions and social roles of women have varied in Indian society, historically and in the various regions, as Jaya Gujral clearly documents. Historians find that women had a great deal of freedom in the Vedic Age, long before the birth of Christ, but the Muslim invasion brought with it purdah, the seclusion of women, and many religions and legal laws of both the Muslim and Hindu cultures restricted life and placed an onus on their gender (Papanek and Minault, 1982). Female infanticide was practiced in several regions, and, according to Miller (1981) there is evidence of continued neglect in rural North India. Child marriages guaranteed that the young wife became socialized into the boy's family, but the custom created many child widows with no offspring of their own to protect and support them. Widow remarriage was forbidden to the higher castes, although practiced among the lower ones because of the need to continue reproduction and the work of many family members. Suttee idealized self-immolation on the funeral pyre of the deceased husband, and those widows who did not go through this had to make themselves physically unattractive and absent from public functions. Widows were called "inauspicious things" and avoided when possible.

As late as the middle of the nineteenth century the situation of widows horrified many colonial Britishers who were, however, usually unwilling to interfere in the local culture or to give this matter high priority. Some attempts were made to change some aspects of this way of life through laws, but these were often unsuccessful, running against both tradition and strongly established religions.

In the early decades of the nineteenth century, some British administrators and missionaries and a few Indian male social reformers cooperated to improve the social and legal status of Indian women. They were most appalled by customs that affected the lives of women most directly and so secured legal sanctions prohibiting infanticide, which was primarily practiced on female babies, and suttee, the sacrificial death of a Hindu widow on her husband's funeral pyre. Their campaign to ameliorate the condition of women who survived such practices proceeded more slowly and focused on the education of women and the advocacy of widow remarriage. Closely linked to these issues was the custom of child marriage, which precluded much education and produced substantial numbers of Hindu child widows but not child widowers—men were allowed to remarry (Ramusack, 1981:199).

Introducing changes too rapidly with externally imposed laws such as the Hindu Widow Remarriage Act of 1856, the colonial powers brought about a revolt by Indian men (Ramusack, 1981:199). Parents faced with the 1929–1930 Sarda Act, making marriage of girls under 14 and boys under 18 illegal, rushed to marry off "three million little girls and two million boys" before it was put into effect (Felton, 1966:168).

The social movement to pass that act involved not only British officials but also leading Hindu women.

Gujral describes here the complexity of the modern joint family and the fact that arranged marriages are still prevalent. However, even though the wife leaves her natal family upon marriage, she returns often for extended periods of time, usually surrounding the birth of a child. Male dominance permeates life and dependence upon a son still concentrates the woman's attention and love on him, not the husband. That is the traditional way of life, still observed in rural areas. Change is occurring, however; sons are moving away from the parents' homes and establishing their own households. Ross found the situation of widows whose sons moved away very difficult compared to that of the matriarch managing her own home with "absolute rule over the family members" (Ross, 1961:95). The daughter-in-law, who is a virtual servant in such a household, has a completely different position if the household belongs to her and her husband, not through inheritance, and the mother-in-law is the outsider.

There is no agreement among Indian scholars as to the kinship disorganizing effect of urbanization and the creation of paid jobs, which decreases dependence upon that unit. However, the situation of the widow who must leave her own home to live in the home of a son is a perfect example of some of the problems inherent in social development that removes traditional sources of support without substitution of "modern" ones, such as social security. As Gujral notes, the early stages of social development often change the customs and obligations of traditional society, which protected widowed women and guaranteed embedment in an economically active kinship work group. Heavy dependence upon a son who migrates or who has turned his attention to his family of procreation can leave a widow to her own devices, while a lack of education and experience outside of the home can make self-sufficiency impossible. Inability to remarry, because of caste or age, combined with the loss of function and status through the death of the husband, leave few options and a potential for poverty. The lot of widows without grown sons has been traditionally uncomfortable, but at least economic supports from kin networks exist. The support systems of widows, according to Gujral, still "hinge on surviving sons and their families who are able to accommodate them in the natural life-cycle of the traditional Indian family."

Korea

Problems associated with the migration of children and of the widow accompanying social development in the Third World is also brought up by Jasoon Koo in her description of the support systems of widows in Korea and by Marsel Heisel in reference to Turkey. Such geographic mobility is a relatively new phenomenon, except for migratory hunting and gathering subsistence groups, which moved together. Industrialization and urbanization have created labor markets that draw people from rural, agricultural areas to mines, factories, and accompanying work centers. We saw that women on Malo do not move in their lifetimes, except at marriage, nor is permanent migration frequent. Indian migrations are from rural to urban areas, concomitant with the migration of brides to the husbands' joint families. Koo writes of two movements: that of adult children—even the oldest sons—to Seoul, leaving the mother without supports in maintaining the land. If she is unable to get sufficient help from other relatives or village neighbors, she may have to follow the son into the city, as part of the migrant family or alone. Migrants can face dramatic change and culture shock if reared in rural areas without formal education or an understanding of the complex urban system. Women are so raised as to not even know how to develop new relationships or find new roles. The children with whom they live are often better educated and have a lifestyle that makes the mother uncomfortable. In return for housing and economic supports, the widow provides services such as care of the children, a pattern also evident among the Asians and Mexicans in California (Clark and Pelman, volume 2).

The location of the son's home in the city is an important factor in the social integration of the widow. If the kinship group stays relatively close together, or rural people from the same village or area live nearby, the widow may actually continue an active social life similar to the one she had before. Many a Korean widow, however, loses her function as the channel of communication and kin-keeper when she moves to the children in the city if she does not know neighbors and the kinship unit is dispersed. Immigrants to other countries often form ethnic communities in which people did not even need to learn the language of the dominant group to get by in their daily round of activities. This was true of the Polish Americans, who formed their own churches, schools, clubs, and economic services (Lopata, 1976). However, ethnic communities changed over time and the older widows became gradually disengaged, not replacing former neighbors, friends, and group members with new suppliers of supports (Cumming and Henry, 1961). This is not the case with Korean widows, in that they have stayed in their own society upon migration. However, their lack of literacy and rural-urban, as well as regional, differences are enough to isolate them from people not from the same home area.

Here again we find that migrating sons may direct their attention to the wife and children, loosening ties with aged parents and weakening their feelings of obligation. The widows who waited all their lives to reach the relatively powerful position of family matriarch may be stripped of it by social change.

Turkey

Marsel Heisel's description of the support systems of widows in Turkey illustrates some of the points made before in this chapter: the difficulty of changing traditions through laws, the importance of sons, and the effects of migration of children for paid employment. Atatürk, the founder of the Turkish Republic, who led the movement to modernize the social and economic institutions of Turkey, gave women all the legal rights available to men 60 years ago. However, in the rural areas and small towns, where men continue to exercise great power and many women are still illiterate and economically dependent on father, husband, and son, progress is slow. The reforms were based on the Swiss Civil Code but conflict with Islamic law, which does not see women as equal to men. Marriage is regarded mainly as a means of having children, who are important on the land since they contribute economically rather than being costly, in contrast to urban areas with extended mass education as in the United States.

The woman's world exists separately from the man's in the majority of households and communities. According to Heisel, this often provides widows with strong support networks. Unless working constantly for bare subsistence in the agricultural areas, women are able to socialize and provide confidante and social supports. Services are exchanged among the women, who thus have relative independence in their own world, more so maybe than is true of women who are in constant interaction with more powerful males.

Turkey is experiencing extensive emigration, planned as temporary for employment, mainly to Germany, but often lasting for years. This has several effects, one of which is the feminization of agriculture or other work if only the males leave. Sometimes the sons take their wives with them, leaving the older generation behind. Sons freed from the father's authority tend to focus their attention on the family of procreation. Elderly widows are becoming increasingly worried that they will not be cared for by the son, who is the main person responsible for the mother's welfare. Unlike the situation of Korean widows, who often join the migrant son, Turkish widows tend to remain in that country. The shift to a foreign and completely different society discourages such movement. In general, according to Heisel, social and economic development and the ensuing changes in family relations tend to decrease a man's feeling of obligation to his parents; however, the social commitment of family members to older kin, as well as the emotional and economic ties, continue to be important among Turks still living in their homeland.

Iran

The Family Law and Civil Code of Iran is based on the laws of Islam. Jackie Touba's study of the support systems of widows in the Tehran area took place just before the 1978 revolution and she was lucky to get out of the country with her family and the data. According to these laws, the son inherits the property and is expected to support the family and relatives, including parents and siblings. As we saw before, this pattern is not unusual in traditional, patrilineal family societies. Polygyny has been allowed in the past as a means of providing supports for widows and children. Here we have the first mention of war as a source of widowhood, which will be discussed at greater length in connection with Israel. The dependency of wives and mothers upon the men of the family is brought about not only by the law, but also by the women's lack of education and knowledge of the world outside of the home. We find migration, more than other sources of change, undermining the traditional family support system. Although families try to migrate to the cities together, the male tends to benefit more by the job-organized economic system, which frees him from his family of orientation, the power of his father, and responsibility for his widowed mother. A strict division of labor makes support by sons very sex segregated, so it is the daughter-in-law and occasionally the daughter, if available, who provides service supports. The absence of social security or other governmental assistance means that the widow is in difficult circumstances if she has no family willing to provide supports.

Israel

Israel is a heterogeneous society. Its population contains a wide variety of religious affiliations, degrees of religious observance, countries of origin, etc. Marriage and divorce are under the jurisdiction of the religious authorities (e.g., Rabbinical courts for Jews, Muslim courts for Muslim Arabs). Jews from different cultural backgrounds may and do "intermarry." Several laws passed by the Knesset (the Israeli parliament) have attempted to abolish the discrimination against women that is entrenched in many religious customs. Such laws are "The Law of Equal Rights for Women" (1951), "The Law of Inheritance" (1965), and "The Law of Monetary Relations between Spouses" (1973).

The economic and social status of widows in Israel depends on the cause of the husband's death. War widows are most privileged; they receive financial aid as well as many free services for themselves and their offspring. Widows whose husbands died as a result of work accidents receive reasonable pensions. The majority of widows, however, whose husbands died of natural causes, receive only minimal support from social security and many of them suffer actual poverty.

Widowhood brings with it a loss of social status in all the societies we have studied, but the degree varies, depending on several factors. One of these is the way in which the husband died and the direction of blame for the death. In India the wife is blamed, for it is her duty to keep her husband healthy. In Israel the loss of status is greater for the "civilian" widow than for the war widow. Israel is still a family-oriented society, and those who live outside of the conventional family framework, even through no fault of their own, are somewhat isolated and looked down upon.

The Philippines

Women in the Philippines, as described by Evangelina Blust, have more egalitarian marriages than any of the groups described thus far. Filipino husbands and wives share authority in the family and both participate in decision making on most family issues. However, the traditional roles of the man as head and provider and the woman as homemaker still persist. The husband, according to the Civil Code, is responsible for the support of the wife and the rest of the family; the wife manages the affairs of the household. Since social welfare services and governmental assistance are very limited, the nuclear and func-

tionally extended family and the strongly established norm of reciprocity among people guarantee a support system even in widowhood.

The group of widows Blust studied in the Philippines receive more
filial support than they expect. These women can support themselves
through a variety of market activities, especially in the rural areas, but
children are one of the main sources of economic assistance. The
importance of the daughter in the support systems reinforces the
woman-for-the-home-and-family norm of the Filipino family. Blust
selected a sample of only those widows who had an available daughter.
We thus do not know how many widows have no available daughter
and if the sons and/or daughters-in-law are more active in such cases.

Australia

Australia is considered the most developed of the societies discussed
in this volume. The standard family form in Australia is nuclear. However,
due to relatively low rates of internal mobility, it is highly likely that a
widowed family will have members of both the widow's and her
deceased husband's family living in the immediate area. There are,
however, no legal or social expectations nor obligations upon either
family to provide economic, emotional, or social support to a widowed
member.

Australia's social welfare policy recognizes a societal responsibility
for both the aged and the widowed. The governmental pension system
is means-tested but was developed with the view that a widowed
woman with young children should not be required to go out to work.
To some extent, the system assumes that an older widowed woman,
who has spent her life out of the labor force, should not be expected to
work; the widows' pension is available at age 50 for widowed women
without children. Consequently, although pensions are low relative to
overall living standards in Australian society, they are available to all
widows subject to a means test. The "gap" that American widows
experience is also faced by Australian widows in that to be eligible for
the pension they must have a child under age 18 or themselves be over
age 50.

Change in women's roles in Australia is occurring, though probably
not as quickly as in the United States. As evidence of this, there are
major differences in the outlook toward employment, in educational
achievement, and in career patterns of the younger widowed women
compared to older women. Younger widows are much more likely to

use their own earnings as major economic supports and expect to continue their work, regardless of whether or not they have children. The older widows sampled usually did not have any work experience since their marriage, had no employment options, and no interest in entering the labor force. This attitude is, of course, facilitated by the availability of widows' pensions.

A major aspect of the situation for Australian widows is a consequence of the immigration program. As a result of active government policy to encourage immigration, a very high percentage of the Australian population, and of the widows in this sample, were foreign-born. Whereas 19 percent of the widows in Chicago had foreign-born parents, 20 percent of the respondents in Australia had themselves been born overseas. This has major implications for the availability of a family support network and for conflicts between the customs surrounding bereavement, mourning, and widowhood of immigrants and the expectations of the Australian society.

Another major difference between the widows of Melbourne and those of Chicago and other societies is the lack of religious control and even support within Australia. While Australian society claims to have an official religion—i.e., Episcopalian—in reality only a very small percentage of the sample admitted to having any strong religious belief, and an even smaller percentage to having a religious affiliation. In this they differ considerably from the American blacks studied by Neale.

Australian widows have an advantage over widows in the Chicago area in that the government provides health care and there is relatively little fear of crime. This is, however, the first society we have studied in which the problem of loneliness is mentioned. The absence of an all-encompassing extended family, village, densely packed neighborhood, or commune can result in social isolation and loneliness, especially after the children leave home and the husband dies. In that regard the Australian widows are similar to the American urban women in the same family situations.

China

The situation of widows in postrevolutionary China is fascinating. The society was strongly influenced on all socioeconomic levels by patriarchal, hierarchal, and Confucian ideology. Sons were a necessity since land passed on to them, they provided care in old age, and were the only ones to participate in ancestral worship. The young bride came to the home of her husband's family and was a virtual slave to her mother-in-law. Marriage was arranged, and the suicide rate of young women was notoriously high.

The revolution and several governments tried to eradicate this ancient and strongly established culture through a variety of methods beyond the mere passing of laws. The extended family was broken up by the government by assigning members to different geographical areas. Land reform collectivized ownership, and work control shifted from families to cooperative work teams on communes. The whole process weakened the son's obligations to his widowed mother, but the commune took over as the support network. Each member contributes to the life of the commune and in turn receives services. According to Denise Barnes, even the young are organized into volunteer teams to help the old, who, in turn, are given jobs as counselors, monitors, and arbitrators, functions requiring less physical strength and greater "wisdom" than other commune work.

Thus this is the only case among all our examples of life-styles and life frameworks of widows where the society has recognized that such women are deprived of the traditional support systems by societal change and has actively substituted for them. The other societies have introduced changes directed toward pushing people toward "development" without acknowledging responsibilities for those members who were socialized into the old system and unable to take advantage of the new life-styles. The Chinese women faced with enforced modernization are still mainly illiterate and accustomed to being obedient and passive outside of their immediate family. The attempt to break up the patriarchy has left them without protectors, except within the new communities created by socialism. However, the revolution has not really emancipated them from the old patriarchal domination, because it built upon it, according to Stacey (1983).

A new problem has been introduced in the lives of Chinese women by recent actions of the government. Determined to control population growth, it has restricted each family to one child. This has resulted in a return to infanticide; girls are allowed to die in the hope that the next child will be a boy, able to carry forth the family obligations only a male offspring can do (Bennett, 1983; Mosher, 1983). This situation documents the difficulty of changing a traditional status system that assigns little value to girls.

Summary

We now have a brief introduction to the life of widows in several societies the world over. We see the highly integrated widow in Malo, Vanuatu, a relatively stable society where individuals know one another from birth and have ascribed life-styles with relatively few alternatives. We see other widows deeply affected by social change, stemming from the behavior of younger generations who, rather than remaining nearby and providing the traditional support systems without which these dependent women cannot survive, have moved away. The widow then must either move to join them or find substitutes. Some widows are able to eke out a living in the informal section, but the new system of organizing work into jobs for pay finds many widows, especially the older ones, without adequate preparation. As societies become transformed by the dramatic changes of industrialization and urbanization and all their accompanying characteristics, personal resources—in the form of self-confidence and knowledge provided by formal education, as well as income, health, and willingness to undertake new social relations and social roles—affect what happens to members at any stage of the life course. This is particularly true of women whose husbands die in communities where this event results in strong disorganization of prior support systems and life-styles. Of course, in some societies the husband-wife relationship is not as important as it is in middle-class America, so that the husband's death may simply disorganize the service and economic support systems while not so drastically altering the social and emotional ones. The presence of larger interdependent units, of which a woman is a continuing member, can be created through other ways than the family: by a society developing communes, by a tightly knit ethnic community, or by a purposely created homogeneous environment such as a retirement community.

A main difference in what happens to a woman when her husband dies appears to be whether she herself must reorganize her support systems and life-styles, as is typical for modern women in urban, more developed centers, or whether her social integration is provided by others. In many societies undergoing major transitions, a gap develops between how a woman was socialized and how she now must live. This is particularly true if she herself must migrate from an area in which she had already developed a more or less satisfactory support network to one in which she is a stranger and lacks the personal resources to build new networks. If unable to change upon widowhood—or if other changes such as neighborhood population shifts or her own migration—she can be forced to gradually disengage unless others provide connecting links between her and outside social contacts. Socialization of women into passivity vis-à-vis the world outside of the home, typical not only of societies with seclusion norms such as purdah but even in America of the not-too-distant past, combined with the failure of societies to replace traditional support systems with new ones can result in loneliness, social isolation, and a very limited life space.

Let us now examine the support systems of the widows described in the various chapters of this book in greater detail, returning later to some more generalized observations.

2 Women as Widows on Malo (Natamambo), Vanuatu (South Pacific)

ROBERT L. RUBINSTEIN

It has sometimes been remarked that in Melanesia—that culture area that includes New Guinea, the Solomon Islands, and Vanuatu (formerly called the New Hebrides)—death is a significant mechanism that reconstitutes or regenerates social, economic, and human relations (Weiner, 1980; Strathern, 1981).[1] In the case of widowhood, as with any death, the loss to society of a valued member acts to threaten significant social relations that have been laboriously and continuously built up over many years, often in climates of psychological and political competition and contention. Both the widow and "society at large" are survivors in an anomalous position: both attached to the deceased and moving away from him at the same time. Depending on the influence and status of the deceased, society—be this individuals, families, or larger groupings such as lineages—must repair the tear in the social fabric, often with a cross-stitching provided by the back and forth of exchange and other actions that prevent the ramifications of the loss.

This chapter examines the "social support," resources, and "social integration" of widows in one Melanesian society, that of Malo Island (Natamambo) in Vanuatu. Here I have placed the terms social support and social integration in quotes to indicate their rather unusual status in a society with a population of about 2,300 in 1979 (New Hebrides Government, 1979), in which many people are related, and in which all persons have grown up and lived their lives with one another in a relatively small (about ten miles by eight miles) island. On Malo, issues of social integration do not really have the same flavor that they do in a large-scale "complex" society. This does not mean that social integration at the individual or group level is not an issue in special ways. Although the term social support or support system is also more an analytic construct suited to large-scale societies, we are certainly able to ascertain those categories of persons who generally make up a "support system" for widows on Malo. Yet in Malo support systems and social relations are always deeply personalized, primarily—but not exclusively—kin-based, and with historical and biographic dimensions. This is a society in which people are born together, live together, and die together. Knowledge of the activities and doings of one another is great, and one of the most interesting forms of knowledge is knowledge of other Malo individuals (Rubinstein, 1981). In such a case, "social integration" rarely reaches a stage in which other Maloese people and groups are not known about. In contrast, in the West one may be entirely ignorant of or tune out the lives, aspirations, and daily doings of numerous individuals and groups, even those who live nearby. Concomitantly, on Malo "social support" is never decontextualized from an historically ongoing, densely packed bundle of human relations and strategies for maintaining, displaying, and portraying the nuances of these relations. There are no "formal or informal services," there are merely relationships.

The Ethnographic Background

The South Pacific island of Malo lies in the northern part of Vanuatu between the larger islands of Espiritu Santo, Aoba (Ambai), and Malekula. Malo itself, oval shaped, has a low coastal strip surrounded by a fringing reef and a high central plateau, capped, on Malo's western end, by Malo Peak. The infrastructure of Malo society is traditional Melanesian (Chowning, 1973), based on mixed yam and taro gardening and pig husbandry. Pigs also form the basis of the internal economy. Today, most weddings and many land transactions and legal cases involve the payment or exchange of pigs. This traditional economy has been increasingly supplemented in recent years by cash-cropping. Maloese own and work coconut plantations and turn coconut meat into copra, from which coconut oil is eventually extracted at mills. Native cattle-raising exists on a small scale but it too is increasing in importance as a means of earning cash.

Although the people of Malo have experienced change from exposure to others during World War II, from missionaries, and from the
attempts to develop a national culture following independence in 1980,
"tradition" still plays an important role in everyday life. Tradition is
labeled *kastom* ("custom") in Bislama, the English-based pidgin language widely used in interethnic situations in Vanuatu in lieu of the
numerous local languages. *Kastom* refers to two distinctive complexes
of strategies, beliefs, and behaviors on Malo. The first is that complex
whole, which includes what are conceptualized as traditional rules
and regulations: rules of land tenure, prescribed kin behavior, rules of
marriage and remarriage, as well as items of folklore and medicines.
The second constellation of things is the *Sumbuea*, or traditional pig-
killing system, which is in its last gasps on Malo.

Modern daily concerns revolve, for the most part, around gardens
and pigs, the raising of children, the increasing needs of a cash-based
economy, the responsibilities of nation-building, and the forming of a
national identity. It is certainly not an exaggeration to say that for most
Maloese these are everyday concerns.

The Engendered Culture

On Malo, the experience of widowhood is fixed in its matrix of gender,
and an understanding of this gender system is crucial to understanding the life of widows (see also Lopata, 1979). In general, on Malo
public life revolves around the activities and doings of men. This has
been the traditional system since pig-killing times and continues in
modern political and social life. Land inheritance is patrilineal and is
culturally and symbolically associated with men. The Maloese say,
"Men stay on the land and women leave it," referring both to sons who
stay and carry on and to daughters who marry out. Land is both an
idiom for and an actuality of the viricentric life. Marriages are conceptualized, at the same time, as relationships between individuals,
kindreds, and relationships between lands. Men are their lands and
lands are their men.

The central kin-land construct is the *buatuivanua*, which I have
glossed as the "land-group," a term that emphasizes, as does its use in
the Malo language, both persons and lands. Land-groups are named,
bounded parcels of lands of various sizes with unique histories that

may contain a variety of kin-based collectivities organized patrilineally and patrilaterally. At one end of this spectrum of collectivities is a named land inhabited by a simple lineage: a man, his sons, and his sons' sons and their respective families. At the other end is a complex land-group: several such lineages who share a named, bounded land, who derive their primary identity from it, and who reckon some kin attachment to one another, either agnatically or through some historical circumstances.

Sets of brothers on the land form basic social units. Same-parent brothers are reckoned to be in a close, collective relationship. However, lacking any more direct kin relationship, men of a complex land-group of the same generation call one another "brother." Brotherly coherence is provided by another kin mechanism: a man and his father's father call one another younger and elder brother, respectively. Thus brotherhood is a quality of close kinsmen, of kinsmen who otherwise share land-group identity, and cross-generationally.

Women—as daughters and sisters—are dispossessed from their natal land at the time of their marriage. As one man put it, "My daughter belongs to me and when she marries, she'll belong to another man." At marriage, exchanges of pigs, yams, and other valuables "place" the bride at her husband's land; they socially fix any of her biological offspring as her husband's children; they establish children's continuing right to their father's land; and they "straighten out" the kin terms affines will now use to "call" one another.

While women no longer "belong to" their father's land or place after marriage, their relationship with that place endures in the visits they make there and in the continued shared interests. For this woman's children, however, her natal land is a special place. It is here they find their mother's parents, figures of indulgence and fun, and their mother's brother, a figure of authority and respect. Furthermore, the mother's natal land is her children's refuge, a place with an indissoluble tie, a place where these individuals may go in times of dire trouble or need.

The "overt" social system—lines of men—form the most visible aspect of Malo social structure. Lines of women form a more covert, underlying structure, which is often visible when the male system fails. Thus, when a man has no male offspring, the land passes through his sister, sister's daughter, or sister's daughter's daughter to the closest male relative (e.g., the sister's son, sister's daughter's son or brother, etc.). Such a line of women born of women is referred to as a man's "breadfruit tree root." More importantly, when a person dies, significant payments are made to persons from the deceased's natal land (if a woman) or mother's natal land (if a man) for the investment they have made in the deceased's life and land.

These complementary social "systems" also suggest a position of structural primacy for the sibling set, despite its being broken up upon the marriage of a sister. Although the overt, male system breaks apart sibling sets, these sets provide a pivotal nexus between types of social organizations.[2]

Marriage and Its Aftermath

From the Western point of view, marriage is the union of two individuals that may involve two families. From the Malo point of view, marriage is the union of two individuals, but it always involves families and represents a complex series of arrangements between persons of two lands. Basic to the notion of marriage is the idea that a transaction must accompany it. A payment must go from the groom to the bride's family (specifically to her father, mother, and brothers). Such a payment acts to socially place the bride at the groom's place—at his land—and to securely place their children there. Regardless of the gender, the children of the wife will now belong to the husband's land. While there can be debate about certain children's legitimacy—at their father's land—and whether their mother was "properly" transacted over or not, therefore making their connection to their father's land uncertain, there is never any question about children's attachment to their mother's natal place—the land from which she came—which is sure and unquestioned. Once the children are older, however, a payment must be made by the father to his father-in-law and others of that land to assure his children's rights to make use of the mother's natal land (to make gardens and use their products, etc.).

At one level such marital and postmarital transactions are interactions between a groom and his wife's father; at another level they are transactions between, on the one hand, a man and his brothers, and, on the other, his wife's immediate kin. At still another level, they represent transactions between a man and his land-kin as well as his wife's natal land-kin. And, at still another level, they are profound relations between named land-groups; when they are discussed in this way, they generally connote a concern with an official version, with history, and with time over generations. Metaphorically, and to a certain extent in reality, a man *is* his brothers, his land brothers, and his land.

Traditionally, and until recent decades, most marriages were arranged, of older men to young girls (age five or ten) and polygyny was practiced. Nowadays, notions of romantic love have dictated alliances of individuals of more equal age and there are few polygynous relationships. Some of these occur in non-Maloese villages.

It is within this general context of gender and land conceptualizations that widowhood should be viewed. A widow is called a *buotinau* in the Malo language; as far as I am aware, there is no complementary term for widower, who remains a "man" or a "person." There are only a small number of widows on Malo at the present time, perhaps thirty. Most are elderly.

When a woman is widowed there are a number of alternatives for her. She may continue to live on her husband's land, at her husband's place, as a widow; she may marry a husband's brother; or, she may marry the son of her deceased husband's cowife. It is also possible that she may be "claimed" by her husband's sister's son as part of that individual's rights in the deceased's property. A further option is that she may remarry another man who is not related to her former husband. Several factors govern the choosing of these alternatives: land relations and contending legal principles, the age of the widow, and the population of potential mates.

A woman belongs "legally" to the land of the man to whom she was married. This is her place, an attachment that has its legal foundation in *kastom* and in the social strength of transaction (because there has been a payment to transfer her and any of her children to her husband's land), and its emotional foundation in her relations with her husband (in the fact that this is her children's place and in ongoing human struggles and activities). Thus, when her husband dies, a woman continues to "belong" to his land and, in a sense, to the men of that land, her husband's "brothers." It is not uncommon then for a widow, a year or two after the death of her husband, to marry one of her deceased husband's brothers, most commonly a "real" brother—a brother with the same parents. Such a remarriage generally occurs when the widow is in her childbearing years, and in fact she may marry a husband's brother who is relatively young and has not yet married. Traditionally, such an arrangement was de facto; the widow already belonged to and was transacted to her husband's place. Today most Maloese would have such a remarriage acknowledged by means of a church ceremony.

Theoretically, however, there exists a contending principle of remarriage. While a widow "belongs" to the men of her deceased husband's land, she may also be thought of as belonging to her deceased husband's sister's son. Indeed, widows are sometimes, jokingly or not, referred to as "*buotinaun* 'So-and-so'" ("So-and-so's widow"), referring to a husband's sister's son, whether or not that husband's sister's son wants her, and especially if the potential match is viewed as incongruous or awkward, and hence humorous in the eyes of others. This labeling, at least, suggests a primacy of the husband's sister's son's right to his uncle's widow, but examples of such remarriages are rare.

These forms of widow remarriage express an unresolved contention between viricentric relations via transactions and the power of connections through women. Another form of possible widow remarriage, the case in which a son (or sons) take his deceased father's cowife (a "mother" but not his actual biological mother) as a wife. In such a case, again, a transaction has already located a cowife on the son's land.

Because of improved health, modern sibling sets tend to be larger than those of the past and the survival rate of set members is fairly high. Fewer younger and middle-aged men seem to die, leaving fewer younger and middle-aged widows. Similarly, in the past men seemed to marry women who were substantially younger than themselves, while more recently this age differential seems to have evened out. Those younger women who are widowed tend to marry deceased husband's brothers, keeping the transactions in pigs "all in the family." However, earlier in this century, in response to the substantially lower population and smaller surviving sibling sets, younger widows were often asked as wives of men of other land-groups. Among the now older living or recently deceased cohort of women, cases of multiple serial monogamy are common. For example, the elderly mother of one informant was now in her fourth period of widowhood. Cases of multiple remarriages have important transactive repercussions. Each time a woman remarries onto a new land (a different *buatuivanua*), the men of that new land should pay men of the deceased former husband's land to transfer that woman from her old home to her new home.

It should be pointed out that individuals are rarely forced to marry or remarry. These various arrangements are generally contingent upon the agreement and acceptance of both potential spouses at the present time. There are two sorts of exceptions, however. The first is that, in the past, young girls were more or less dealt as wives by their fathers to other men. Such deals often involved taking the daughters long distances (for example to another island) so that they would have difficulty returning home. Or, if such deals were made on Malo, and a young girl returned to her parents' home after fleeing her husband, physical force was used to make the girl stay at her husband's place. In recent times, in the only instance of a heavily pressured marriage I am familiar with, a marriage between a man and a certain woman was agreed upon and the pigs gathered and guests invited. At the last possible moment the girl ran off to another man. The men of the girl's land were forced (by tradition, public opinion, and the chiefs) to come up with a spur-of-the-moment replacement who went through with the wedding, "because the pigs had already stood."

Instances of remarriage to one's husband's brother and also of serial monogamy have quite different implications for a period of widowhood and for the support one receives in late life. A woman who remarries a deceased husband's brother tends to stay on that land after her second husband dies; it is the place of her children and it is her home. In some cases, dying men, in a kind of living will, gather the family and instruct them to permit the wife to continue to live on the land and use the gardens. However, in the case of multiple serial monogamy, a woman might have sons attached to three or four different lands and daughters with three or four natal lands and three or four lands onto which they have married. Although a widow in such cases "belongs" to the last land to which she was transacted, her options in temporary residence and in "visit and stay" are much greater.

Social Support in Widowhood

The death of an individual sets off a period of intense activity that, when the deceased is a married man, involves the widow and, always, other close family members and other mourners. Traditionally, if the deceased was an important man in the pig-killing system, special ceremonies marked the tenth and hundredth day after his death. His widows covered their bodies in ash, were expected to "sit" and sleep at his grave site until the one-hundredth day, to restrict the types and amounts of food they consumed, to cry and wail daily, and to not wash nor don normal dress. Currently, the most intense period of mourning lasts to the tenth day, when a ceremony, called "Tenth Day" is held. At this occasion wealth—in the form of yams taken from the deceased's gardens, his pigs, and his money—is given out to those who have come to mourn. More specifically, larger shares of this wealth are given by the survivors to the deceased's matrilateral kin—those from his mother's natal land, including his mother's brother. It should be recalled that since a man and his son's son are brothers, a man's mother's brother and his mother's brother's son's son are also brothers in respect to one another; payments may therefore be made to a relatively young man—an older man's mother's brother's son's son. Such payments are made for a variety of reasons, such as to honor mourners and to pay them back for their investment and support of the deceased. But payments to matrilateral kin are made specifically to close an account; their "lending" of a natal person to the land of the deceased and his father.

During this mourning period society draws together to help patch the social tear. This is true even to the extent that relatives from the other side of the island, or those who are living on other islands, and who have not been to visit in months or years, come to mourn. These persons stay for several days or until the tenth day. Local relatives, friends, and other mourners come daily, bringing food, and helping to cook for the crowd. The close family—widow, children, siblings, nieces, and nephews—mourn daily by wailing a stylized song of mourning with a doleful cadence and with words selected by each individual to tell of his or her relations with the deceased. Often, survivors dream of or experience the spirit of the deceased, which lingers, visiting its corporeal haunts and usual pathways, before it departs.

On the tenth day, after the distribution of the deceased's wealth, most of the mourners depart, leaving the widow and her immediate family. A kind of veil of privacy then falls. This period, the few months following the Tenth Day ceremony, can be the most difficult for a widow. Grief remains as she decides what her options are. One older widow noted, at the time of her last husband's death, that she had buried several husbands, had survived them all, and was obviously no good for men, so that she would not remarry. Besides the question of remarriage, widows must face a variety of other important issues involving possible residential moves, disposition of property, and future activities.

If a widow is elderly and does not remarry, she will, as we have noted, tend to remain at the place of her deceased husband. For the rest of her life her children and grandchildren will be her main supporters and care-givers. As has been so often noted for the West (Shanas,

1981a, 1981b; Brody, 1981), children are the primary providers of care and support for elderly widows and other elderly individuals. The same appears to be true for many non-Western societies (Rubinstein and Johnsen, 1984). On Malo, this is certainly the case. But rather than sons and daughters specifically, it is usually sons' wives who carry the care-giving burden for widows, primarily because daughters have married away from the land at which their elderly mother is living and because there are considerable restrictions on the care-giving interaction between a mature man and his mother (see below). Generally, Maloese distinguish two levels of social help. The first is the cooperative help of kinly good fellowship and mutual concern (*tuania*, "help"), as when a man and his wife, along with his elderly widowed mother who resides on another land, make a garden together or may work together to prepare one another's garden land. The second is care (*mataci*, from *mata*, "eye"), the support, watchfulness and personal care over one—such as a child or an elder—who is weak or infirm.

If a widow has no children, she is definitely at a disadvantage. If she has daughters who are married out into other lands, or if she has sons who are not yet married, she is also at a disadvantage. Nydegger (1983) has noted that in Third World societies, the position of elderly persons without children is often quite bad. While this is not precisely true for Malo, there is some degree of truth in such a generalization. Generally, all widows have children (albeit not children who are their own); but, in the case of a childless widow, it is sisters' children and children of land relatives who theoretically should provide help. However, the strategic interests of these individuals may be elsewhere, and they may fail to respond to needs in specific instances.

The widow without enough support may need to adapt by taking over types of activities that were traditionally performed by a husband, such as heavier garden work—male activities including climbing trees and the like. There is some social stigma attached to the taking over of gender-inappropriate tasks, although an allowance is made if the need is clear. In such instances a widow is said to be "taking on the work of two" (certainly an honorable description in a society that values ability to work hard and long) or "taking on men's work" (a less-honorable estate for women).

Support can vary depending on the number of children and grandchildren. It further varies on the marital status of the children. Having married sons is an important resource for an elderly widow. Support further varies on the flexibility of daughters' marriages. It is said that a daughter's care-giving tasks should primarily take place at her husband's place; but within the context of particular marriages and relationships, there is greater or lesser flexibility in how a daughter can spend her time. Quality of support, of course, depends on the number of people for whom support and care are being provided by a given person. Malo is another society with "women in the middle" (Brody, 1981), in that women work daily in their gardens, cut copra for cash, take care of their children, and are burdened with increasing tasks of care-giving as people live longer. The degree to which a widow receives support also varies upon the traditionalist and modern orientation of each family. For example, traditionalists will not permit a mature brother and sister to garden together and will be circumspect about the types of garden activities that mothers and sons can perform for one another; certainly, such rules preventing certain types of help act to significantly deplete the pool of possible helpful manpower.

Specific acts of care-giving are also subject to rather strict rules, particularly when a care-giver is looking after a person who is deemed sick (ronjo) — normally a temporary state — rather than someone who suffers from a chronic injury or illness such as a bad leg, circulation problems, or arthritis. Tables 2.1 and 2.2 give a general summary of such care-giving rules. These rules have several important effects on the lives of widows and others. Men (e.g., widowers) generally have more coresident givers of care than do widows. A man will receive personal care from both a mature son and a daughter-in-law, while a woman can only receive personal care from her son's wife. (Daughters generally reside elsewhere, and even if they can provide care will do so only when their own family commitments have let up.) The fact of the matter is that on Malo a grown man should not even enter his mother's house or personal areas, nor should he touch her; he should keep away from her home in times of illness.

People take such rules seriously. For example, a man I knew, a core member of the modernist faction, did not visit his brother (really a father's father's brother's son's son), who was bedridden and unable to speak because of a stroke, because that man was his "brother" and therefore he could not visit him when he was sick, enter his home, or even talk directly with him.

Given a typical homestead, then, at which an elderly couple resides close by to a son and his family, the daughter-in-law gives care and help to both parents-in-law, while the son gives care to the father but not to his mother. If the elderly father dies, the daughter-in-law contin-

Table 2.1   Care-giving Relations of a Man, Malo, Vanuatu

Relationship	General Rule
Mother	If the mother is sick, a man cannot go inside her house to aid her. A mature man never goes inside his mother's house. If there is absolutely *no one* else to care for her, then a son will do it. In general, the son's wife will care for her husband's mother. A mature man cannot touch his mother.
Father	It is permissible for both a man and his wife to care for his father.
Brother's wife	It is permissible for a man to care for his brother's wife only if he and she are old.
Sister	Never. (*"Tambu! Tambu!"*) A man cannot care for her, even if both are old.
Brother	Care-giving forbidden. When a brother is sick, a man cannot, in theory, enter his house, talk to him directly, nor even inquire directly about his well-being.
Father's father	This individual is classed as an "elder brother" and subject to the same rules as a brother. A woman can look after her husband's father's father. If there were no closer care-givers, a man could do this.
Father's mother	Care-giving permitted.
Mother's father or mother's mother	"There is no law." This is a loose and free relationship.
Mother's brother	Never. Touching or physically going near him will result in a fine.
Mother's brother's wife	Care-giving permitted, but somewhat restrained.
Son-in-law/father-in-law	"Looking after" permitted, but not likely.
Mother-in-law	Forbidden.
Brother-in-law	Forbidden.
Sister-in-law	Permitted, but not likely.
Spouse	Frequent.
Children	Permitted. After daughters marry, however, they are usually someone else's concern.
Son's son or son's daughter	Forbidden. They are siblings.
Daughter's daughter or daughter's son	Permitted.

Table 2.2   Care-giving Relations of a Woman, Malo, Vanuatu

Relationship	General Rule
Mother	"Looking after" permitted.
Father	Permitted.
Brother's wife/ son's wife	Both are called by the same term. Care-giving is permitted.
Sister	Permitted.
Brother	Care-giving forbidden, absolutely.
Father's father	He is a "brother;" therefore forbidden.
Father's mother	Permitted. Same as with men.
Mother's father or mother's mother	"No law." Same as with men.
Mother's brother	"Looking after" is never permitted. This is an extremely difficult and charged relationship.
Mother's brother's wife	Permitted, but restrained.
Son-in-law	No care-giving permitted.
Father-in-law	Frequent.
Mother-in-law	Frequent.
Brother-in-law	Permitted.
Sister-in-law	Permitted.
Spouse	Frequent.
Children	Sons permitted, to physical maturity only. Daughters permitted.
Son's daughter or son's son	"Looking after" permitted, but relationship is not as close as with grandchildren through the daughter.
Daughter's daughter or daughter's son	Permitted.

ues to give care to her mother-in-law, but the son now has no care-giving tasks he can perform. While in these cases the elderly mother may also receive help from her son's children, the elderly father could not receive personal care from them, since they are "siblings." (A man or woman and his or her father's father are siblings.)

Besides help from immediate children and children-in-law, widows may receive support from children of land relatives. This form of support is especially significant when older widows have no children of their own or children who are not in a position to give them support. Here, then, is a kind of rule of substitution similar to that described by Shanas for the United States: failing immediate kin, siblings' kin; failing siblings' kin, land kin. This is a rule in its most skeletal form, and, no doubt, has some sort of mental reality for Malo persons. However, the strict order of this rule of replacement is often compromised by disagreements with and alternate commitments of close kin and the alternate commitments of siblings' children and other land kin. And as always, in a place where psychological and political strategies of various sorts are important aspects of interpersonal relations, such strategies may not always include the provision of aid. Depending on the individuals involved and the strategic interests of those individuals, the moral efficacy of kin connections can range from the weak and ineffectual to a strong type of self-sacrifice. Generally, however, the moral force of kinship does currently operate to engender help and care-giving activity, even in cases when older widows have few close kin to provide for them. Given continued cultural change, however, the effectiveness of certain types of kin relations may fail.

Personal Resources in Widowhood

The personal resources of widows depend very much on the gender system (again) and on the relative age and life experiences of each widow. From the point of view of what the sociocultural system of Malo allows women to have, there are certain classes of important property they cannot own, most specifically land. While they may have use rights to and may make money from productive trees such as coconuts, because women do not possess land they never really own them. Thus, a significant form of wealth is denied to women. Women can own pigs—although these are generally held and used in a common arrangement with their husbands—for common tasks such as making marriage payments. Women may own money; many women, including widows, participate in copra-making groups, which hire their services to native plantation owners. I knew two older widows who took advantage of a child's residence in a town to stay there and to acquire paid work whenever they could. One older widow is a shaman of some repute, divining the supernatural causes of illnesses for a small fee.

That the relative age and life experiences of widows produce a differential in personal resources is primarily due to the fact that knowledge is an important social resource and a value of considerable importance. Knowledge, particularly of traditional life, of traditional medicines and spells, and knowledge of land affairs and land boundaries are important and valuable domains (Rubinstein, 1981). I have heard older, knowledgeable widows testify at land litigations, a rather unusual inclusion of a woman in a public activity. In such a role, widows become actors in important public arenas and can play an important part in shaping public opinion.

Older widows (and married women as well) sometimes act as "initiators" of sexual experiences for young men. I have collected data on several instances of such affairs between older women and young men. Such surreptitious alliances may be uncovered by a third party and circulate as public gossip, or they may be hidden but "told out" by the widow as part of a deathbed confession.

All in all, however, the resources of women—in their lack of access to substantial property and public clout—are considerably less than those of men. As members of groups such as the women's church group, women have some power within such restricted arenas, but even a recent suggestion that a woman could act as a church elder was disparaged by many. Widows, deprived of whatever voice they may have in decisions through the absence of a spouse they might privately influence, may even have fewer resources. Resources of widows, specifically as occupiers of a social position or role, are negligible; resources of female individuals, be they widowed or of another status, may vary considerably depending on what they make of what they have and on the "plasticity" of the particular social segment with which they interact.

Social Integration

According to Rosow (1967:9), social integration results from "forces" that place persons into the social system and "govern their participation and patterned association with others." Such a social constellation has three dimensions: social values, formal and informal group memberships, and social roles. Thus, people are tied into their society essentially through their beliefs, the groups that they belong to, and the positions that they occupy. Generally within sociology, and also within its gerontological permutations as "disengagement" and "activity theory," social integration has been treated as a quantifiable entity. We do not have specific data here to present on the "number of roles" or the "number of groups active in"; rather, I will discuss in a general way each of the dimensions of social integration as it exists in Malo in respect to widowhood.

Social Roles

Widowhood creates vulnerabilities in ties that eventually must be reproduced. The widow's role complex consists primarily of former roles in extension: mother, grandmother, sister, worker. The absence of a spouse creates major difficulties in the effective continuation of many relationships, in that the productivity of the marital unit is halved. Participation in the exchange system or the economic support system —the raising of sufficient pigs for the marriage transactions of as-yet-unmarried sons, and of yams, for numerous exchange events, including weddings—must continue. If a widow does not remarry, her deceased husband's brother may act further as a "father" to her children, redoubling his efforts to acquire pigs for them when they are in need. As we have seen, the death of a mature man requires the immediate reduction in his wealth, as relatives, especially those from his mother's land, are given part of the inheritance. Such an "expense" can leave the family depleted and with diminished adult manpower. A death, then, fosters a greater dependency of a widow's children on her husband's brothers as providers.

While the role of wife is now missing, for the older widow who has children that role may have counted for little more anyway than the roles of mother and worker while the husband was alive. On a day-to-day basis the widow may continue to garden, cook, and clean for a large number of people, of whom the husband was just one more. This does not suggest a lack of disaffiliation or grief, since grief is a part of the widow's life. It means, however, that there are components of roles that continue unchanged, at least as far as work goes. An older woman who does not remarry is reintegrated back into the family in a new way, although many of her old practical roles continue. The new status, however, consists of a degree of anomalousness and outsideness. This is probably the first time since she was young that the woman has been unmarried. She is now an unmarried adult woman, a rarity. When her husband was living, she was there on the land, with him and because of him. Now she is there, because of him, but he is gone. Such a woman who continues living at her husband's place after his death may be said to be living *ana tambun tamanatuna*, "at the graveside of her husband." Certainly, without a spouse, a woman is in an anomalous position, but it is a position that, given the proper support and acceptance, is quite tenable, and there are widows who have retained this status for decades, finding the idea or opportunities of remarriage not to their liking.

The role of widow is one that is currently being carved out. Both demographic and genealogical data suggest that there were fewer widows in the past as women tended to remarry or take up residence with a man of her deceased husband's land in a quasi-marital relationship. Women did not "live alone." Traditionally, a young or middle-aged man might take an older widow as a wife-of-sorts, to live with him and his other wives. The modern widow, the individual who continues to live at her husband's land after his death, to continue unmarried, to possibly have affairs (children may be born years after their social father dies and still be his child), to live as a kind of semioutsider, is a new sort of person, the product of changing times and circumstances.

Formal and Informal Group Memberships

For both men and women, formal group membership is an important part of social life. For a woman, membership in several types of groups is possible: the church itself and the church women's group, political parties, copra-cutting "companies," the cooperative society, a bank account (a kind of "membership" in a larger grouping). Widows can and do participate in all these, although again the institutions or social segments these groups represent are primarily controlled by men. Numerous informal groupings exist, which are primarily based on kinship and proximity.

Social Values

To what extent does society value widows? How does such an evaluation influence "social integration?" Answering these questions is, to a large extent, contingent on specifying what society consists of. Above, we referred to a problem in assessing to what extent political factions together formed a single "society" or two widely disparate groupings. In a sense, the point was moot in that whether Malo is one or two societies, widows are equally "integrated" into both. In the question raised here, to what extent does society value widows, we necessarily must deal with another possibly bifurcated society: a society that is either wholly or possibly dichotomous on the basis of gender differences—men and women inhabit profoundly different experiential worlds. The problem of the integration of men and women into one sociocultural system is an issue only recently being discussed in the Melanesian literature. It becomes difficult to discuss "society's" estimation of whether an entity is valued or not if society consists of two large blocks characterized by profound differences in experience, knowledge, practices, and assumptions. I am unable to say whether men and women value widows distinctively, but this seems to me to be a fundamental question that requires further investigation, especially regarding the possibility that women may see a period of unmarried mature adulthood (when the children have grown) as a kind of blessing—an anomalous social position over which the male system has little control. Indeed, the only time I ever heard men discuss a woman in a position of authority—over a piece of land as a land manager—was when two men, both leaders of the traditionalist and modernist factions, respectively, agreed that a certain older widow (who was an only child) was indeed the rightful proprietor of a piece of ground. The extended periods of widowhood characteristic of modern times may provide a degree of structural anomalousness that may be exploited by certain individuals to their advantage.

Most Maloese prefer to operate "within the system." Only a handful of individuals never marry, and these for reasons of what are defined as serious physical or mental infirmities. One high-school-aged girl noted that "if a girl is not married by 17 or 18, you're considered 'over the hill.'" Changing social circumstances have brought some new opportunities to women: high school, work in town, a career in teaching, a delayed marriage. What individuals will make of these remains to be seen.

Yet, within the internal system on Malo, widowhood, due to its very nature of being outside within, may provide a significant position for women to gather and use power. While a woman "belongs" to a place, she is a "free" woman in the sense that no spouse is effectively in charge. She occupies the only adult position for a woman for which she is not stigmatized for being unmarried. While she may not own land, she may have administrative control over it, as well as over her family. It will be interesting to watch what women can do in this circumstance in the future.

As the pace of social change increases, it is likely that change will occur in aspects of the gender system and, as a consequence, in the lives of widows. It is difficult to predict precisely these changes, but I expect that women will be able, due to increased educational opportunities, to achieve an increasing number of technical and managerial positions. While the ownership of land by women seems unlikely in the immediate future, it will exist as a possibility only when the national or local government follows a policy of placing legal gender equality above customary land rules, an ordering that seems unlikely to occur. Having tangible cash or landed property will go a long way toward increasing the power and public influence of women in general and of widows in particular.

Conclusion

I have reviewed the circumstances of widows in one small island society that is increasingly characterized by social and economic change. The analysis has suggested that understanding opportunities for widows must, first and foremost, be placed in the context of those sociocultural factors that contribute to the construction of gender definitions and relations and, therefore, to definitions of possibilities for women in Malo society. Increasingly, however, as Malo and Vanuatu enter the world community, opportunities and possibilities for all will be shaped by world economic forces. Whether widows on Malo will join a growing number of poor widows throughout the world, and eventually a category of poor elderly, remains to be seen.

3 Widowhood in India

JAYA SARMA GUJRAL

The Indian Setting

India is such a diverse country, with such enormous differences among a multiplicity of regional, religious, linguistic, and socioeconomic groups, that generalizations are very difficult. History records that waves of conquerors from Central Asia brought both cattle and the Indo-Germanic languages to India some four thousand years ago. The Hindu religion developed as a synthesis of the old and the new within the subcontinent, giving it a loose framework for a common culture with many regional differences. Islam came to the northern parts beginning around the 11th century with the Persian and, later, Afghan conquerors. Christianity is said to have arrived in the fourth century A.D. and Kerala, at the southwest corner, has had a Syrian Christian community from very ancient times. At present the population of India is 82 percent Hindu, 12 percent Muslim, and 6 percent other minority religious groups.

India entered the world economy with the establishment of sea routes. The legacy of the British rule left an integrated legal system, the civil service, one of the world's longest railway systems, the English language, and an educational system based largely on the British.

India is the second most populous country in the world after the People's Republic of China and is judged to be one of the poorest. However, there are enormous differences between the rich and the poor. India remains largely rural, with the majority of the population

(69 percent) still dependent upon agriculture (Government of India, 1982). The modern industrial and service sectors account for only about 5 percent of the jobs in the country. Climatic and other geographic differentials account for an uneven distribution of agricultural production and natural resources. The process of modernization and social development is very slow.

Population Composition

The study of widowhood, as a social phenomenon, must be placed within the context of the complexities noted above. Women's status is generally low, but varies by many factors (Government of India, 1978). The problems of widowhood have become acute due to the social and economic dependency of women on households that, with modernization, are changing functionally.

Women remain at a disadvantage in their ability to reap the same benefits as men from the process of modernization. In the early stages of development, the family structure does not change as rapidly as does the social and economic environment. Therefore, women who are often bound to family and household experience social change with a "time lag." However, customs and obligations of a traditional society that protected widowed women to a certain extent are now more quickly cast off by menfolk, especially when economic changes force such decisions on them at an ever-quickening pace. Unless the community and public policy enable women to "catch up"—with help in education, training, job opportunities, enforcement of laws of inheritance, and a rudimentary social security system—the individual and the family will have to cope as best as it can with the problems women face on losing their menfolk. While divorce is rare, separation is common, and separated women face similar problems as the widowed.

The 1971 census estimates 23 million widows of all ages as compared to 8 million widowers in India (see table 3.1). The absolute number of widows has increased from 22 million in 1951 (Government of India 1974:77). In 1961, 10.8 percent of the total female population was widowed in contrast to 3.7 percent of the male population. The percentage widowed has increased with age for both sexes. A larger percent of widowers were concentrated at younger ages among rural residents, while those aged 45 and above congregated at urban places. For the country as a whole, the ratio of widowers to widows decreased with age. There were 60 widowers to every 100 widows at ages 10–14 years compared to 30 widowers per 100 widows at ages 60–64 years. Child marriages still existed as late as 1971, which accounts for the young age of some of the widows and widowers.

Compared to other countries, including America, India does not have an excessively high widowhood rate (see Lopata, 1979:35). One of the reasons for this is the high mortality of women in the country. Miller (1981), in *The Endangered Sex*, documents female infant neglect and infanticide, especially in northern India. Being born a female has absolutely negative consequences in India throughout the life course, especially during childhood and in the reproductive years. The census has recorded falling sex ratios—the proportion of females to males in the population—from 1901 to 1981, from 972 to 935. Death rates have also been falling, although they are still high in rural areas. Kohli (1977) suggests that development of public health activity accounts for most of the mortality variation among states. This includes, for example, malaria control, followed by availability of hospital beds (Kohli, 1977:139). According to most observers, the large sex differentials in mortality in India must take into account the differential access to public health and medical care. Gopalan (1985) estimates that less than 20 percent of the Indian population has access to health care, even of the most

Table 3.1 Percentage Distribution of Widowed Persons by Sex, 1971

Age Group	Rural			Urban	
	Males	Females		Males	Females
10–14	0.03	0.07		0.02	0.03
15–19	0.18	0.37		0.05	0.23
20–24	0.74	0.95		0.31	0.71
25–29	1.40	1.94		0.69	1.51
30–34	2.35	4.06		1.26	3.46
35–39	3.09	7.17		1.63	6.25
40–44	5.03	14.34		2.90	13.46
45–49	6.45	20.31		3.94	20.93
50–54	10.42	36.28		6.67	37.73
55–59	12.50	40.52		9.07	43.72
60–64	18.12	62.21		14.69	63.98
All Ages	3.2	7.9		1.9	8.9

Source: Census of India, 1971; Series I—India, Part II—Special.

rudimentary variety. Given the low literacy among females in most parts of India, the large distances, and poor transportation, as well as the very low status of women, it may be hypothesized that women are at a tremendous disadvantage in gaining access to health care.

The Socioeconomic Situation of Women

Marriage

Almost all women may expect to marry in India. Agarwala (1973:54) estimates that only 1 or 2 percent of females remain unmarried by the age of 35 years. Also, marriage, and the age at which men and women marry, are seen as less dependent on economic and political conditions than in other countries (cf. Hajnal, 1965), especially northwestern Europe and America.

Given the prevalence of almost universal marriage, the status change involved at marriage is significant in the lives of all Indian women. The wedding ceremony is accompanied by conspicuous consumption, with large expenditures by the bride's family of origin. There are very specific rules among Hindus as to suitable marriage markets, the most important being exogamy regarding village of residence and at least four degrees of patrilineal kin, and endogamy within the caste. In urban areas, class differentials have added another dimension to the complexity of choice of marriage partners. Higher education and better jobs are sought for in bridegrooms within the same caste, with a compatible educational attainment by the bride. Dowries often make up for other qualities lacking in the bride or her family, especially in northern India (Government of India, 1974).

While research into differential socialization of boys and girls is in its infancy, it may be remarked that Indian culture stresses the tenuousness during childhood of a girl's relationship to her parents, her village of birth, and people in her environment. Girls are encouraged to withhold their commitments until marriage, when these can be transferred to the husbands and in-laws. This is especially important as marriages are arranged and should ideally occur before the girl attains puberty, although consummation takes place only after puberty has been attained. A Child Marriage Restraint Act was passed in 1929 (known as the "Sarda Act") that raised the minimum age of legal marriage to 14 years for girls and 18 years for boys. The act was amended in 1949 to further raise the age for girls to 15 years (Agarwala, 1973:55). In 1971, the mean age at marriage for Indian females had risen from approximately 12.7 years in 1901 to 15.4 in rural areas and 16.8 in urban areas (Government of India, 1971). Northern states, especially the Hindi-speaking ones, still have extremely low marriage ages —between 14 to 14.8 years. Southern, and northeastern states, with matriarchal traditions and higher female education, have higher marriage ages for females. In Kerala, in southwestern India, the average age is 18.6 years, while it is 20.9 years for the northeastern state of Nagaland.

Although a new bride has a very low status, in time she slowly improves her status in the life cycle of the family, especially if she bears male children. Children born within a marriage acquire membership primarily in the patrilineal line, except in the southwest and northeast, where a matriarchal culture prevails. Daughters may inherit property on an equal basis as sons from the father according to the Hindu Succession Act of 1956 (Gupte and Divekar, 1963) and from the husband on his death according to the Hindu Marriage Act of 1955 (Saha, 1965). However, tradition allowed women rights only to moveable property, and enforcement of the law depends on a woman being able to stand up for her rights where inherited property is in question, and then only if she can count on cooperation from her children and other family members. Usually, her status improves in non-property-holding households with her contribution to family income through paid labor, especially in the rice-growing areas of the Indo-Gangetic plains, the southern coastal belts, or the lower valleys of the Himalayas and the northeastern hills. Certain indicators for higher status are lower prevalence of the dowry system, higher ages of marriage, and of course, higher rates of participation in the labor force.

Few women of the upper castes work in the fields. However, there are large, and growing, groups in all regions of India who do not own land but who are agricultural laborers; the rural work activity of women consists mostly of this type and is highly seasonal. Peak activity depends on the type of crop as well as the time of planting and harvesting. Women are favored employees of tea and coffee plantations and also work on construction projects, carrying loads, etc.

Modernization of agricultural production has been hypothesized as having a negative effect on women's status (Boserup, 1970:53). In India, as in other Third World countries, this can occur because of the decreasing participation of women in the labor force. The census of 1971 does record a sharp drop for women, but that may be mainly because of the change in definition of economic activity (see table 3.2). Prior to that time, any economic activity was included; but, with the 1971 census, only people in the formal labor force were included. This shows what a high proportion of women worked in the informal labor force, especially in rural areas. Some authors have noted that mechanization has often meant less work for local agricultural laborers, especially women, as has the greater inputs of migratory, seasonal, more skilled workers from other states and localities. An interesting aspect of ongoing modernization that needs to be studied is whether benefits accrue to the older or the younger generation. Women may be beneficiaries as mothers but losers as participants in the labor force.

   Caldwell's (1982) theory of intergenerational wealth transfers posits that in traditional peasant societies wealth flows from the younger to the older generation. Children, from a very young age, contribute labor and earnings to the household while consuming very little. As adults, they provide economic security during their parents' old age. With modernization (or, as Caldwell prefers, "westernization"), especially along with the western values transferred through the educational systems adopted from colonial powers in most developing countries, the direction of the flow of wealth changes toward the younger generation. Not only is education costly for parents, but foregone earnings and labor inputs of children while they attend school are seen as additional burdens. So, while children are highly valued in traditional societies, and, hence, fertility remains high in such societies, modernization should bring about a change in the value of children and fertility rates as the direction of wealth flows changes (Caldwell, 1982:339). As a corollary to this theory, Caldwell maintains that in periods of

Table 3.2   Work Participation Rates, 1961–81 (in percentages)

	1961		1971		1981	
	M	F	M	F	M	F
Total	57.16	27.93	52.61	12.13	51.23	14.44
Rural	58.30	31.42	53.62	13.44	52.21	16.49
Urban	52.37	11.16	48.82	6.68	48.18	7.57

Source: Government of India Census of India 1981; Series—1 India, Paper—3 of 1981—Provisional Population Totals: Workers and Nonworkers (Statement 1, p. 3)
Note: 1961 figures include "secondary work" done by those labeled in 1971 and 1981 as "nonworkers," and, hence, part of the decrease in participation rates (i.e., "proportion of workers to total population, *not* the proportion of the labor force to total population") between 1961 and 1971 to 1981 is due to this redefinition.

transition, when family size is likely to be large due to falling mortality rates contrasted with previously high fertility, parents use certain strategies to ensure that wealth and benefits still flow in their direction. Before children rebel against norms prescribing family obligations, parents benefit from remittances sent back to the extended family from paid jobs in the modern sector or urban areas; in fact, parents may encourage migration of some children to reap benefits from modernization and economic change (Caldwell, 1982:361; see also Willis, 1982).

This aspect of the theory may be particularly relevant to an understanding of the social situation of widows in a still largely rural society such as India. With larger numbers of surviving widows, especially those of older ages who have no other institutionalized avenues of economic support, younger generations are likely to carry a greater burden of dependent mothers and other widowed kinfolk when the age structure of the population is controlled. This situation can last many years before the economy is able to institute public means of intergenerational transfers such as the social security systems in more developed nations.

Widowhood

As her children grow older, a woman establishes her position within the household. Her highest status is reached when her sons marry, and she can relegate day-to-day chores to her daughters-in-law. While widowhood diminishes a woman's status (e.g., she no longer appears in such public functions as religious ceremonies that she would do as a wife), she retains her power as a mother-in-law. Although she may depend economically on a son, she rules within the household as manager of household resources and production (see also Vatuk, 1980:146–48).

Some authors have reported the special relationship of affection and deference between Indian mothers and their sons (e.g., Goode, 1963:374). The traditional norm is for the widow to continue living either in the extended family with all her children and other kin of her deceased husband or with one of her sons, most probably the eldest. Here, she is expected to be treated with respect by her daughter-in-law and her grandchildren, while dependent on her son for her welfare. Daughters, once married, carry no financial responsibility for parents but maintain affectionate relationships with parents and brothers; they expect

to visit these family members accompanied by their children at regular
intervals.

Hence, the problems of widowhood and survivorship hinge on the
women who do not have any of the traditional bases of support. If a
widow has no surviving sons, or her sons are unable to support her,
she becomes the responsibility of other members of her husband's
kin. While in the traditional society, there existed the obligation of
looking after all women in the extended household, we know little
about the actual treatment of widows in the past. Anecdotal evidence
strongly suggests abuse of both younger and older widows who did
not have surviving sons as protectors.

In the modernizing society, where the extended family obligations
are slowly changing, looking after dependent women who are not
immediate members is becoming an economic and social liability. In
rural areas, where women are more likely to be members of productive
units, the widowhood of extended-family womenfolk is more easily
accommodated than it is in urban areas, where fewer women work
and where more men are dependent on wage and salary earnings. The
differential impact of modernization on problems of widowhood is
little known. While support systems along traditional lines are probably still working, stresses and strains are appearing in Hindu society,
both in the north and the south.

Remarriage

The studies by Agarwala (1967) and Dandekar (1962) for areas around
Delhi and Poona in western India confirm that younger widows with
fewer children, belonging to castes other than the highest, remarry
fairly often. The surveys, conducted by Agarwala in Delhi (1967) and
around Poona by Dandekar (1962), showed that 25–38 percent of widowed females remarried. Of those widowed a second time, between
6.7 and 31.2 percent remarried a second time. Remarriage rates varied
from zero percent for Brahmins around Delhi to between 41.1 percent
in western India and 62.5 percent in Delhi for scheduled or lower-caste
widows (Agarwala, 1966:91, table 7). A more rigorous analysis of data,
controlling for age at widowhood, number of children at widowhood,
and caste, showed that the prevalence of a Brahminic influence in
certain cities independently depressed remarriage rates within their
spheres of influence, even in rural areas (Agarwala, 1967:134). Among
groups who follow the levirate system, whereby a brother or other close

relative of the deceased husband marries the widow, the informality of remarriage and, therefore, lower cost, increased remarriage rates con- siderably (Agarwala, 1967:131). Also, time spent in the widowed state was shorter for groups who followed the levirate system than among those who allowed remarriage, but encouraged a period of mourning (Agarwala, 1966:89–90).

Among most groups in India remarriage is probably seen as the best solution for younger widows. Kapadia (1966:177), in an informal survey, found mostly positive opinions about widow remarriage. Among reli- gious minority groups, Christians, Sikhs, and Muslims have always allowed remarriage, and the levirate system has been followed by the latter two religious groups in northwestern parts of the Indian subcontinent. Among the majority Hindu population, remarriage was forbidden for Brahmin widows and strongly discouraged among all the higher castes. Such practices as "suttee," the self-immolation of widows on the pyres of their dead husbands, were practiced, however, only among the warrior and other higher castes of the north. Brahminic tradition prescribed a complete change in the life-style of widows, which was intended to make these women sexually unattractive and unavailable. Shaving of the head, wearing only white clothes, eating of a completely vegetarian diet, and other practices may be explicated by these motives. Among the majority of the Hindu population of lower caste, and among the tribal peoples of India, remarriage of widows allowed the reinstatement of widowed women in productive activity and reutilization of their reproductive capacity.

Agarwala's (1966) analysis of time spent in effective marriage may indicate a higher propensity toward remarriage of widows. However, since his analysis was based on the effect of both widowerhood and widowhood, it is difficult to estimate the independent effect, if any, of a lessening of time spent in widowhood alone. Hence, it is not at all clear whether a time trend toward more remarriage can be discerned in modern India, given that mortality has been falling differentially in favor of males.

There are two competing theories that are relevant in an analysis of time trends in remarriage of widows. Modernization theories indicate that, with economic and social changes within a society, more resources become available for education, legislative action, and improvement in living conditions of the population. These changes, together with tech- nological change in methods of production, influence the options open to households and individuals, thus inducing psychosocial changes and the emergence of "modernity" in persons exposed to such modernizing agents as education, industrial or other work in the modern sector, and the mass communication media (Inkeles and Smith, 1974). Variance in indicators of modernity between groups would be accounted for by differential exposure to such agents or by differential intensity of reformatory action. Modernization theory would predict higher remarriage rates over time and changes in the family and kinship systems within the society.

The other theory is that of "sanskritization" advanced by M. N. Srinivas (1967). In brief, he sees that the caste system allows collective mobility to a group that emulates the rituals and characteristics of the dominant caste within a certain region. A group, such as a subcaste or "jati" that wishes to be recognized as a higher caste or subcaste due to the material or power privileges accruing to these higher-status groups, follows a strategy of copying the values and life-styles of the subcaste enjoying the highest position in the area of residence. This effort at collective mobility has been particularly noted among occupational groups who have already acquired material well-being and wish to consolidate their position in the ritual hierarchy of the caste system, which has governed social position to such a large extent in India (Srinivas, 1967). The "sanskritizing" tendency has been observed in some parts of India as a result of various political and social movements in the wake of democratization and search for political constituencies.

While no specific studies are available, recent accounts in newspapers of widow-burnings may point to a trend of limited reinstatement of values discouraging the otherwise normal practice of remarriage in various parts of northern India among castes that are materially prosperous but ritually low in the caste hierarchy. Also, the higher concentration of widows in urban settings, where per capita income is higher than in rural areas, may reflect this effort by individual households toward upward mobility. Or, it may indicate urban residence of widowed women who, for some reason, have had to form single-person households in these areas. Vatuk (1982) cites several studies of living arrangements of older persons that show widows at older ages living alone. If these hypotheses were to be proven true, then remarriage rates could well decline within groups enjoying increasing material benefits due to socioeconomic change or pursuing strategies of political integration and participating in the struggle for power within a region. Studies are needed to test the conflicting trends predicted by the theories of modernization and sanskritization, especially for local areas and urban places (see also Rosen, 1967).

Conclusion

What becomes increasingly apparent from the various considerations above is that traditional family strategies and the reality of the widow's social situation and support systems are likely to come into conflict during a period of transition, although present demographic structures, as well as other social and economic conditions, may delay any actual changes for some time to come. However, the anomaly of the widow's situation was, perhaps, felt even in the past, and gave rise to such violent customs as self-immolation and the isolation of widows. Prevention of child marriages and the Widows Remarriage Act of 1958 (Gupte and Divekar, 1976) were efforts by reformers to use legislative action to intervene on women's behalf. However, the values of society have changed, or are changing, very slowly in India; under such conditions, laws are difficult to enforce.

Women who are widowed, whether young or old, need certain options, among them economic security for themselves and their children, and an assured status in society. Traditional Indian society tried to accommodate both goals through remarriage of younger widows among the service and lower castes, but exaggerated conceptions of purity and loyalty were expected of higher-caste women (Kapadia, 1966). The influence of Brahmanic traditions among all sections of society in certain areas had negative effects even on the otherwise normal strategy of remarriage. In a patriarchal household, Indian women performed such extremely sex- and age-specific roles that loss of the role of wife could not be made up for some length of time in the life cycle of the household. While the role of mother is venerated in Indian society, actual child rearing is shared by siblings, grandmothers, and others within the extended kin household. Women had to wait until their own sons grew up and took the place of the older patriarch as head of the household to be reinstated, to some extent, in their status. This loss of status with widowhood was mitigated among women who were valued for their work or income contribution. This fluctuation of women's status over the life cycle of a household seems to hold even today, although regional and other variations are natural in such a diverse society as India. Modernization is expected to diversify roles among women as well as men. Whether this happens within the Indian household probably depends on such factors as education, job opportunities, changes in family structure, and forms of social security available for older age groups, among whom widows are concentrated.

Social relationships are extremely bound by the family in India, and women have traditionally functioned to maintain home production in a subsistence economy. Among the service castes, this role did not change with widowhood as the household could ill afford to maintain the welfare of a nonproductive member. Among the higher castes, however, the loss of status at widowhood was essentially due to loss of function. Hindu widows were not supposed to cook, or, for instance, take part in various regular functions such as religious ones in West Bengal. This loss of function of particular members could be accommodated by households with above-subsistence resources, but little is known about the psychosocial effects of such loss on the widow herself.

The effect of urbanization on widowhood, if any, is also not clear. Rates of urbanization in India are low compared to other developing countries and to the advanced Western countries at comparable stages of development (see Bose, 1973). Evidence points to overrepresentation of widows in urban places, and to single-person households formed by older widows with tenuous family connections in urban places (Vatuk, 1982). If this were true, then the thesis derived from sanskritization would not hold as it posits a collective effort on the part of social groups toward upward mobility. The situation may be different in rural areas, where caste networks may be more strongly integrated into the social and political systems.

The support, both economic and social, that widows received in India, and continue to receive, seems to hinge on surviving sons and their families, who are able to accommodate them in the natural life cycle of the traditional Indian family. This obviously contrasts very sharply with the American widows studied by Lopata (1979) and Hyman (1983), who report on the self-sufficiency of American widows. Given the constraints to employment of women in other than the agricultural sector, the complete lack of any system of social security places Indian widows in a dependent position on the households of the younger generation. The actual situation of the support system between generations in the life cycle of the Indian family needs to be studied, with special reference to differentials over time and between groups in the various regions of the country.

Given the options open to Indian women, the importance of remarriage of younger widows is obvious. While remarriage is probably more widespread in India than was thought (Agarwala, 1966, 1967; Vatuk, 1982), studies that controlled for similar variables, or were conducted on an all-India basis, are obviously needed. Age at widowhood, number of children, and caste have been seen to be crucial control variables (Agarwala, 1967). Other factors, such as land or other property ownership, and work or labor-force status should also be considered.

Finally, very little is known about widowhood in south India. Most studies on widowhood and widow remarriage have considered the situation in northern India. It is obviously important to compare these two culturally different parts of the country.

4 Widows in Seoul, Korea

JASOON KOO

Literature on widowhood in various societies helps us to create a descriptive model for the consideration of the social integration and support systems of widows in any one society. In premodern societies, a strong extended family system is common and offers material protection and emotional supports to the widow and her children. The widow also fulfills a useful function within the family. If she is an elderly widow with a grown son who has become the male head of the family, she is often able to retain a life-style similar to that before the death of her husband because she stays in her own house. Many aspects of more modern societies contribute to the precariousness of a widow's position. In highly industrialized, urbanized societies, the widow can count on few ascribed family and community supports. In societies in the process of changing from traditional to more modernized forms, the norms of behavior and the actual conditions of widowhood are changing. We expect that widows in such societies may also experience some ambiguity of status since they are caught between the relative security provided by ascribed roles of the traditional culture and the unsettling forces introduced by modernization. Women living in modernizing societies, who were socialized into traditional support systems but have become deprived of them through social changes, are most apt to be without adequate supports (see also Lopata, 1979; Cowgill and Holmes, 1972; Goode, 1963).

This chapter examines the support systems of widows in Korea, a modernizing society. It contrasts urban and rural widows and hypothesizes that there is some similarity between those in Seoul and Chicago, as studied by Lopata (1979), but that there is less similarity between those in rural Korea and the widows in either city. The rural environment provides a traditional, more structured and ritualized role for the widow than does the urban environment. On the other hand, because Korea is a society still in the process of modernizing, even the urban widows, many of whom were socialized in rural areas, have a traditional set of expectations as to their support systems and ambiguous sources of support.

The Research Setting

Korea is an ancient oriental country with a history of 4,318 years. It has been influenced strongly by Confucian philosophy, has been an agrarian country with rice as the predominant crop, and, until the early twentieth century, was a kingdom. It was annexed by Japan from 1910 to 1945 and was then partitioned in 1945 into North Korea—under Soviet control—and South Korea—under domination by the United States—to facilitate the Japanese surrender at the 38th parallel. After the Korean War (1950–53), the demarcation line remained the same.

The population of South Korea is about 40 million, with an annual growth of approximately 1.5 percent at the present time. In 1983 65 percent of the total population was living in urban areas; the literacy rate was 90 percent. Korea has shown marked industrial expansion since 1963, promoted by the government, and the modernization of South Korea has been accelerated. Economic growth during the 1960s and 1970s improved the general condition of life but has also caused a wide rural–urban gap, as well as a status gap between different income groups.

The Traditional Korean Family

The main characteristic of the patriarchal family system is the continuity of the paternal family generation after generation. Ideally the patriarchal family is a large one because more than two generations live together in one house. The affinity of family members, filial piety, and chastity of women have been considered essential values.

It was a son's duty to provide old-age security for his parents and to look after them even after death through the family memorial rites called *chesa*. The oldest son remained in the paternal family home and assumed the responsibility of caring for family property and the elderly parents. The father preserved the property and then bequeathed most of it to his eldest son. In actual situations, eldest or only sons could not free themselves from the traditional obligation toward their parents; children were subordinate to their parents.

Grandparents were persons to be respected greatly by their grandchildren. Because of their age, they had the right to break some of the forms of etiquette insisted upon for others in the family. Because of the great importance of grandchildren, particularly grandsons—as leaders in the worship after death (*chesa*)—grandparents tended to be much less strict with grandchildren than were parents. The interpersonal behavior between parent-in-law and daughter-in-law used to be that of absolute superior and subordinate. Emphasis upon filial piety and respect for parents and elders is still the central theme of Korean moral education.

Women's Traditional Status

Traditionally, at the age of six a girl was isolated completely from the opposite sex, forbidden all social activities, and confined within her home. Her essential virtue was submission to a succession of lords: first, to her parents, then to her husband, and finally to her own eldest son. When she was given away to her bridegroom, she had to thoroughly learn all the traditions and expectations of her husband's family. She seldom visited her own parents unless there was an emergency or an important event of the life cycle, such as a wedding, birthday, or funeral. In most cases, she did not keep track of her own brothers and sisters. It was even believed that marriage within visiting distance of her natal family could lead to conflict. This is the theme of a common Korean proverb: "the toilet and in-laws better be far from the house." If the wife were to have within visiting distance a refuge to which she could return, with close relatives there to support her grievances, the possibility of domestic discord and strife between the two families was believed to be too great.

Severe grounds for divorce aimed at making the woman dedicate her life to the entire extended family of her husband included: disobedience to her parents-in-law and/or conflict with her sister-in-law; failure to bear a son, since she was responsible for the family lineage of her husband; adultery, which was equated with the behavior of animals;

mere jealousy toward her husband's family, especially toward the female members; an incurable disease or hereditary disease; gossiping or excessive talkativeness leading to family strife; and larceny. However, there were three means of avoiding divorce that were determined culturally and bound by Confucian tradition to protect the helpless, weaker sex: if she had served three years of mourning for the parents of her husband; if the husband's family had been poor at the time of marriage but later became prosperous; and, if she had no place to live after her divorce.

The Traditional Status of Widows

It was not proper for a widow to remarry, since being a chaste and modest woman was a traditional virtue. The widow who returned to her parents was expected to leave her children behind to grow up in their own father's lineage. At the death of her husband, the deceased husband's patrilineage had to guard a widow and her children from outside contacts. If her sons were young, the dead man's father and brothers took care of his property; the widow received whatever share was considered appropriate for the support of herself and the children. The right of inheritance for women was denied; widows never inherited property.

In the higher social classes, a widow was expected to weep for her deceased husband and to wear white mourning dress the rest of her life. It would have been immoral for her to do otherwise. The king who reigned from 1469–94 excluded children of remarried widows from competition at the public examination and from admittance to any official employment. Such children were looked down upon as illegitimate. Once a girl was engaged to her unknown bridegroom-to-be through arrangements made by her parents, she was required to remain single, like a widow, until her death if her bridegroom-to-be died before the marriage ceremony took place. Faithfulness of wives and widows was an imperative family virtue in Korean society. A vermilion arch, monumental gateway, or memorial stone was often erected at the edge of a village to praise a virtuous widow who, being exemplary, remained faithful to her husband's memory and her old parents-in-law.

The Changing Family

Many Korean family sociologists suggest that the modernization of Korea is altering the traditional extended family system, propelling them toward a form of the nuclear family (Cho, 1975; Choe, 1963; Choi, 1975; Ju, 1963; Kim, 1976; Roh, 1972). According to the census reports, the nuclear family unit increased from 66.8 to 71.9 percent of all households in nine years, 1966 to 1975, while the extended family decreased from 23.3 to 13.1 percent (Korean Economic Planning Board, 1966, 1978). Single-person households increased from 9.9 to 15.1 percent during this period. These data show major changes in Korean traditional family units.

In addition to this change of structure, many other changes are taking place in the Korean family as an institution. Marriages, earlier arranged by parents, are increasingly a matter of mutual preference of the bride and groom themselves. The young couple also is gaining control of where they live, and marriages are becoming neolocal rather than patrilocal. Studies of urban families have shown that relations between husband and wife are more socioemotional; kin ties are loosening and close contacts are maintained only within the direct lineal descent lines, usually involving persons in no more than three generations. Attitudinal studies show that young couples prefer residential separation from their parents as soon as possible after their marriages, and they insist on selecting their own marriage partners (Chung, 1972).

Current Legal Status of Widows

It is necessary to point out that industrialization and urbanization are instrumental in transforming the authoritarian, large, stable, rural family system into a more equalitarian, relatively independent but unstable, nuclear family, which affects the status of widows in Korean society. The traditional role and status of widows are changing under the impact of modernization. One important change has been that today there is no legal prohibition against remarriage by widows. However, a widow should observe a six-month waiting period after her husband's death. The waiting period is to assure that she is not pregnant by her first husband when she remarries. In actual fact, widows rarely remarry, while widowers almost always do. The right of the widow to hold the deceased husband's property has been recognized. Since 1960, when the civil law was amended, and for the first time in history, the right to inheritance has become available and applicable to women. Legally, the inheritance right of a wife has been interpreted in the following manner if no will has been made: the wife is entitled to inherit the same share as the net estate of her eldest son.

The Study

The research reported here[1] was conducted in the summer of 1980 in Seoul, the second largest city in Asia, and in two villages in predominantly agricultural provinces to the south of the city. Seoul's population is now around 9.5 million, and 22 percent of the total Korean population live there. The sample was stratified to give a representation of widows in two age groups. The age of 60 was used as the cut-off point for the groups since it has strong meaning in Korean society, being the completion of five 12-year cycles and the beginning of old age. A total of 400 widows were interviewed, two hundred of whom lived in Seoul and the other 200 in rural villages. One hundred in each location were 60 or older, the other 100 were under 60. The theoretical overview led us to hypothesize that differing patterns of support systems existed between rural and urban widows, rural widows having traditional support systems and Seoul widows having ambiguous sources of support (see Koo, 1982). The research instrument was modeled on that used by Helena Lopata (1979) in her study of widows in Chicago.

Profile of the Respondents

A descriptive profile of the personal and background characteristics of the respondents will help the reader interpret the complex analysis of their support systems.

Education. In Korea, only in the last 35 years has education become compulsory for girls as well as for boys. Not only has there been a rise in the number of elementary schools, but the number of high schools for girls has increased very rapidly. In the traditional rural environment, the education of women was not believed to serve any useful function. But recent rapid urbanization has been accompanied by increased literacy and education. It is evident that younger generations are receiving more education than did their forebears. Younger widows showed a high percentage at all levels of education beyond elementary school: 21 percent of the younger, but 61 percent of older widows received only some elementary education; 37 percent of the younger and 12

percent of the older widows had gone to junior high school; 24 percent of the younger widows went to senior high school, compared
with only 5 percent of the older widows. A considerable proportion of
the younger widows also had at least some college education. None of
the rural widows went beyond junior high school, let alone to college.

Occupation. Women in Seoul have diversified occupationally as the
national economy has developed. Only 26 percent of younger and 44
percent of older widows were not working outside the home. Urban-
type occupations such as professional, clerical, service, business, crafts,
and sales were reported, with the greatest number employed as sales-
women or service workers. Most rural widows were farmers or farm
laborers; none was in an urban-type occupation. Over 80 percent of
our respondents had not been employed before widowhood because
they had stayed at home to take care of the children and keep house.

Income. Respondents were asked to estimate their own monthly
income. The median income for younger widows was about 105,000
won (approximately U.S. $150) and for older widows about 12,620 *won*
(approximately U.S. $18). Seoul widows had a median income three
times higher than that of the rural widows. The average monthly earnings of all urban workers in Korea in 1978 was figured at 159,600 *won*
(approximately U.S. $228) (Hahbdong, 1980). The present income situa-
tion of widows in Korea has been generally bad, falling far below the
average. It must be kept in mind that a large number of widows are
engaged in low-paying jobs and that younger widows are faring worse
than older widows. The income of younger widows often supports a
household containing several children, while the income of older widows more often than not maintains only a single person. Older widows,
however, are more likely to indicate that they do not have *any* income;
34 percent of older widows contrasted with 15 percent of younger
widows reported that they received no monthly cash income.

Characteristics of household. Most of the widows surveyed were
living with children. The large majority of the younger widows were
living with unmarried children, while the older widows were living
with married children. More rural (12 percent) than Seoul (4 percent)
widows were living alone, which may be because their families have
moved away, with the widows being left behind. None of the rural
widows lived with a married daughter, while 10 percent of the Seoul
widows did. There was not a single household in which a widow lived
with her parents- or siblings-in-law.

Place of residence before widowhood. Data concerning place of residence before widowhood indicate a high degree of geographical mobility for Seoul widows: 65 percent of the younger widows and only 35 percent of the older widows resided in Seoul when their husbands were alive. Twenty percent of the younger widows came to Seoul from rural areas after the husband's death and 15 percent came from other urban areas; 41 percent of the older widows came from rural areas, 24 percent from other urban areas. Ninety-three percent of the rural widows had resided in rural areas.

Support Systems of Widows in Seoul

In this section, we present an analysis of support systems available to widows in Seoul. Four types of support systems were included in the analysis of the present arrangement of the widows in our sample at the time of our interview: economic, service, social, and emotional. Since our respondents were interviewed at least one year after the death of their husbands, we also tried to reconstruct some of the problems that occurred immediately following being widowed. In an effort to reflect the real situation as the women saw it, the questions on support systems were completely open-ended.

Early Problems and Support Systems in Widowhood

We asked the respondents what problems were the most difficult for them immediately after their husband's death. A majority of the widows reported financial matters as the most difficult; many mentioned that they needed money to buy food and pay bills and that they —especially the younger widows—were left as the only breadwinners in their household. It is probable that more older women already depended to some extent on children before becoming widows. More rural than Seoul widows reported financial difficulties.[2]

The second most frequently mentioned problem faced by our respondents after their husband's death was emotional, including grief and loneliness. Older widows more often than younger listed this as their greatest difficulty. Older widows lost not only companionship but also the crucial long-standing life role of wife. Seoul widows were more likely to experience emotional problems than were rural widows.

Another problem was child rearing. About one in seven reported that it was difficult for them to raise children alone. It had been the father's job to discipline the children; Korean children respect and fear their fathers and it was rare to find children who were hard to handle. Traditionally the widow's father- or brother-in-law became a substitute authority figure. If the children were small and these in-laws were inaccessible, a widowed mother might indeed experience difficulty in rearing and socializing her children. High geographical mobility and weakness of the extended family, especially in Seoul, may have aggravated this difficulty.

In answer to the question about what kind of help they received with these difficult problems, the responses varied, such as receiving food, money, advice, loans of money, assistance with children's education, or with farming, comfort, and so on. However, most help was given in nonmonetary forms—i.e., help with farming or comfort. Surprisingly, 31 percent of the younger and 36 percent of the older widows said they did not receive any help at all.

Respondents were asked which people gave them help with their most difficult problems. "None" said 30 percent of the younger widows and 36 percent of the older widows. If they had received help, children were named most frequently. Siblings and siblings-in-law were more significant resources for the younger than for the older widows. In-laws were more often helpful to rural than to Seoul widows, but even among rural widows only half received help from this source. In general, only half of the Seoul widows received aid from their family and kin, and Seoul widows seldom thought that their neighbors were helpful. Friends were mentioned as a source of help by 9 percent of the younger and 3 percent of the older widows. Professionals, agencies, or government did not appear in the support systems of Seoul widows.

We asked the widows four questions about the absence of support systems since widowhood: (1) was there any kind of help they wished they had received; (2) were there any persons or groups they wished they had received support from; (3) was there any reason for the failure of supports; and, (4) were there any mistakes they had made.

About half of the respondents designated at least one additional type of support that they had needed, with the majority saying they could have used additional financial aid, especially for their children's education. This finding is not surprising given the widespread parental concern of Koreans for having their children highly educated. This is not simply a new trend caused by either modernization or widowhood, rather it is something that can be traced from the Confucian tradition in Korea. Through passing an examination that required a long period of study, one became a high-ranking bureaucrat in traditional Korea and brought wealth and glory to one's family. Koreans believe that education is the most vital factor in one's success. This traditional idea is reinforced in the modern setting, where the educated actually can get better jobs as well as social respect. Parents who cannot support their children's education up to their ability feel that they have not performed one of their major duties as parents; it also makes them feel insecure about their own welfare in old age. Comforting, making decisions, helping with farming, and legal aid were also reported as needed supports but were noted too infrequently to warrant statistical analysis.

Surprisingly, more than half of the widows who felt that they needed more help said that there was no one to whom they could turn for such supports. Children and siblings-in-law were most frequently charged by the widows as the persons who failed to help them. This result indicates that many Korean widows still expect support from children and in-laws. Young widows mostly named siblings-in-law, while older ones designated children or siblings-in-law. The majority of our respondents said that they were reluctant to ask for help from other persons since these others also had their own problems. However, about one-third of the Seoul widows viewed the failure of others to help them as sheer unwillingness. More widows in Seoul than in rural areas noted the failure of in-laws to help them. The lack of involvement of siblings-in-law in the lives of Korean widows goes against the traditions of Korean society. It is not surprising to find that many Korean widows, especially younger urban ones, expressed hostility toward siblings-in-law, primarily brothers-in-law: "Nowadays, the in-laws are useless."

In modern societies, we can assume that women experience great changes after the husband's death; they must reorganize their lives on many levels. But when we asked our respondents what mistakes they had made in their lives since widowhood, the majority (six in ten) could not identify any particular mistake. The specific mistakes were largely child-related matters or selling the house or land. There was a younger–older variation in the pattern of the mistake reported. Child-related matters such as not sending children to advanced school or a son's failing marriage were most frequently reported by the older widows. It is interesting to learn that many older widows think they could have selected better daughters-in-law if their husbands had been alive. Over a fourth of the older widows considered these matters as the major mistakes they made after their husbands died, while only a tenth of the younger ones did so. A fifth of the younger widows regretted that they did not send their children to advanced school, and a tenth said that they should not have sold the house or land. More rural than Seoul widows regretted that they did not send children to advanced school. During the interviews, some younger widows said that they wished that the government would give scholarships to their children. These data reveal that support for children's education is important in the lives of Korean widows.

Four Support Systems at the Time of Interview

This part of the chapter provides a profile of the support systems of Seoul widows at the time of our interviews.

Economic supports. The economic support in Lopata's (1979) study included gifts of money, food or clothing, or help with payments for rent or mortgages, as well as for other expenses such as medical help or vacations. Since all of these supports really are part of the aggregate income, we asked our respondents the sources of their family income and the percentage attributed to each category at the time of the interview. The reason we asked about family income, instead of the widow's personal income, was to obtain a broader perspective on the financial expenditure of the family on the widow's behalf. We must keep in mind here that the majority of Korean widows live in a joint household with various members of their extended families.

Seven sources of economic support were mentioned by our respondents: own earnings, children's income, investments, rent from house or rooms, welfare payments, veterans' family pensions, and contributions from the late husband's relatives. Most respondents reported a single source of family income (younger, 70 percent; older, 83 percent), while the remainder had two sources of income. Most of the Korean widows were economically dependent on children or their own earnings. The most frequent source of family income for the younger widows was own earnings, while the older widows usually were dependent on children. Thirty percent of younger and 2 percent of older widows depended solely on their own earnings. By contrast, many more of the older widows reported that children were the sole providers of family income (younger, 25 percent; older, 75 percent).

The modernization of life in Korea is evidenced by the fact that some of the widows were able to get jobs and earn monies for their support. The actual support patterns of the family showed that about one-third of the widows had shifted the source of their family income from their own earnings during the early part of widowhood to those of their children at the time of the interviews. As an older respondent explained to us (she had been widowed for 33 years and had one son and one daughter): "I had been the only breadwinner. Now my son is making pretty good money. He doesn't want me to work and I just stay home. But do you know what has happened? I'm nothing better than a housekeeper. My daughter-in-law is working at a university. I have to take care of my two grandsons and the house during the daytime." There were quite a few older widows who said that children were supporting them but that they had to take care of grandchildren (21 percent). Investments, rents, veterans' pensions, and welfare payments were least likely to be the sole source of support for Seoul widows. Korea does not have a social security program.

For the widows who had two sources of family income, children's and their own earnings again were the primary sources. More younger than older widows reported their own earnings as the primary source of the family income (younger, 13 percent; older, 3 percent). Children were named as the primary source by 13 percent of the younger and 6 percent of the older widows. Only 1–5 percent of widows were obtaining their primary family income from investments, rents, pensions, or the in-laws. When we combine figures for single source and primary source, 43 percent of the younger and 5 percent of the older widows relied on their own earnings for their family income.

In fact, a majority of widows have had experience as the major breadwinners of their households since widowhood (younger, 64 percent; older, 47 percent). Interestingly, these figures are much higher than those of studies done by Nuckols (1973) or Amundsen (1971) in the United States. Nuckols, in his study of widows in Boston, Houston, Chicago, and San Francisco, found that only 40 percent of the women who were interviewed after two years of widowhood reported their major source of income was their own earnings; Amundsen found that if a woman was widowed, the chances were one out of three that she would have to go to work. Basically, this research reveals that Korean women increased their independence by seeking employment after their husband's death. American widows often obtain Social Security, which makes working for pay unnecessary.

The gender of the children was important to the economic support of the widow's family. Sons were major contributors to the family income for the older widows. Sixty-four percent of the older widows said that sons were the primary earners of family income, while one in ten reported daughters as main contributors to family income. For the younger widows who listed children, both sons and daughters were named almost equally (17 percent). This finding suggests that the younger widows had unmarried daughters who were contributing family income until they got married. Interestingly, rural widows rarely reported daughters as contributors to the family income.

Our findings do not agree with what Lopata (1979:334–35) found in her study of Chicago widows. Few Chicago widows relied on children financially. Furthermore, about 60 percent of the Chicago widows had more than one source of income, the main source being Social Security. About three out of four widows received regular income from Social Security, either directly or through benefits coming to the children or other dependents in the household. Income from a widow's own job was reported by one-fourth of the Chicago widows, and one-third had income from interest or savings. Other sources besides these were Veterans' Widows Pensions, employee pensions, private insurance, and public assistance or welfare.

It is clear that Korea is far behind in developing social security for widows. Children still are primarily responsible for the support of the older widows. If the widows are younger, the support patterns for them show a trend away from dependence on husband's kinsmen and toward the widows themselves or their children. Moreover, at the present time, four out of five widows do not have enough income to be self-sufficient.

Service support. We asked the respondents what kind of service support they received during the last year, from whom, and how many things they received. Service support was defined as those things people do for each other in daily life, or in solving special problems. These included household repairs, help with housekeeping, child care, sick care, helping make decisions, and legal aid. In terms of service, we could not establish any criteria for need, but only recorded whether or not a widow received any support of this kind and from whom she received it. Over a third of the widows reported that they received some such service supports during the last year. The number of such supports received by the women averaged 1.9 for younger widows and 1.6 for older ones.

Services given to widows most frequently involved sick care—24 percent of the younger and 36 percent of the older widows received some such help. Older women probably needed more sick care. Help with housekeeping, child care, decisions, legal aid, and prayer were reported by less than 4 percent of our respondents. Since most of the widows were living with children, either married or unmarried, they did not count normal housework by other members of the common household as service support. However, the widows did regard sick care by a household member as service support, with children most frequently named as contributors. Other contributors, such as siblings, siblings-in-law, neighbors, and friends were reported less frequently. Our findings here are consistent with what Lopata found. Help given to Chicago widows most frequently was sick care, and the main contributors were children (Lopata, 1979:80).

Social support. Social support consists of invitations to participate in social activities.[3] We asked our respondents if other people had invited them to participate in social activities during the last year and, if so, what kind of social activities, who asked, and how many times. The majority of our respondents were invited to at least one social occasion. However, 38 percent of younger and 30 percent of older widows reported that they did not get any invitation. Almost twice as many Seoul than rural women lacked invitations (34 compared to 18 percent). The mean frequency of supports in a one-year period was 5.5 for younger widows and 6.2 for older widows.

The specific activities reported were: sight-seeing, tours, birthday parties, lunches or dinners, concerts, exhibits, playing cards, and picnics. The most frequent invitation was for birthday parties, and more rural than Seoul widows received such invitations (rural, 84 percent; Seoul, 49 percent). Traditionally, Koreans have recognized aging with pomp and ceremony. Birthdays have been celebrated. The sixtieth birthday invariably has been the inspiration for the biggest party the family and kin can afford. Usually relatives and friends come from far and near. If the family is wealthy, it has to be prepared to lavishly entertain guests from the entire neighborhood. The likely reason for the rural–urban variation in birthday party activities is that urban people are giving up this traditional celebration while rural people still observe it. Not surprisingly, the main participants at these affairs were neighbors. In contrast, the hosts were children, siblings, and friends for urban widows.

Lunch or dinner was the second most frequently mentioned invitation by the respondents. Again, more rural than urban widows received these invitations (rural, 30 percent; Seoul, 14 percent). Traditionally, eating and drinking were an important accompaniment to almost every social occasion. People in the village were constantly being treated by others and reciprocating to the best of their ability. On those occasions when large amounts of special food were prepared, neighbors, friends, and others to whom the household was obligated were likely to be invited. This custom still persists in rural areas. However, in the urban area, these kinds of friendly, informal relations are rarely seen among neighbors.

The sight-seeing tour was the second most frequent social activity for the older widows (25 percent) and lunch or dinner for the younger ones (18 percent). Travel agencies in Seoul have now arranged a special tour called a "filial tour" for older people who want to take trips to visit famous temples, scenic spots, or islands with a group of friends or other older people. It is viewed as an act of filial piety. Going to concerts and exhibits, playing games, and celebrating holidays were rarely reported.

Overall, neighbors were the main source of social support for rural widows (rural, 76 percent; Seoul, 7 percent) and friends for Seoul widows (rural, 11 percent; Seoul, 43 percent). Family and kin were less important in providing social support than they were for economic and service support. The importance of friends to the social support of Seoul widows agrees with what Lopata found in her Chicago study (1978:84).

For Seoul widows, socioeconomic status was most strongly associated with the extent of social support given. There are some good reasons why support is related to the widows' economic status. For example, a telephone is a convenience for making contacts. However, almost half of our Seoul sample did not have one. Also, the main activities the Seoul widows enjoyed were touring, birthday parties, and lunches or dinners, and these involve expenditure either at the initial occasion or when one reciprocates, as is expected.

Emotional supports. The widows were asked what persons were closest to them at the time of the interviews, whom they most enjoyed being with, to whom they told their problems, who comforted them when they were depressed, who made them feel important, to whom did they turn in times of crisis, and who most often made them angry. Obviously, these questions are interrelated and overlap much as real life experiences overlap and merge into each other.

Children were the major source of emotional support and were ranked highest in each category. This finding shows that the mother role is the basis of a Korean woman's psychological security. The second most frequent source of emotional support came from grandchildren. They contributed mostly to feelings of closeness and enjoyment of company and somewhat less to problem-solving and assistance in crises. More older than younger widows said that grandchildren were close to them. Friends were important mainly to the younger widows, one-third of whom reported they told their problems to friends; only one-tenth of the older widows did so. Seoul widows were more likely than rural widows to find friends helpful.

Siblings were reported by over one-fourth of the younger widows as the persons to whom they told problems and to whom they turned in crisis. Siblings-in-law and parents-in-law were not significant for them in times of crisis; in fact, older widows seldom named siblings or siblings-in-law. It is interesting to find that a fourth of the younger rural widows reported that siblings-in-law were the persons they felt closest to, told their problems to, and turned to in a crisis. It is probable that after the husband's death, the widow pushes her role of daughter- and sister-in-law into the background. As the number of nuclear-type families in the national figure indicates, more and more Koreans, especially young urban people, tend to establish nuclear households separate from their parents. Thus, after the husband dies, the family remains a separate household with the woman as head. Some Western sociologists, such as Peter Marris (1958), in his study of London widows, and Helena Lopata (1979), in her study of Chicago widows, have found similar results. They found that the involvement of in-laws in the life of a widow and her children was minimal.

Daughters-in-law were important persons only to the older widows; however, they did not feel they were closest to in-laws. Forty-four percent of elderly widows named daughters-in-law as the person who most frequently made them angry. The data indicate that the relationship between widow and daughter-in-law is fraught with conflict. The mother-in-law/daughter-in-law relationship has traditionally been one of tension and strain. The daughter-in-law came to her husband's home in a subordinate role, with her mother-in-law in a position of absolute authority over her. In fact, one of the mother-in-law's main duties was to train the strange newcomer into the ways of the household so that she in turn could take over its administration. In other words, she had to see that the daughter-in-law became identified with her new family in such a way that its continuity would be maintained in all its traditional details. It was a relationship in which the daughter-in-law owed the husband's mother complete obedience and respect. As the women of the household were seldom apart, the daughter-in-law often feared and hated her mother-in-law, who, in turn, was jealous of the daughter-in-law as a rival for her son's affection.

The feelings of hostility between the two women probably have been overemphasized in the literature. However, this helps to explain the conflict that is likely to ensue between them when the family structure changes; the closer husband/wife relationship characteristic of a nuclear family directly conflicts with the former affectionate mother/son relationship. In the current situation, another factor is that the daughter-in-law now has more education, self-confidence, knowledge, and experience, and thus is much harder for the mother-in-law to control. Daughters-in-law have learned new theories of child care, housekeeping, and personal behavior. They know more about the outside world.

The stress may be aggravated for rural women who break up their housekeeping after the death of their husbands and move into the homes of married sons in urban areas. They lose many functions and are likely to be considered by modern daughters-in-law as meddlesome. This challenges the mother-in-law's previous supreme position as adult adviser and source of knowledge and tends to enhance the friction between the women when they live in the same household. A widow who is dependent on her son for support is under pressure to give up some of her traditional authority. Living in the son's urban household, she no longer has a claim on a joint family estate, and the daughter-in-law is freer to assert her independence — and her husband is likely to side with her rather than with his mother. The daughter-in-law sees her mother-in-law as a guest in the household or as someone who helps her look after the house.

Moreover, the daughter-in-law now retains closer ties with her own family of origin. Her own blood relatives tend to become her advisers and thus compete with the mother-in-law in her traditional position as trainer and consultant. The beleaguered mother-in-law must even share her grandchildren with her daughter-in-law's relations. All of these factors highlight a crucial change that is now going on in the relationship between the two. The older widows have fallen in status and, as a result, are bound to encounter difficulty with their daughters-in-law. It is striking to know that the city of Seoul reported that about 250 runaway grandmothers were under the care of the City Day Care Center each week; of them, 85 percent were widowed mothers-in-law (*Chosun Ilbo*, 1976; *Dongah Ilbo*, 1976). Now many Korean mothers do not want their daughters to marry the eldest son of a widow. The mothers say, "I don't want my daughter to have trouble with a lone mother-in-law." Other persons were not significant as emotional supports for Seoul widows.

Children Involved in Emotional Supports

Our data show that Korean widows are much more strongly attached to their children than to any other person. This is because a woman's role as mother has been more important than her role as wife in the traditional Korean family. Traditionally, a Korean woman could be described as first a dependent upon her father before marriage, then her husband after marriage, and then her son in widowhood. This was a basic sociological fact, not a stereotype. The continuing implications of this fact can be seen when it is realized that the males in those three dominant male roles always were much less dependent upon the woman for the stability of their own personalities. A wife did not find full satisfaction in the conjugal bond because of the traditional restrictions and because of the lack of motivation for the husband to make the emotional commitment. Besides, interaction with other women in the household such as mother-in-law and sister-in-law often was not congenial. In this situation, the woman found a socially accepted and gratifying escape in her role as mother. Therefore, a young wife built her own small circle of security with her children, in particular with her sons.

There are several explanations for this close tie between mother and son. First, the male child insured continuity of the family lineage, and the mother achieved status by bearing a son. The future of the woman's marital security was achieved by having sons. Thus, the woman who had given birth to a son had removed one potential excuse for divorce. Second, formally, the woman had no rights in the property of her husband's family. If her husband died leaving her a widow, then she could expect maintenance, but she would always feel that she was a dependent and not a person who belonged legitimately. It was only the relationship to a male that could give the woman a sense of right. Thus, the son confirmed her status as a member of the family and provided insurance against the possible loss of status due to widowhood. Therefore, widowhood did not alter the woman's dependent status, it just shifted it from husband to son. She could not alienate or sell her share of the property.

Third, within the patrilineal extended family, the mother was the only person who would accept the young son without judging him. The mother was his main confidante. The son told his mother all his troubles, and she acted as an intermediary between him and his father. The possibility that the mother might mean as much to the son as vice versa made this mother/son relationship more important and gratifying to the woman than her relationship to her husband, which could be one-sided. Thus, she used the son's early years to bind him to her by teaching him that he owed his life, security, and position to her.

The direct implication of this excessive importance of a son in the life of the woman possibly devalued the daughter. The mother could be close to her daughter, but she would be closer to her son. The son was her future support. The daughter could not give such support even if she wished, because she herself would remain a dependent.

In Korea, most accounts of socialization, child development, and the mother/child relationship refer implicitly or explicitly only to the development and socialization of the boy, and to the mother/son relationship. There is a striking lack of systematic description about the mother/daughter relationship.

In modernized societies, on the other hand, not only has this mother/son relationship become less intense, but there is considerable evidence that the mother/daughter relationship is stronger and more persistent. Young and Wilmott (1957) described the daily visiting and mutual aid of working-class mothers and daughters in East London. Peter Marris (1958) found in his London study that daughters were most likely to find enjoyment and affection with their mothers, while adult sons saw their relation to their mothers primarily as obligatory and tended to feel less close to their mothers than they once were. Townsend (1967), in his London study of the aged, found that daughters were the chief source of aid to their widowed mothers and that the youngest child often was closer than the eldest son. This is substantiated by Lopata (1979), who found that daughters most often were listed as the source of comfort when the widows felt blue and as being emotionally the closest. Also, the oldest son was least likely to be identified as the closest child. Both Townsend and Lopata gave two reasons for this: (1) in a situation where the household structure is nuclear, adult daughters look to their mothers for advice, for aid in childbirth and child care, for friendship and companionship, and for financial help; (2) sons leave home and become involved in jobs and outside relations, including those of husband and father. Eldest children especially can move away with less compunction because younger siblings are still living with or near their parents. Townsend pointed out that by the time most English women became widows, their eldest children were attaining the status of grandparents; sons and daughters who had reached their fifties often were grandparents themselves. They had their attention divided between aged parents and the oncoming generations.

Here we tentatively can hypothesize that due to the modernization process the traditional preference for and favoritism toward males is becoming weaker in Korean society and this in turn is changing the emotional support system of widows. Daughters are beginning to appear just as important as sons in the emotional support system of widows. We asked our respondents to indicate each child separately in their emotional support system so that we could specify the sex and birth order of the children. Our data reveal that sex and birth order of children are important variables in determining who provides emotional support to the widows.

Regardless of a widow's age, oldest sons predominated as the persons to whom they felt closest, whom they enjoyed most, who comforted them, who made them feel important, to whom they turned in crisis, and who also most often made them angry. However, oldest daughters were listed more frequently than other sons. The data suggest that oldest sons still are most important for the Korean widows but that in the urban area daughters are gaining in importance.

During our interviews the respondents sometimes asserted that the oldest sons were important to them because they were the ones they could count on. It is an obligatory concern that in fact makes it possible for the widows to count on them. Obligation is functional for subjective closeness. However, when the need for help becomes acute, as in the case of a widowed mother, an added strain is put upon the relationship. There is an expected level of support and those who fail to meet these expectations become the targets of the widow's anger —these usually are the oldest sons. Twenty-six percent of older widows named the oldest sons as the person who most frequently made them angry. For younger widows, other sons made them angry as frequently as oldest sons.

Seoul widows found daughters supportive, with almost half of them reporting that daughters were closest. Daughters were most likely to be the persons who comforted them when they were depressed. This was the only emotional support category in which daughters outnumbered sons (younger, 51 percent; older, 42 percent). All of these findings suggest that probably the traditional mother/daughter relationship is changing during the process of modernization. Seoul widows found daughters more supportive than did rural widows.

The mother/daughter relationship in the Korean family has not been as clearly defined as the relationship between mother and son. As the daughter was only a temporary family member, her role was that of a child or young girl. She was an economic liability. The daughter owed complete obedience to her father as head of the family. But as most of her activities were centered in the home, her mother was her chief supervisor and disciplinarian. Her mother also had the responsibility of training her for her future married role. However, she was not the mother's most important responsibility, for the mother's duty lay first of all to her parents-in-law, then to her husband, then to her sons, and finally to her daughters. On the other hand, the mother's close intimate contact with her daughters, their mutual household interests, and the fact that she did not owe them much may have allowed a warm informal relationship to develop between them. The bond of affection remained after the daughter left for her husband's home if there was contact. However, the mother was not expected to have much influence over the daughter after the girl's marriage. The daughter often married into a family from a distant area and afterward had few contacts with her family.

Now daughters who set up a nuclear family after marriage are free from the control of the mother-in-law. They also count less on guidance and help from their mothers-in-law and so are more likely to turn to their own mothers. If the father died at an early age, mother and daughter may have developed a close relationship. Meanwhile, the strain in the mother's relationship with her son and daughter-in-law increased, for she not only lost her power to control him when she moved into his household, but also had to accept a less-important position in his affections. The close mother/daughter tie in the nuclear family may somewhat compensate the widowed mother for the transfer of much of the son's affection from her to his wife. These data suggest that the changing relationship between the mother and daughter may be rivaling that of her relationship to her son. Perhaps it can best be summed up in the words of an older Seoul respondent who was living with her only son:

I am angry with my son. It seems to me that he does not care about me any more. I am also sick quite often because of old age. Whenever I am sick, he just asks me whether I went to a neighborhood drugstore. [In Korea people can buy any medicine without prescription.] He never thought of taking me to a doctor. But when his children and wife are sick, he does. I have had backaches for a long time. I have a daughter who is living in Yongdungp'o. It takes about an hour for me to go to her house by bus. I go to her house often. Once I stayed with her for ten days. My daughter asked me to stay with her until her brother came to take me home. Finally he came and asked me to go home. He felt guilty about having left me there so long.

Here again we can see the strain between the oldest son and the widowed mother. In the three-generational family, one of the common problems of a man is the conflict of loyalties in his mind: on the one hand, loyalty to his mother to whom he owes so much, and, on the other hand, to his wife, who is his consort and who leans upon him for support. The indication of increasing importance of daughters in the emotional support of urban widows probably reflects the failure of some sons to live up to traditional expectations.

Conclusion

It is obvious that in Korean society many cultural myths continue to be sustained regarding the prevalence of traditional welfare and protective functions toward women whose spouses have died. True, the widow's fate is viewed as a particularly severe tragedy, and she elicits sympathy and compassion. But these sentiments are not always translated into protection and support. In modern times, it appears that with the loss of her husband she also loses the protection of the in-laws in her husband's home. When a man dies and leaves behind a wife and young children, the widow has to earn not only her own livelihood, like widows living in single-member households, but must also support her children until the eldest son becomes the chief earning member. It is the mother who is responsible for the care of the young children and getting them married.

This precarious condition is highlighted in Seoul as a result of the increasing integration of family members into the cash economy.

Traditionally, it was uncommon for a woman in the Korean family to accept employment outside the home. Most women were not employed before widowhood. They had to stay home to take care of the children and keep house. This conforms to the traditional norm of restricting women to their domestic functions. The changes in family structure and functions as well as economic pressures apparently have resulted in traditional obligations being discounted. The husband's death eliminates a portion or all of the income. There is no insurance or social security for widows, and those who do not have a source of financial support face severe economic crisis. Basically, this research has found that Korean women have increased their dependence on themselves after their husband's death by seeking employment. In fact, it is probable that widows in the urban areas of rapidly modernizing societies, such as Korea, face even greater ambiguity and more difficult adjustments than those faced by widows in more highly modernized societies.

Most Korean women have been socialized to be passive and dependent. They have been trained to automatically expect support systems to be available in the form of a constantly present family and an unchanging neighborhood. They have been supported economically and emotionally by husbands, sons, and patrilineage. However, society is changing—becoming more urbanized, geographically mobile, socially individualized, and requiring voluntary engagement by members in a complex of available social roles. Women must learn to play more independent roles. This necessitates changes in the structure of male versus female authority. Korean women must be prepared, as individuals, to meet disruptions in their lives as the society changes, as their roles are less ascribed, less predictable, and in some respects, less secure.

5 Women and Widows in Turkey: Support Systems

MARSEL A. HEISEL

Introduction

Among developing nations, and particularly among Muslim nations, Turkey stands out for the scope and thoroughness of the social, cultural, and economic reforms affecting the status of women and the speed with which their emancipation has been pursued. Turkish women have all of the legal rights available to men and have been taking part in the political, economic, and professional life of the country in increasing numbers since the birth of the republic 60 years ago. Of all Muslim countries, Turkey has the highest number of women graduates in all levels of education. In Turkish universities the proportion of women among academic personnel has for many years been far ahead of Europe (Abadan-Unat, 1981:26). Currently in Turkey 20 percent of all practicing lawyers and 15 percent of all practicing physicians are female, an achievement equal to or higher than that of Western countries such as France or the United States (Öncü, 1981:183–84).

Despite this remarkable progress, the majority of Turkish women remain disadvantaged citizens, caught between the divergent, and often contradictory forces of traditional and progressive values. Particularly in rural areas, the emancipation of women has been much slower than predicted in the early days of the Atatürk revolution. Only about a third of them are literate (Timur, 1974), they are financially dependent on their husbands even when they do much of the agricultural work, and they remain under strict surveillance of male relatives, with little opportunity to develop the types of independent behavior often needed to cope in the modern world.

The family has always been the main, if not the only, source of social, personal, and economic support for women. However, since 1950 Turkey has experienced exceptional sociocultural and economic changes that have had a major impact on all levels of society. Rapid population increase has made it difficult for families to subsist on small plots of land, mechanization of agriculture has reduced the need for women to work in the fields, and the expanding highway networks have facilitated rapid urbanization, quadrupling the population of major cities such as Ankara and Istanbul. The rural-to-urban migration, as well as the migration to Europe in the 1960s and early 1970s, has produced complex changes both in the family and in the community, in many cases altering the roles and interrelations between men and women and among generations.

In general, women have been the beneficiaries of rapid social change as it has produced hitherto unavailable opportunities for freedom, status, self-expression, and self-control. For many women, however, progress may also entail the breakdown of the support systems on which they depend for their very existence or expect to depend when future needs arise. Women beyond their formative years, and especially older women and widows, are particularly vulnerable to the many complex problems of development. For example, in a society where a woman's security, beyond her husband, depends on her sons, migration of the sons or even the emancipation of a daughter-in-law can create serious problems for an older woman.

Turkey, a country considered by many a showcase for social development in the last 60 years, offers an excellent background in which to explore the social situation of women and widows as it relates to development. What are the implications of social and economic development on the lives of women? How do changing social conditions affect the support systems and coping capabilities of women such as widows who become marginalized while caught in the process of national change? What are the effects of tradition, legal status, or special circumstances such as migration on the resources available to them? What is the nature of the social and personal resources available to women and widows in urban centers, villages, and rural areas? How has the changing social structure or the changing family situation affected the support system of women whose lives become disorganized upon the death of the spouse? Empirical social science research in Turkey, in spite of its relatively recent origin (Kâğitçibaşi, 1982a), provides many interesting insights. While there appear to be no studies on widows, available research on the social situation of Turkish women in general makes it possible to seek answers to some of these questions and to understand, or at least to speculate on, the position of widows.

Turkey: The Country

Turkey occupies 301,000 square miles, an area about twice the size of California, at the strategic junction of Europe and Asia, directly across from Africa. Most of the land (97 percent) lies in Asia, encompassing the Anatolian peninsula, and 3 percent is in Europe. The population, estimated at 50 million for 1985 (United Nations, 1984), is 98 percent Muslim and speaks Turkish. The modern Turkish republic was proclaimed in 1923, after a war of independence that lasted for four years and tried to salvage an independent Turkey from a dismembered Ottoman Empire after World War I. Some historians see the Ottoman period, which lasted over six centuries (1299–1918) and at its height spread over significant parts of Asia, Europe, and Africa, as a time when the position of Turkish women deteriorated from its early pre-Islamic state (Afetinan, 1962).

The Islamic family laws adopted by the Ottomans greatly limited the rights and freedoms of women: women had no say in choosing their husbands, and a man had the right to polygyny (up to four wives at a time) and to divorce his wife whenever he wished by merely stating that he was divorcing her. A woman received about half as much inheritance as a man, but the property laws granted her power to deal with her own property as she pleased (Afetinan, 1962:28).

The introduction of the harem life, copied from Persia and Byzantium to the Ottoman palace in the fifteenth century, with the ensuing architectural division of houses into harem (women's section) and *selamlik* (men's section), isolated city women from any contact with men except their husbands and a very few close relatives, and confined them to domestic tasks and rearing children (Afetinan, 1962:26–28). They went out clothed in a loose wrap (*çarşaf*) or coat (*ferace*) and had their faces veiled with a *yaşmak*, which left only their eyes uncovered. Women in villages and rural areas, who supplied a great portion of the farm labor, were not as isolated within their sex since they often had to work with men in the fields; they did not cover their faces unless they met a strange man.

The first political and social reforms of the Ottoman Empire in 1883 —the Tanzimat period—had a deep effect on the constrained life of the elite city women who were often privately educated at home to learn Arabic, Persian, and French. These reforms were also the first steps ever taken toward the emancipation of women in a Muslim country. The first girls' schools were opened during this period and a new class of educated women emerged (Afetinan, 1962:37). It is important to note, however, that education was primarily for elite urban women, which deepened the chasm between urban and rural women, a disparity still very much in evidence. The early reforms did not change the Islamic family law and women remained largely subservient to men.

It was the War of Independence, 1918–23, under the leadership of Mustafa Kemal Atatürk, and the unprecedented reforms enacted to propel the country into westernization that radically changed the course of life for Turkish women. As stated by Eren (1963:180), "The successful emergence of the Turkish woman from the seclusion of the harem is, no doubt, one of the greatest achievements of the Atatürk Revolution."

At the basis of Atatürk's reforms was the replacement of the Sheria, the Islamic law, with the Swiss Civil Code. These legal changes, enacted in 1926, greatly improved the position of women by abolishing polygyny and unilateral divorce by men, making it possible for women to sue for divorce and demand alimony, requiring women's consent for marriage, allowing them to marry without parental consent after the age of 18, and giving women equal rights to private property and inheritance. By 1934, women also gained complete political equality with the right to vote for, and be elected to, the national parliament (Eren, 1964). Legally, today's Turkish women have complete equality with men.

Demographic Characteristics

A country with exceptionally high fertility, Turkey's population doubled between 1950 and 1975, going from 20,809,000 to 40,025,000, and has reached 50,000,000 in 1985. In spite of the current decline in fertility, the population is expected to reach 100,000,000 in 2022—an almost eightfold increase in the first century of the republic. Turkey is also experiencing a shift from being a predominantly agrarian nation in 1950 (79 percent rural and 21 percent urban) to an equally rural and urban population in 1985, with a projected dominance of urban population (73 percent urban and 27 percent rural) in the year 2025 (United Nations, 1984).

Even though natural growth is higher in rural areas, the rate of growth is highest in urban centers because of rural-to-urban migration. As a result, squatter settlements called *gecekondu*, which literally means "set-at-night" and for the most part are illegally built shacks, have proliferated in the outskirts of large municipalities. It is estimated that 84 percent of squatter settlements in Turkey are inhabited by migrants from rural areas (Karpat, 1976:2). Among the population of the three major cities, 59 percent of Ankara, 45 percent of Istanbul, and 33 percent of Izmir live in *gecekondu* areas (Kongar, 1976).

Since World War II, up to which time women had a lower life expectancy than men, the decline in mortality has been faster for women. Currently, life expectancy at birth is estimated at 62.8 years for women and 58.3 years for men. This gain has been much greater for women in cities, with considerable improvement in all coastal areas. Life expectancy for women in rural areas lags about three years behind that in cities and is lowest in the central and eastern provinces, where infant mortality in general, and mortality of female infants in particular, remains exceptionally high (Erder, 1981). There is a 10 percent surplus of males in the 0–15 age group (Çillov, 1974), an unusually high number that is probably due to the underenumeration of females before the age of puberty and reflects the low status of girls in the family.

Distribution of the population by marital status consistently shows the number of those widowed and divorced to be rather small. About 10 percent of the female population over 15 years of age is widowed and 1 percent is divorced. (Çillov, 1974; Census of Population, 1975; 1980). This is lower than in the United States, where the proportion of the total female population has remained around 14 percent since 1970, when it reached its peak (Lopata, 1979:35). The situation in Turkey can be attributed to the high incidence of remarriage of those widowed or divorced (Çillov, 1974) and the very low rate of divorce, this latter in spite of the fact that Turkey has one of the most permissive divorce laws in the world, granting complete equality to women and allowing divorce on grounds of incompatibility (Levine, 1982).

In spite of the very low proportion of widows in the population,

both the number and proportion of widowed women sharply increase
after age 50. Even though this increase is partially the result of higher
mortality rates of middle-aged men, it also reflects the decline in remarriage of women once they get beyond their childbearing years. Widowhood among elderly women, as would be expected, is rather high.
Analysis of the distribution of population by age and marital status for
the Turkish Census of 1975 shows 30 percent of the half-million women
60 to 64 years of age, and 50 percent of the 1 million women aged 65
and over, to be widowed (Turkish Census, 1975), proportions not very
different from those in the United States (Lopata, 1979:36).

Family Structure

Typically, the rural Turkish family has been described as a large,
patriarchal, extended family household that is becoming nuclear as a
result of pressures from social change and urbanization. Recent studies,
however, question this assumption, showing that the majority of Turkish
families live in nuclear, not extended, households. In spite of the nuclear
structure of families, however, the relations among kin, particularly in
the sphere of mutual support, appears to resemble that of extended
families.

In 1968 the staff of the Hacettepe Institute of Population Studies
conducted a survey on family structure and population problems in
Turkey, based on a nationwide multistage probability sample of 4,500
households. Cross classification was done by five geographic regions
and community size. Family was defined as a group of related persons
living in a shared dwelling unit—following the definition adopted by
the United Nations—and four types of families were distinguished: (1)
nuclear, consisting of husband, wife, and their unmarried children; (2)
patriarchal extended, consisting of husband, wife, and unmarried children as well as married sons, their wives, and their children; (3) transient extended family, husband, wife, and unmarried children living
together with widowed parent(s) and/or their unmarried siblings; (4)
dissolved family, a household in which one spouse is missing due to
separation, death, or other circumstances (Timur, 1981:59–63).

In an analysis of survey results with regard to family structure, Timur
(1981) found that 60 percent were nuclear, 19 percent patriarchal
extended, 13 percent transient extended, and 8 percent dissolved.
Comparison of family type by place of residence (metropolitan, large
city, city, town, and village) showed 68 percent of metropolitan families

and 55 percent of village families to be nuclear. The patriarchal extended family comprised one-fifth of families in small towns and one-fourth of those in villages with population less than 2,000. In rural areas, nuclear families predominate among farm workers and small farmers, while extended families are more prevalent among those who own at least middle-sized farms and large landowners. Even though a very large proportion of peasants (75 percent) in this survey aspired to live in an extended family, which they considered an indication of prosperity and prestige (Timur, 1981:66), there is no evidence that, within the last century, the proportion of extended-family households in rural Anatolia has been any higher than it is now (Duben, 1982:93).

There is some evidence, however, that the relative proportion of extended and nuclear households is related both to geographic area —being highest in the east—and level of development. Hinderink and Kiray (1970) compared four villages at different levels of development, using criteria such as level of agroeconomic development, relative isolation, farm analysis, and standard of living. In the least-developed village, Oruclu, 41 percent of households had a patrilineally extended family structure, and 55 percent were nuclear. There were no households headed by women, and no single women or men living alone. By comparison, the proportion of extended families was 29 percent in Keçiören, a village in an intermediate stage of development, and 18–13 percent in the two most-developed villages. However, relatively recent emigrants to Yunusoğlu, the most-advanced village, had much tighter extended families than earlier settlers, with complete authority of mother-in-law over daughter-in-law (Hinderink and Kiray, 1970:174).

Surveys in urban areas appear to be confined to *gecekondu* settlements of mostly rural migrants, where the family structure is predominantly nuclear (Karpat, 1976; Kongar, 1976; Şenyapili, 1981). What is important to note in these studies is that the Turkish family, whether rural or urban, appears to be a dynamic entity often in a state of flux, changing from nuclear to extended or transient and then back to nuclear, adapting to the needs of its members and to economic conditions. The young married son usually begins conjugal life in his father's household, then establishes a separate house to which the elderly parents, or a widowed parent, may move at a later date. Moreover, in spite of nuclear-family-type households, members have extended-family-type interactions; they provide material support when needed, help each other in times of crisis and conflict, tend to live in proximity to their kin even when they migrate, and socialize predominantly with them and have a strong sense of family solidarity (Kiray, 1974). In the urban *gecekondus*, friendships formed at work and neighborhood relations appear to be slowly substituting for exclusive reliance on kin (Kongar, 1974). But the "functionally extended family" and the strong kin ties still persist (Kâğitçibaşi, 1982:5), as does another important characteristic of the Turkish family: the status difference between men and women with male dominance and control.

The Status of Women in the Family

In her analysis of women in Turkish society, Coşar (1978:125) notes that "A Turkish woman is branded at birth because she is not born a boy." The birth of a daughter is a disappointment to the family. A woman's status and security in life are still very dependent on her ability to produce sons who will strengthen the family lineage and also take care of parents in their old age. A girl child has no value on either account and is often referred to as "guest" in the house, as she will be taken away by strangers at marriage, when she will join a different family. She will remain much of a stranger and a second-class citizen in that environment also until she has a son and improves her position. In a recent national survey with a representative sample of 2,300 persons, 84 percent of respondents reported that they preferred sons to daughters. Reasons given for wanting a son, in order of frequency, were as follows: financial and practical help while sons were young, help in old age, carrying on the family name (especially important to fathers), companionship and love (especially important to mothers), and religious and social obligations (especially important to fathers), (Kâğitçibaşi, 1982b,c). In the case of widowhood, the most important source of support for a woman would be her grown son since she would be assured of a place in his household until her death. The premium placed on sons reinforces the vicious circle that perpetuates the low status of women from the time they are born.

Girls are socialized from early life into being obedient, dependent, adaptable, and, particularly, sexually modest and "chaste," qualities best achieved by sexual segregation. The extent to which male–female relations are controlled, however, depends to a considerable degree on socioeconomic background and urbanization. Upper-middle-class women in large cities, particularly the unmarrieds in the younger generation, mix quite freely, not only at school and work but also in social situations. In peasant villages and small towns, where the majority of women still live, the rigid social norms applied to women keep them from taking advantage of the Atatürk reforms and confine them predominantly to biological and domestic roles. It is important to understand their situation.

Studies of villages (Sterling, 1965; Magnarella, 1974, 1979; Mansur, 1972) show that girls are virtually segregated from boys before they approach puberty and remain under strict control of male relatives throughout their lives. The sexual segregation, control, and subordination of women needs to be understood in terms of the traditions of Islam, which, in spite of the secular basis of the Turkish constitution, still permeate male–female relationships. In the core of this tradition is the concept of "*namus*," or honor. The honor of a man is dependent on the sexual purity of his women—his mother, sisters, wife, and daughters. He is shamed if they become sexually tainted and even minor sexual suggestions may render a woman impure. Consequently, the behavior and relations of women are delimited by social norms designed to preserve the family honor. Young women are seldom left alone and are married soon after puberty. One of the qualities necessary in a bride is honor—assurance that she has never looked at a strange male since childhood (Sterling, 1965; Magnarella, 1974). She becomes somewhat freer of male control in her later years, when she ceases to be sexually vulnerable (Keddie and Beck, 1978:2).

Most girls in villages are married by the time they are fifteen. When the Family Law was first introduced in 1926, the legal age of marriage was 18 for men and 17 for women, but this was lowered soon after to 17 and 15, respectively, as it became evident that few people complied with the age requirement (White, 1978:55). In the study of four villages by Hinderink and Kiray (1970), the proportion of unmarried women among those aged 15 and above was 15 percent in the least-developed villages and 17 percent in the most-developed one.

Parents arrange most marriages, particularly those of daughters, sometimes without their consent. Timur's (1981) analysis of the 1968 national survey on family and population problems showed that among married women respondents, 78 percent of the marriages had been arranged, 67 percent with their consent and 11 percent without their consent; 13 percent had made their own choice and 9 percent had eloped. In contrast, half of the men had made the decision for themselves. Marriage among relatives is favored, as it strengthens kinship ties, and is rather common, in the order of 30 percent in Turkey as a whole and 36 percent in villages (Fişek, 1984:267).

The reason for the high percentage of elopement is primarily the bride price, which is still a common practice in rural areas. It is valued as a symbol of the girl's chastity and represents compensation to the bride's family for the loss of her labor (Kâğitçibaşi, 1982:7). Poor young men who are unable to pay the bride price, or who have no kin able to give financial assistance, resort to the socially tolerated practice of elopement—or *kiz kaçirma*, "kidnapping of girls" in literal translation —which, as Sterling (1965) pointed out, becomes a cheap way to get a wife. Bride price is by no means confined to the countryside, but the incidence tends to increase as one goes from metropolitan areas to villages. It is estimated to transpire in one-fifth of marriages in metropolitan areas and in two-thirds of village unions (Fişek, 1984).

Among the functions attributed to bride price is providing support for the wife in case of divorce or widowhood. In rural western Turkey, where agriculture is highly mechanized, the bride price has been on the decline (Timur, 1981), but substitutes in the form of gifts of gold coins or ornaments to the bride remain. Mansur (1972) reports that in Bodrum, a modern village on the Aegean Sea, upon marriage a groom provides a house as well as gold pieces and gold bracelets. The gold is a guarantee for the bride against the future and is preferred to money in a bank. Village customs permit women to sell the gold at their own discretion, but an attempt by a husband to sell his wife's gold is a cause for divorce. Most women wear their gold pieces on their person as a necklace, strung around a ribbon.

Civil registration at marriage has been required since 1926 and must precede a religious ceremony. However, in rural areas this has been a far from universal practice. Polygyny, which was never widespread, was also prohibited with the acceptance of the Civil Code but still exists in certain areas. The Turkish Assembly has periodically passed laws to legitimize the children born to unregistered or polygynous unions, pointing to the large numbers who do not comply with legal requirements (Kâğitçibaşi, 1982:6; White, 1978:56). On the other hand, in his study of Susurluk, a highly developed western village, Magnarella notes that 86 percent of his respondents said a civil ceremony should be performed. He was particularly impressed with women's knowledge of the law, and gives as an example a 75-year-old illiterate peasant woman who told him that civil marriage amounted to financial guarantee: "If the husband dies, his wife and children automatically inherit the estate. If he is negligent in his duties, his wife can sue for support. If he ejects his wife, she can get alimony. According to her, no wise woman should marry without it." (Magnarella, 1974:124).

Support Systems of Widows

The family is the main support system of widows in Turkey. However, the economic, service, social, and emotional support systems available to them, which are individually discussed below, are also dependent on factors such as location and social class and are greatly influenced by the continuous social changes that accompany national development.

Economic Supports

There is no doubt that the legal changes and radical social reforms of the 1920s and the technological and agricultural modernization of the 1950s and 1960s have had a major impact on changing the status of women and the economic position of widows in Turkish society. However, even though legal restrictions have been removed, structural inequalities, cultural biases, social limitations, and Islamic traditions have created obstacles to women's progress and still continue to do so. Many Turkish social scientists appear to conclude that the majority of Turkish women are treated as being inferior to men, that major inequalities between men and women still persist, and that the progress of women, particularly of those living in rural areas—whether measured in terms of educational level and labor force participation or status within the family—has been slower than expected or assumed to be (Abadan-Unat, 1981).

The Turkish Civil Code gives a widow a choice of half the estate in trust or one-quarter in full possession if children survive, otherwise both of these rights (Sterling, 1965:123). She is also entitled to a survivor's benefit if her husband was the recipient, or potential recipient, of social security or some similar pension system. Survivor pensions are the same as old-age pensions and are payable to widows of any age (USDHHS, 1983).

A widow loses her benefits upon remarriage but regains them if the marriage ends in divorce. A widow entitled to benefits from more than one husband receives the highest of possible allotments (Ekşioğlu, 1984:55).

The social security system for agricultural workers is of very recent origin, and few rural women qualify for any survivor's benefits. Given the high rate of inflation, the bride price, mentioned earlier, can scarcely be thought of as a source of economic security for a woman who has lost her husband. A young widow is likely to find economic support in remarriage, but for a widow beyond her childbearing years the most important support system is her sons and the commitment of the family to support elderly or widowed parents. The condition of widows with no sons or near kin willing and able to assume responsibility may be rather precarious.

Few widows can rely on their own earnings since participation in the labor force, either before or subsequent to widowhood, is still limited to small select groups of women. This condition is primarily due to major disparities in the educational attainment of women in various segments of the society, depending on factors such as geographic location, level of socioeconomic development, or social class. Although the female literacy rate has increased from 5 percent in 1927 to 48 percent in 1975 (Özbay, 1982), half the women are still illiterate. This tends to be true mostly in underdeveloped villages and among the lower classes. The large gap between male and female educational achievement is now decreasing in urban centers. In fact, women tend to have negative attitudes toward education for members of their gender (Özbay, 1981:175–78).

Studies of women and work in developing societies show that, excluding the unpaid agriculture work on family farms, participation in the labor force increases rather sharply with education (Youssef, 1974), and this applies to Turkey. Labor-force participation for women aged 12 years and over was 1 percent for illiterates, 5 percent for primary school graduates, 12 percent for secondary school graduates, 30 percent for lycée (high school) graduates, 56 percent for graduates from vocational schools, and 70 percent for university graduates (Kazgan, 1981:148–49). Women constitute about 11 percent of the urban labor force (Kazgan 1981:124). The rural-to-urban migration has not greatly changed the picture of employment of women in cities, since few living in *gecekondu* neighborhoods are working for pay. Among factors reinforcing low employment rates are the absence of child-care facilities and the inadequate support of female kin, who are likely to have remained in the villages (Kandiyoti, 1977). Except for the very educated professional women, the majority of workers are single, divorced, or widowed. Women in agricultural labor under the status of "unpaid family member" are deprived of personal earnings, the results of their work accruing to the male head of the family.

In terms of economic situation and future prospects, the gulf between rural and urban women, and between the social classes, is considerable. The consequences of development, such as migration and urbanization, as well as lower fertility and increasing life expectancy, can be expected to alter in the future the level and type of a widow's dependency on her family, as well as the response of family members to a widow's needs. Increasing education would make her more independent in towns and cities.

Service Supports

As in the case of economic support, the family is also the main, if not the only, service provider to the widow. In his study of two villages Sterling (1965) reports that, because of the high death rate, there were a good number of widows and widowers, most of whom remarried. The death rate has considerably declined since the date of his research, but the high remarriage rate of widows seems to persist. Sterling's work merits attention because it is among the very few that offer any information on widows. Moreover, as already indicated, since the status of Turkish women outside metropolitan centers has tended to remain the same, the study provides valuable insights about widows in rural areas.

A table of distribution of 319 households by household composition, comprising a total of about 2,000 persons in the two villages, shows nine households where a widow was living with her children and six households where she was living alone (Sterling, 1965:38). Interestingly, Sterling (1965) calls the family of these widows "fragmentary households," while he treats a widower as if he were a married couple and includes the two families composed of father and his children within the general heading of "simple households." The reason given for this classification also describes succinctly the social status of a widow: "A wifeless man and his children form an autonomous domestic unit in a way that a husbandless woman and her children do not" (Sterling, 1965:36).

Sterling reports that most young widows remarry because life for a woman without a man is difficult and also because they are in much demand as producers of sons. A woman depends on her husband for basic support, and particularly for tilling the fields and defending her.

Upon widowhood, she may remain in her husband's house, under the protection of his father and brothers, or she can return to her own father or brothers, who will arrange for her remarriage. Often, the widow marries within the husband's kin. Most polygynous marriages occur when a man takes in his brother's widow. Such illegal unions are based on the rationale that he would be the best stepfather to her children and also on the fact that he can thus retain his brother's land. Otherwise, she might marry a stranger and he might find a stranger tilling the plot next to his own.

A widow's children may remain with her husband's kin or her own, or they may go with her to her new husband, depending on circumstances. Villagers are aware that according to Muslim law a child belongs to its father's lineage, but they attach little importance to this matter (Sterling, 1965:196–99).

It is much easier for a widow with sons to remarry than it is for a widow with daughters. Sterling mentions one widow who had four daughters and remained single. She declared herself against husbands and independent, but the author expresses doubt that anybody would marry a woman who had failed four times to produce a son. Her father farmed the land as a sharecropper and she relied on him for outside contacts (Sterling, 1965:197).

Grown sons are the biggest asset to a widow. If they are old enough to work, the sons remain together on the land until they and their sisters are all married. In such a situation the widow is unlikely to remarry (Sterling, 1965:41). Older widows are sure of a place in their son's household until death. The old widows living alone in Sterling's villages were all childless, or at least sonless (1965:114). The villagers considered living alone one of the worse fates to befall a woman, making her dependent on the charity of neighbors who have no obligation to help (1965:174).

Not all widows necessarily live with their sons, but they expect to be cared for and supported by them. In areas where it is customary to provide a separate dwelling for a married son, women often continue living in their own home after the death of the husband. Mansur (1972) reports that in Bodrum, while widowers move into the house of their children because they don't know how to manage on their own, few widows do so. They prefer to end their life in their own home. She notes that these elderly widows seem neither lonely nor neglected. Their children and grandchildren live close by and all they have to do, if they need any help, is open the door and ask somebody for assistance.

Judging from the very little information available on the elderly and widows, the social commitment felt by the children appears to be rather strong. Depending on circumstances, the widowed parent is provided with cash, shelter, food, and clothing in a matter-of-fact manner. In one survey, when asked how many people lived in their house, after giving the number, respondents often added, "but I also provide for my mother living in another house" (Hinderink and Kiray, 1970).

Even though the predominant family type is nuclear, living with a son in old age is the ideal norm. When respondents in a national survey were asked if they would like to live with a married son in the future, three fourths of them answered in the affirmative. The proportion of those who said yes varied with the place of residence, ranging from 90 percent in rural areas to 30 percent in the cities of Istanbul, Ankara, and Izmir (Timur, 1981:68). For widows living with married sons, the very important mother–son relation can easily be construed into an opportunity to exercise harsh authority over the daughter-in-law. But the primary authority in the household is sex and not age. Adult men treat their mothers with respect and accept the duty to care for them. But, according to Sterling (1965), it is the son who is superior and who gives orders—even to his mother.

While a widow can count on relatives for economic and service support, there is little to encourage her should she wish to retain independence and self-determination. There are few, if any, social and voluntary organizations to which a woman can turn for help, a condition that makes the plight of widows with no relatives on whom to rely particularly acute.

Voluntary organizations do not flourish in Turkey. An illustration from Mansur's (1972:228) study in Bodrum can be considered typical of their fate: upon being formed, the Women's Association in Bodrum registered some 60 members and the money collected was used for circumcision festivities for eight little boys whose parents were poor. Thereafter, the board did not know what it was supposed to do and the association remained dormant. Mansur (1972:219) also observes that villagers in Bodrum make a sharp distinction between family members and outsiders—*el* in Turkish, a concept denoting all those not included in the family. Close interactions are all within the family and someone considered family is always preferred to an outsider.

The failure of civic groups can perhaps be explained with this twin concept of "family" and "stranger" that permeates the culture. Problems are expected to be dealt with from within the "family." Outside assistance is neither expected nor welcomed and is considered an interference that should be constrained, whether offered or received. Much as this attitude keeps the family bonds strong, it also reinforces women's dependency and inhibits the development of social or personal resources that women, and particularly widows, may need in order to cope with changing life situations. Moreover in Turkey, as in other developing countries, the many social changes experienced in the last two decades—particularly rapid population increase, migration, and urbanization—have greatly stressed the capacity of the family to cope with its many problems, disrupting the security system of such marginalized members as widows.

Social Supports

Sexual segregation is a predominant characteristic at almost all levels of Turkish society. Men and women live in two separate worlds, have separate social networks, live separate social lives. Consequently, the loss of a husband does not necessarily diminish a woman's participation in social activities.

A woman can rely on female companionship and emotional support at times of crisis, and certainly during the illness and death of a spouse. In rural Turkey death is an occasion of much visiting among women, not only immediately after its occurrence but also in subsequent months when religious ceremonies are arranged. As the death of a spouse becomes imminent, close relatives, friends, and the village Imam gather in his room to pray and read from the Koran, waiting for his death. The morning after the person has passed away, the Imam comes to the home of the deceased again to read the whole Koran. For seven nights after the burial, female relatives and friends go to the home of the deceased, where they join his wife and female relatives in prayer. The Imam comes again to the home on the fifty-second night for special prayers. Women gather annually on the night of burial to read the Koran and the Mevlut for the deceased (Magnarella, 1979:53–56). Mevlut meetings, where prayers are spoken and chanted and the story of the birth of the Prophet is read by a woman, are very popular among village and town women (Mansur, 1972). They are often held for the soul of a dead relative, but they are similar to visiting, with sweets and lemonade served after the meeting, providing a social and therapeutic medium for a widow during her mourning. Death, like birth, circumcision, and marriage, is an occasion for women to leave their home and mingle with other women, a practice that offers much comfort to the bereaved.

Women of all ages move in a female network of relatives and neighbors, a network that is an important source of interaction, support, comfort, mutual aid, information, and entertainment. Village studies report that women tend to be gregarious and that they seldom appear to be alone or lonely. In villages, and even in many urban neighborhoods, house doors are always open to other women and children. Daily chores such as fetching water and work in the fields, or domestic activities such as sewing and embroidery, are done in the company of other women.

In small towns, where women have more leisure time and social stratification is more rigid, formal visiting days provide a framework of contact among women of different ages, marital status, or social class (Aswad, 1974; Benedict, 1974). Even well-educated urban women share social activities with husbands in the evenings and on weekends main-tain a network of female social relations, usually relatives, neighbors, or former classmates, with whom they spend much of their free time (Kandiyoti, 1981, 1982). Thus, most social interactions of women are not lost with widowhood; in fact, they may even be strengthened after the death of the husband, when more time is available for female friends.

Emotional Supports

Marriage in the rural context is a social union characterized by divi-sion of labor, the segregation of the sexes, the male's superiority, and the lower status of the female partner. This union does not encompass the notion of romantic love or companionship between husband and wife. Women are submissive, work in the fields, look after the house and children, and associate with other women. They are seldom allowed to leave the village, unless they are visiting their relatives. Men, on the other hand, are free to come and go as they please. They do the heavy labor, such as tilling the fields, carry out all official interactions with the outside world, and spend their leisure time in the company of other men. They command authority and make all important deci-sions for the family.

Based on this segregated conjugal role relationship and the two separate extrafamilial social networks in which husband and wife operate, Olson (1982) developed the concept of "duofocal family structure" to describe the Turkish family. In a "duofocal" context, instead of a single center of intrafamily relationships there are two foci, with the husband and wife each being the focus of his or her own separate and unisex network. This separation provides women with a social sphere, albeit a narrow one, in which they can escape from male dominance and develop psychological independence from men.

A duofocal society obliterates many of the factors that produced loneliness and desolation in the Chicago-area widows (Lopata, 1979), as a husband's death does not disrupt a woman's social network of female friends. However, the advantages of such a social structure on the affective sphere is counteracted by the limits imposed by it on a widow's behavior and her opportunities to develop personal and economic resources — resources extremely important to the emotional well-being of a widow in a changing society.

The value of social segregation has been romanticized by some scholars to the point of claiming that it provides a kind of freedom and emancipation for women unequaled in the Western world (Fallers and Fallers, 1976; Olson, 1982). Such interpretations overlook the fact that sexual segregation also acts to keep women from taking full advantage of opportunities for personal development and perpetuates the unequal status and subordinate position of women.

The situation of widows epitomizes the encounter of two contradictory forces operating in a sexually segregated society, accentuating both the positive and negative consequences of a duofocal family structure. The strong affiliation with a female network, beside providing the widow with emotional support, promotes psychological independence from men and from the memory of the deceased husband. Thus it facilitates a widow's speedy reorganization of her life. The subordinate position of women, however, drastically reduces her options for a socially independent life; her very survival depends on her bonds with a male who will support and protect her, whether it is a new husband, grown son, or her own father or brother.

Since women do not depend on their husbands for a social life and have close ties with other women, a widow can rely upon virtual continuation of companionship and social networks after the death of her spouse. Upon widowhood, Turkish women are likely to experience immense warmth, sympathy, and support from their female kin, friends, and neighbors. On the other hand, particularly in small towns and villages, the consequences of social limits imposed on women from childhood—low status, low education, restricted mobility, dependency, and subordination to men—all converge to make it very difficult for a widow to continue her life without the support and protection of a husband or a male relative. The risks of such dependency for widows can best be understood in light of socioeconomic development and changing family relations in Turkey.

Social and Economic Development: Impact on Women and Widows

In the last 20 years or so, components of development—such as factories built in towns, rural-to-urban migration, and migration abroad—have greatly influenced the life of Turkish families and Turkish women. As a result, the number of nuclear families has increased, employment opportunities for women have spread even to small towns, and family relations have changed. Many women, particularly those in the younger generation, tend to welcome the change, but others have to struggle with social situations for which they have no preparation. Still others, particularly the elderly and widows, are concerned about being left alone and with no support.

Change in Traditional Family Relations

Kiray (1976a) reports that in Ereğli, a small coastal town on the Black Sea, the increasing number of nuclear families has helped to bring husband and wife together. Particularly among the younger generation, with higher income, there is a lessening of sex segregation, increased companionship between men and women, and emerging patterns of social interaction such as husband and wife going to the movies or visiting together. This development has brought a concurrent change in the relationship between a grown son and his parents, with major consequence on the support system of the elderly and widows.

When the son moves out of the household to start an autonomous family and also becomes financially independent, there is an erosion of the authority relation traditionally expected to exist between father and son. In the typical case, the independence of the son from the father's authority is achieved through the mother, who mediates between them as conflicts of authority arise. She negotiates the son's freedom in a way that allows the father to pretend he still has authority over the son, and in doing so strengthens her bonds with her son, on whom she has lavished love and attention since his birth—and on whom her ultimate security depends.

However, as the son rejects the father's authority he also becomes free to accept new values, such as siding with his wife rather than with his mother when conflicts arise between the two. As the son loosens his family ties, parents often fear that they can no longer rely on him in their old age. As Kiray (1976a:266) reports, "The intense insecurity and fear of being left alone in old age, and having to depend on strangers, can be strongly felt in Ereğli. Society has not yet provided any new relationships or institutions which would obviate this insecurity." Nevertheless, one form of adaptation, of particular interest to widows, has already emerged: a change from reliance on sons toward reliance on daughters in old age. While in more isolated parts of Turkey it is still disgraceful for parents to live with their daughter and son-in-law, in Ereğli, at the time of the study, such an arrangement existed in about 8 percent of the nuclear families and half of those were widows living with their daughters (Kiray, 1976a:266).

The change in social conditions is even more apparent in towns with rapid urbanization. An example reported by Magnarella (1974) is Susurluk in northwest Anatolia. Susurluk was a peasant village of about 4,000 persons until a sugar refinery was built there in 1955, and the population tripled by 1960. Young men soon found themselves with more education, more skills, and more capacity to earn money than their fathers, which greatly reduced the domination of the patriarch. The change also increased the opportunities of women for employment and gave them more freedom of movement. Women started to shop in the market on their own, and many were taken by their husbands to the movies or the town park. Wives became partners in family decisions. In a survey with 127 married men in town, about one-third said they always consulted their wives in important family decisions while only 15 percent said that they never did so. Nuclear families and separate households became the rule—those remaining in extended households were mostly poor families who could not afford separate households or kins who were at the time jointly engaged in family business. In spite of these changes, both emotional and economic ties with older kin continued to be important.

Family Change in Metropolitan Areas

The most change in family relations and support systems has occurred in metropolitan areas, especially in places affected by migration. Families in metropolitan areas are mostly nuclear and small. The large urban house, which in the past accommodated large families with widowed mother or father and even other widowed relatives, has virtually disappeared. Urban households have changed to the extent that it is even possible to encounter a group of working single men living together, or even men or women who chose to live alone (Kiray, 1984:71).

Transitions in the urban family have not changed much the roles of men—they are still the primary earners and control family finances —but they have added new roles for women. Many women work, and many have taken over functions previously performed by husbands, such as children's school and bureaucratic matters, without any reduction in their domestic duties or substantial gain in their social status. The often-heard complaint of metropolitan women is that they still lack equality with men (Kiray, 1984:73).

Migrant women to the city appear to retain the inferior position they held in the village. Karpat (1976) reports that when questioned in depth, women in the *gecekondus* showed resentment against the low status assigned them, and many welcomed the interview as an opportunity to express their discontent. Nevertheless, their responses also revealed important changes regarding themselves and their family relations. A frequent reason given by women for migrating from the village was the desire to get away from their mother-in-law's interference in family life. When asked "Who should choose your husband?" 47 percent of the single women interviewed said only herself; only 14 percent would accept a husband chosen unilaterally by the parents. The majority of the women in the *gecekondu* are very satisfied with life in the city (Karpat, 1976; Kongar, 1976): they are happy to have a chance to work, they like the easier life and greater choice of food and clothing. They maintain some contact with the rural communities they left but hardly anyone wants to go back. Even children are rarely sent back to their grandparents, and in those rare cases the stay is very short (Kiray, 1976b:219).

Just as there are few older widows living with their married children in the *gecekondus*, it is also difficult to imagine a *gecekondu* widow going back to the restraints of her village to be supported by male relatives. There are no studies to date on the condition and support systems of either *gecekondu* widows or on the widowed parents rural-to-urban migrants leave behind.

External Migration and Family Change

Migration abroad presents an even more complex situation for families, having profound effect both on individuals who migrate and on those who remain behind.

Migration from Turkey to Westen European countries, mostly to the Federal Republic of Germany, started in 1960 and reached its height around 1975. Migration of workers abroad was not a temporary affair to earn cash, but the result of basic changes, particularly rapid increase of population, that made it almost impossible for peasant families with little land to subsist through agriculture. Abadan-Unat (1976) reports that while in the beginning the Turkish migrant population was almost entirely composed of men, the proportion of women grew substantially over the years to make up almost one-fourth of all Turkish workers in 1973. In the beginning of 1974 there were 615,827 Turkish men and 135,575 women working in West Germany. In 1972, 82 percent of the men were married, about half of whom were living with their wives. Of the women, only 22 percent were married, and 88 percent of those were accompanied by their husbands. Turkish couples in Germany tended to be jointly employed (Abadan-Unat, 1976:6–10).

What sets the immigrant family apart is that the various members of the nuclear family are often dispersed and there is continuous change in the composition of the family. Wives from the village join their husbands abroad, sometimes get a job there, and may remain for a year or two, leaving some of the children behind and taking some of them along, depending on circumstances (Kiray, 1976b). Kiray gives as an example the case of a woman who lived in Istanbul with her husband and mother-in-law. Both husband and wife were originally from the village but had already cut all their ties with it. The wife obtained a job in Cologne first and was able to procure the necessary permission for her husband to join her. The mother remained in Istanbul. Within the year they had a boy and asked the mother to come and look after the child. Subsequently, the mother refused to stay in Germany and returned home. The child was put in an institution in Cologne, joining the parents during weekends. This did not seem to work very well, and in the fourth year the boy was left with an elderly couple in Istanbul, who kept him for a fee while the parents still worked in Germany (Kiray, 1976b:218).

This may be an extreme example, but it illustrates how external labor migration, more than other aspects of social and economic development, breaks down the reciprocal support system between generations, and specifically between a widowed older parent and her grown children. It is not only sons or daughters who are not available for the care of their elders; older parents or widowed relatives, who traditionally helped with the care of young grandchildren, are not as willing or able to do so in foreign lands or in the absence of parents.

Together with the radical changes in the family, external migration has also brought many new roles and responsibilities for women. Turkish migrant women have not only adjusted well to their new roles and the demands put on them, but in the process of fulfilling those roles they have also considerably improved their status in the family. The wife of a migrant family occupies a crucial place; it is she who holds the nuclear family as a unit, and "home" is where she resides and keeps the family belongings. Those who return to the village while the husband is still abroad tend not to go to the extended family, but rather set their own home; financially, this is made possible with remittances sent by the husband. Thus, from being a subservient person dependent on husband and kin, many women have become the independent decision makers of a nuclear family. They are left on their own resources to deal with the day-to-day problems of the family; they have responsibility for the management of cash income sent from abroad; they have to deal with secondary institutions such as banks and post office; and, they have to make decisions concerning the work to be done on the land owned. In addition, they are the authority figure for the children. All this has changed their position vis-à-vis other family members, including husband and mother-in-law, and has brought them status and sophistication (Kiray, 1976b).

Abadan-Unat (1974) notes that among Turkish migrant workers the social adjustment process is faster for women than for men. She attributes this to the eagerness of women to benefit from the economic and social emancipation and the greater ease with which they accept innovations. Her studies of migrant workers in West Germany showed that women were much more likely to consider friendship between men and women possible and much more likely to admire the equality between the spouses and the relaxed behavior in leisure time of German families.

Yenisey (1976) provides information on changes in female migrants on their return home—e.g., they resent the lack of freedom in dress and conduct in rural Turkey and they are annoyed at the social control and gossip. While there was much cooperation between husband

and wife when they were both working abroad, women find their men much less supportive upon their return. For many it is difficult to return to the village life-style, and the family tends to relocate in a large city.

Migration abroad appears to have achieved for the independence, status, and self-sufficiency of village women more than what legal reforms were able to accomplish. Nevertheless, it is important to recognize that this change could not have occurred without the basic legal reforms that women already possessed. Their emancipation, however, may cause an impairment in the support system of some widows.

Conclusion

Even though the nuclear family predominates in Turkey, extended-family relations are extremely important in both rural and urban areas and among all social classes. In general, the family constitutes the basis of economic, service, social, and emotional support systems for widows, and a widow has a place for life in the household of a grown son. However, mobility and migration are weakening these family ties.

The life situation of widows, like the life-style and status of other Turkish women, can be expected to differ considerably depending on social class, education, geographic area, and size of the town where she lives. In a society where the social situation of women is as divergent as it is in Turkey—where almost a third of the physicians in metropolitan centers are women while half the women in villages are illiterate—these variables are particularly salient.

Widows in the most advantageous position are probably the elite metropolitan, well-educated women who have been able to take full advantage of the legal and social reforms that grant women full equality with men. In terms of economic resources and possibilities for controlling their own lives, their situation would be rather similar to the Chicago widows. They would also have the additional advantage, however, of close family bonds and continuous friendship ties with other women to provide them with emotional support, sympathy, and assistance.

A systematic comparison of Turkish widows with those in a developed country, such as the well-researched Chicago-area widows (Lopata, 1979), would not appear to be very meaningful because of lack of comparable data and because of the fundamental difference in the two support systems. While many of the Chicago-area widows maintained themselves on social security benefits, supplemented by paid employment, few widows in Turkey, except the well-educated, upper-class metropolitan women, possess these economic resources. A more useful basis for analysis might be found within the premise of social and economic development of the country and a widow's life situation.

In less-developed parts of Turkey, as in other developing countries, the main source of economic security for a widow is still a new husband, if she is young, or her children, if they are grown and male. However, as an area develops and women have access to formal support systems and opportunities for work and for financial independence, it seems plausible to expect a decline in reliance on children as the main source of security in widowhood. There is some support for this hypothesis in a cross-national study undertaken primarily to study the relation between the value of children for parents and fertility behavior of couples (Kâğitçibaşi, 1982b,c). One aspect of the study, the old-age security value of children, could be applicable to widows.

Investigation of the value of children across ten countries—eight developing countries, including Turkey, and two developed countries, including the United States—shows that the perceived old-age security value of children decreases with socioeconomic development. Based upon nationally representative samples of married women under 40 years of age, 8 percent of the American respondents gave "old-age security" as a reason for having children, while the comparable proportion was 77 percent for Turkey, 50 percent for Korea and Singapore (which are more developed than Turkey), and 95 percent for Java and Indonesia (countries less developed than Turkey). Within Turkey, couples in rural and less-developed areas are much more likely than their urban counterparts to ascribe old-age security value to their children; this value progressively decreases as one proceeds from underdeveloped toward developed areas. "Security in old age" was mentioned as a reason for having children by all respondents in the least-developed areas, by 73 percent of those who lived in somewhat-developed areas, by 61 percent of those in developed areas, and by only 40 percent of those in metropolitan centers (Kâğitçibaşi, 1982c). The results of this study imply that an increasing proportion of widows in the future will expect to rely on resources other than their children for economic support.

Conditions of development that in the last three decades have caused significant social and economic changes in the country—namely, urbanization and migration—are also changing family relations and the position of women in the family and in society. How much of an effect such social changes will have on the life of widows, and whether this effect will be generally positive or negative, will probably depend on the cohort to which the widow belongs. Younger village women who are taking part in this social development are gaining independence and self-assurance, and in the process life and work experience as well. If widowed, they will be able to rely on their own labor and social security for support and act as head of their own family, taking control of their own destiny if they wish to do so. However, these same conditions that foster the true emancipation of women in their younger or middle years may at the same time be the source of a harsh predicament for older women.

It is the generation of older widows, caught in the initial phase of development, that is most vulnerable to the exigencies of social change. This is a generation with little or no education, little status except what is gained through motherhood, and has expected throughout life to be fully supported and cared for by an accommodating son and daughter-in-law (or in some cases a daughter) in old age. Development has not been part of the older generation's culture; migration of the young, women joining the labor force or striving for their rights —particularly younger women reaching for companionship and equality with their husbands in a nuclear family—are a new phenomena. Having no resources for old age except what is vested in the relationship with their sons, these older women would be rightfully apprehensive of their children's nuclear household in a distant geographic area, afraid of being left alone and destitute at the mercy of strangers in their old age. Much as the Turkish family shows every sign of continuing its responsibility to older parents, these concerns appear realistic. Moreover, there may be major discrepancies in what the two generations perceive as being the appropriate care and support of a widowed parent. Succeeding cohorts of widows, those now in their middle years or younger, will be better equipped to cope with their life situation because they will have actively participated in some of the social changes, and they will be able to benefit from policies developed to redress the inequities of old age in a traditional society. In Turkey, as in other developing countries, many elderly widows are caught in the middle of social development, with few resources that will enable them to cope with the demands of a changing society. There is need for policies and support systems that will alleviate their hardship without hindering the small advance in status the younger women are slowly beginning to achieve.

6 The Widowed in Iran

JACQUILINE RUDOLPH TOUBA

In many non-Western societies that are in the process of rapid social development but still adhere to many traditions, status passages, especially in family roles, are marked with complex rituals. The ending of a marital status and role relationships due to the death of a spouse, especially a husband, is considered a major event and is surrounded by numerous family and community ceremonies. In Middle-Eastern societies, where the extended family is still firmly intact and women are much younger than men at marriage, the complexity of social supports is organized to insure the smooth transition of a wife into widowhood.

Widowhood in Iran

One Middle-Eastern society that has been undergoing major societal eruptions, and thus expanding the already large number of widows, is Iran. Iran is at the crossroads between the Middle East and the rest of Asia and identifies with both areas. It is located south of the USSR, east of Turkey and Iraq, west of Pakistan and Afghanistan, and north of Saudi Arabia across the Persian Gulf. Iran was a constitutional monarchy ruled by the Pahlevi dynasty until 1979, at which time the regime changed and the Islamic Republic of Iran was established under the rule of the Ayotollah Khomeini. Following two years of internal turmoil, the country was invaded by Iraq in September 1980, beginning a war originally unprovoked by Iran but that was later utilized by the rulers, who consequently rejected Iraqi peace proposals. Even before the revolution and the war, the proportion of widows in the population was extremely high, due primarily to the early age of marriage for women. Married women in Iran have, traditionally, been destined to widowhood for almost a third of their lives.

From the 1976 Iranian census it is clear that a major proportion of surviving women 45 years and older were widowed, and that the proportion was higher in urban than in rural areas. For example, in the age group 45–54, 18 percent of the urban and 15.4 percent of the rural females were widowed. The proportions increased with age, to 40 percent of urban and 37 percent of rural females in the age group 55–64, and to 66.6 percent in urban and 60 percent in rural areas for females past the age 65 (Statistical Center of Iran, 1976: Table 7). The overall sex ratio for widowers to widows was 17, or 17 widowers for every 100 widows.

As a result of the turn of political events, there has undoubtedly been a dramatic increase in the number of widows in the younger age groups. In addition, there are also increasing problems for older widows because so many of the male youth of the country died during counterrevolutionary activities or at war, thus severely cutting into the traditional support systems for widows, the aged, and the sick.

Rites de Passage

Specific rituals mark the passage from the status of wife to that of widow. At the death of a spouse, the widow and all her family are immediately expected to wear black as a symbol of mourning. All arrangements for the funeral are made by the male members of the immediate and extended families. The widow is comforted by the female members of her family. Often her immediate family will go to her home and take over all the household responsibilities—she is expected to be so emotionally overwhelmed that she will be unable to cope with the events. The funeral will follow the death as soon as possible: the same day or, at the latest, the next day, since embalming is not practiced. At the cemetery there may be a separate area in which the women can gather and wail until the burial ceremonies are completed.

The mourning rituals, where condolences may be paid by close friends and family, take place after the funeral and in the home of the deceased. The widow and her immediate family are expected to receive persons paying their condolences for a number of days. All who visit the home of the deceased are also expected to wear black clothing. At specific intervals, a religious man (mullah) may chant from the Koran, and wailing among the women will be loud and continuous. In most cases the men and women are seated in different rooms; tea is served when religious chanting does not occur. There will also be a specific ceremony held at a mosque for those who are not close enough to the family to pay their respects at the home. At this ceremony in the mosque, women and men sit in separate rooms and a sermon is given by a mullah. This ceremony, called *khatmeh*, is announced in the newspaper if it takes place at a specified time in a large city.

The ceremonies in the home continue all day for seven days. The widow is expected to receive condolences for the first week following the death. On the seventh day the widow, the immediate family, and close friends visit the grave of the deceased, where another ceremony is performed. Between the seventh and fortieth day, the widow and her immediate family are expected to repay the visits of all who paid their condolences at her home, an activity that keeps them busy during that period.

The widow continues to wear black, as does her family, at least for forty days; usually the immediate family continues to do so for one year. In some cases, the widow wears black until the family decides that she may take it off. At that time, another member of the family will bring a new piece of clothing of another color and encourage her to take off her black. Those who receive the widow are also expected, out of respect, to wear black, but only for the time of the visit. In addition to wearing black, the widow should refrain from makeup and cutting or dyeing her hair for at least 40 days and often for one year. She is expected to withdraw from social or recreational activities for the time agreed by her family or her community.

All of these activities are outward expressions of reverence toward the deceased and of proving the widow's grief to the community. She is expected to have periodic religious ceremonies said in her home for her friends and family to revere the deceased. She should also make periodic visits to the grave site, where appropriate ceremonies take place; the family will stay with the widow for that day and perhaps longer.

Legally, the widow must refrain from remarrying for a specific time period, called *eddeh*, which lasts four months and ten days, unless she is pregnant, in which case it is until after the birth of the child (Civil Code of Iran, Section 1154). Traditionally she is expected not to remarry and, in fact, would have little opportunity to do so unless the specific local community defined it as an economic necessity. During the mourning period, the new status of the widow is firmly implanted in her mind. After the 40 days she begins to experience some of the changes that the death of her husband means for her.

Role Changes in Widowhood

Traditionally, married women in Iran have been dependent on their husbands—legally, economically, socially, and psychologically. Until the 1960s, a husband could divorce his wife any time he wished, and only he could initiate divorce, except for very restricted and specific reasons. Even though changes were written into the Family Laws of Iran, difficulties remained for the woman in initiating divorce since it carried such negative social stigma (Nassehy and Touba, 1980). Thus, a woman whose marriage was arranged by her family had no alternative but to accommodate herself to the role defined for her by tradition and by her husband's interpretation of that role. However, since she had been socialized to accept her position, dependence on the husband and yielding to his direction was considered normal.

While obtaining a divorce has been relatively easy for men, a number of things work against its occurrence. Islamic law and tradition apply pressure on a husband to treat his wife fairly and with compassion. At the same time, the extended family also applies pressure, since difficulties affect the whole family. This involvement of the family stems from the fact that marriages are arranged by the parents or other family members to strengthen and expand extended-family ties. First-cousin marriages have been considered a means of accomplishing this and a way of keeping wealth and power within the kinship group. It has been practiced for generations and has been considered the rule rather than the exception. Romantic love has never been a part of mate selection, for it has always been the extended-family unit that has been given consideration.

Traditionally, the woman has been expected to begin the role of mother and housekeeper early in life, a role further strengthened with the establishment of the Islamic Republic. In the past, girls were married at puberty; there was no restriction on the minimum age for marriage until 1935, when the minimum age was set at 15. However, even then it was possible for a girl to be married at 13 with parental consent and the agreement of the court. In reality, in rural areas a girl might be pledged at a much earlier age, with the marriage ceremonies waiting until she reached the official age. Although 15 is considered to be an ideal age for marriage by many, there are women who marry later, especially those in urban areas who are educated (Maroufi, 1968).

When a girl marries at such a young age, she usually has no opportunity to develop a sense of independence. Since her husband was most likely much older than she, the pattern of dependence would be established from the beginning. Managerial and decision-making roles, as well as contact with the larger community, are left to the husband. Women have had little or no experience in dealing with complex organizations, nor have they been aware of larger events outside their social community. Of course, in the latter half of the twentieth century, the situation changed for a small proportion of urban women who were able to gain education at the elementary level or above. However, this is still likely to be true only for those 35 or younger. In rural areas, illiteracy is still high among women aged over 25 years, which further isolates them from the larger community because of their lack of knowledge of the national language.[1] Nevertheless, rural women, who make an economic contribution through weaving or participating in agriculture, may have more say in daily decisions than their urban counterparts, although the husband is still in command of family affairs and important decisions (Touba, 1974, 1975).

With the death of a spouse, a woman must suddenly deal with a society in which she has little or no experience. In the case of Iran, she will most probably continue to be dependent on males, those in her own immediate family if they are available. This almost certainly happens during the 40-day period following the death of the spouse. The woman's own father and brothers will make the immediate decisions if they live nearby. When these relatives are not present, an uncle may be substituted. If sons are of age, they will help make decisions along with the older male relatives.

Economic Aspects of Widowhood

While a woman is married she enjoys the economic and social status of her husband. However, after his death her status changes drastically, not only because of a loss of income from the breadwinner, and her link to complex organizations in the larger society, but also because of the laws of inheritance.

Islam formally defines the proportions of inheritance that should be given to various members of the family. Originally, it was intended that all members should be cared for and that one person could not decide to disinherit his family if he so chose. The children were to be given first priority, and the sons would receive more than the daughters since they would support their own families and perhaps other relatives. Parents, siblings, and other relatives receive a part of the estate, and the widow receives a comparatively small share of the total estate, should there be one. The Family Law and Civil Code of Iran is based directly on the laws of Islam concerning inheritance and are defined as follows by Nagavi (1971):

> Section 913. In all the cases mentioned in this division each of the spouses who survives the deceased spouse shall receive his/her prescribed share, which shall be: One half of the whole estate in case of the husband, one-fourth in case of the wife, provided that the deceased has left no children or children's children; one-fourth of the estate in case of the husband, and one-eighth in case of the wife, where the deceased has left a child or children or children's children; the residue shall be divided among the other heirs according to the provisions of the preceding sections.

> Section 906. If the deceased has left no children, or children's children to whatever degree removed, each of the parents when surviving alone, shall inherit the entire estate (of the deceased). In case, however, both the parents of the deceased have survived him/her, the mother shall receive one-third and the father two-thirds (of the estate). If there is a relative along with the mother (partially) excluding her from inheritance, she shall receive one-sixth of the estate, and the rest shall go to the father.

> Section 907. If the deceased is not survived by any of the parents, but has left one or more children, the estate shall be divided in the following manner: if the child is the only child left by the deceased, whether a daughter or a son, the whole estate shall go to him/her; if there are several children but all of them are sons or daughters, the whole estate shall be divided equally among them; if there are several children, but some of them are sons and other daughters, each son shall receive twice as much as a daughter.

Almost every possibility is spelled out as to who shall receive what portion of the estate, whether heirs are of the first category—husband, wife, children, parents, or children's children—the second category —grandparents, siblings and their children—or of the third category —aunts and uncles.

In case there is more than one wife, since Islam allows up to four under certain conditions, it is stipulated in Section 942 that one-fourth or one-eighth of the estate of the deceased, which is the share of a wife, shall be divided equally among them.

It is also important to note that a wife can only inherit certain properties, and then only the value. For example:

> Section 946. A husband shall inherit from all the property of the deceased wife, but a wife shall inherit only from the following properties of the deceased husband: 1. movable property of any kind or description, 2. buildings and trees.

> Section 947. A wife shall inherit from the value of the buildings and trees (in the estate of the deceased) but not from the build-ings and trees themselves.

This means that a wife can only receive her share of the property after it has been sold; she has no claim until then.

Because of the inheritance laws, after the death of a woman's spouse, she owns only a very small proportion of the home in which she lives and any other property. Thus, while a wife may feel that she is the ruler of the internal affairs of her home, after widowhood legally she is not since her children and other relatives actually own the greater part of the estate. In addition, the length of time it takes to settle an estate may mean that the widow has no economic means of her own on which to survive. In that case, she becomes completely dependent on her adult children or kinship group. Since she only inherits the value of the home in which she lives, she must wait until it is sold before she can receive her share.

Recently, the government of Iran ruled that all members of the imme-diate family must be present in the country to settle an estate. Thus, if one member left the country after the revolution, those remaining cannot settle the estate and the widow cannot receive her share. Similarly, because the government has put restrictions on the sale of property and severely restricted the market for property, the widow may still not be able to receive her share of an estate even when all members necessary are present in the country. Those women who may have been economically quite well-off could become practically penniless as widows unless they have an income and wealth of their own.

Pensions have been available to a small proportion of the population —e.g., when the breadwinner of the family was a government employee. If a woman were to be widowed, she could receive her husband's full pension if there were no underaged children or elderly parents, unless she remarried; in that case, she shared the pension with the children and parents of the deceased. In addition, a widow who did not remarry could receive part or all of her father's pension after his death depending on the other surviving relatives. This sounds like a major support, but we must point out that only a very small proportion of the population have been government employees. Furthermore, after the revolution, the pensions of many were cut off if the husband had had any political connection to the previous regime. Nevertheless, the pension system has continued; the recipients are just a different group. In addition, the families of men killed in the war against Iraq, in fighting against those opposing the present regime, or in the fight for the Islamic Republic, are also receiving some sort of government remuneration, even if the deceased were not a breadwinner.

Traditional Support Systems

Traditionally, there have been a number of support systems, both formal and informal, that came to the aid of the widow. Formal systems have included religious and civil law, and the informal systems have rested with the kinship group—*taiyefeh*, or *khandan*, as it is called in the cities (Behnam, 1978), and the family of procreation.

Religious Law

For centuries, support for the widow in Iran was regulated through the religious and normative laws of the society. The institution of polygyny in Islam was designed to provide support for a widow and her children. At the time of the establishment of this institution, wars were being fought and men killed in large numbers, leaving many widows and children without support. Polygyny was a method of solving the problem, but only if all wives could be cared for equally.

While polygyny was practiced for other reasons—such as economic necessity, especially in some tribal areas—it is important to recognize that the institution was originally intended to provide a system of support for the widow. However, after warfare as a way of life subsided, polygyny remained even though it no longer fulfilled the function for which it was originally intended. The support shifted to the *taiyefeh* or *khandan*.

Civil Law

Legally—that is, according to the Civil Code of Iran—the husband's family is officially designated to be a part of the widow's support system, even if it only concerns the children. For example, in Section 1199 of the Iranian Civil Code, it is stated that,

> After the death of the father or in case of his inability to maintain the children, the liability for maintenance shall devolve upon the paternal grandfather in the order of closeness of their degree. . . . In case the paternal grandparents are not alive or are not able to accept the maintenance, the responsibility goes to the widow.

But,

> If the mother of the children is deceased or unable to maintain the children, the liability shall devolve on the maternal grandfathers and grandmothers and paternal grandfathers and paternal grandmothers who are (otherwise) entitled to maintenance by the children in the order of closeness of their relationship.

However, despite the stipulation of responsibility of extended family members for the support of the children of the deceased, no direct provision is mentioned for the support of the widow. In some cases, however, the widow benefits, as when the husband's family chooses to support the household of the deceased.

Unfortunately, no statistics are available to allow a definite statement as to the degree to which the law has been followed or evaded. If the paternal grandparents do not accept their legal responsibility, it is unlikely that an illiterate widow would even know that such a law existed, let alone how to bring the case to court.

While another law establishes the responsibility of a parent for one's own children, this refers to children under age. However, Section 1200 of the Civil Code does legally establish the liability of children for the maintenance of their parents.

The Kinship Group

Family has a collective meaning in Iran. In addition, use of the concept of *taiyefeh* (often translated to mean kinship group) is more appropriate for understanding the Iranian family than simply using the term family. Traditionally, the *taiyefeh* in Iran has provided a sense of solidarity, unity, sense of belonging, security, and support for its members. It has been considered the most important form of social organization and therefore it has been desirable to enlarge it while, at the same time, maintaining its power and prestige. This has been accomplished through first-cousin marriages. Through such a custom not only is wealth kept within the *taiyefeh* but ties are strengthened and proximity of family members is insured (Khazaneh, 1968). Therefore, even though patrilocal residence patterns may have been practiced, in reality the bride would remain relatively close to her own family, which at the same time would be her husband's family. This concentration of *taiyefeh* members in geographical proximity can be found both in villages and in large cities. In fact, cities in Iran were built up on the basis of the *taiyefeh*; the section in which a *taiyefeh* resided was referred to as a *mahalleh*, which was often named for its important leader.

This buildup of physical areas has served a number of important functions. Beyond the political, it has had a social function. A total support system, consisting of economic, service, social, and emotional support, has been available to all the *taiyefeh* members. Daily interaction was insured so that feelings of isolation were not prevalent. Children grow up feeling as though they are a part of a group. In addition, this solidarity has meant that crisis situations are not individual problems but rather are the concern of the whole *taiyefeh*, since all members are tied together economically, socially, and emotionally. For example, if a husband and wife are having marital difficulties, it becomes the concern of the whole family; a split between individuals, in fact, would mean lesion and dissension for the whole *taiyefeh*.

Behnam (1978) mentions that a sense of unity among *taiyefeh* members can be seen in agricultural work, as well as times of celebration and crises. He states that "The expenses of weddings, circumcisions, and burials have been the responsibility of all group members." He also indicated that *taiyefehs* are still functioning as they did in the past in a number of provincial areas, both urban and rural. Similarly, *taiyefehs*, with their collaborative helping, were found operating in Tehran in the mid-1960s (Vieille, 1965; Vieille and Kotobi, 1966), and have been playing an extremely important welfare function during and after the revolution (Touba, 1982).

Death, as one particular crisis situation, has always been a group phenomenon, with elaborate rituals in which all *taiyefeh* members participate. If the deceased were a male head of household, thought has to be given to the maintenance of the household by all the family. As a result, the widow's problem is one for the whole group, not one that she must solve alone, at least when the *taiyefeh* functions as it did in the past. Most likely the widow's husband was her first cousin, or another relative, so that the husband's family is, in fact, her own as well, and the family of orientation of the deceased will be expected to assume responsibility for the household. If they do not do so, informal pressure will be brought to bear by the *taiyefeh* to fulfill their obligations. When the widow has been living in the *mahalleh* of the *taiyefeh* of which both her own family and her husband's family are members, her living situation can be easily arranged and the support system remains intact.

Sometimes the protection of the widow is accomplished by the brother of the deceased marrying her and raising his brother's children. The brother of the deceased often considers it his duty to look after his brother's family, even if he is much younger than the widow. Also, a new kin marriage could be arranged, since dishonor to any one person would affect all the members of the group. Remarriage could be accomplished relatively easily because of the existence of the institution of polygyny. However, the cases mentioned above are more likely to occur in villages and tribal areas than in the cities.

Family of Procreation

Islam requires that children should obey their parents, respect them, and fear them, just as they fear God. Ghazali, an Iranian religious philosopher, said, "God almighty has said to Moses, 'All persons obeying their parents but disobeying me will be qualified as obedient, and all persons disobeying their parents but obeying me will be qualified as disobedient'" (Nassehy and Touba, 1980).

As mentioned previously, children are legally responsible for their parents but usually have not been told of their legal obligation. Rather, they have been socialized as to their normative responsibilities, which amounts to the same as those stated in law. Children have been taught to respect and love their relatives and to be concerned about their welfare, and have been well-schooled in their obligations to their *taiyefeh*. Sons, particularly the oldest son, have been socialized to assume the authority of the father if he is disabled or deceased. Thus, a son grows up expecting to one day contribute to the maintenance of his parents and female siblings, should they remain single, become divorced, or widowed.

The mother status, being the most important one for a woman, has offered her prestige and a strong emotional relationship with her children, particularly with her sons. The mother–child relationship is different from the father–child relationship because the father has been the symbol of authority—the mother, on the other hand, has been regarded as the symbol of love and security. Mothers, therefore, expect to one day be dependent on their sons. Since husbands are usually much older than wives, the chances of a woman becoming and remaining a widow are much greater than the chances of a father becoming and remaining a widower.

Brides, too, have been socialized to expect that when they marry they will join a household with a mother-in-law and/or sisters-in-law, grandparents, brothers-in-law, etc., or else that these relatives will eventually join the household of the couple should they establish neolocal residence. The obligations of children to parents, siblings, and other *taiyefeh* members to each other have been considered a part of their normal life cycle. The whole orientation and value attached to family unity, security, and maintenance has been part of their cultural heritage.

Changes That May Have Affected the Traditional Support Systems

For the 25 years before the revolution, the urban areas of Iran were given development priority. Thus, social facilities were also first made available in the larger development poles, which were urban areas slated for combined economic and social development in the Five Year Plans. These facilities were to become available only later in the smaller provincial cities. At the same time, changes were occurring in rural areas, such as land reform, introduction of different credit systems, implementation of agricultural innovations and mechanized agriculture, and introduction of mass communication and improved transportation. Migration, which began during World War II, continued as a result of the larger societal changes. This meant an influx of urban and rural migrants to the larger development poles and movement of rural migrants to the smaller provincial cities.

Separation of generations occurred physically, but there are indications that *taiyefehs* still function in the rural areas and provincial cities. However, the population pressures in the capital, Tehran, and lack of space in the old *mahallehs*, as well as changes in educational, occupational, and economic status of *taiyefeh* members, meant the breakup of the old areas. Whether it meant the breakdown of the support system of the *taiyefeh*, however, is another question.

Migrants from the provinces flocked to Tehran. While the initial migrants left their kinship group behind, subsequent migrants went in search of their *taiyefeh* members for help in locating employment, in finding housing, and for provision of a support system to substitute for the one they left behind. Often members of one *taiyefeh* settled in a nearby neighborhood, if not on the same block, as other members. However, it was the male in search of employment or a better life in the big city who was seeking out his *taiyefeh*. Females who accompanied their husbands would be most likely to have left their own *taiyefeh* completely behind unless the couple were first cousins. Nevertheless, the female members of the *taiyefeh* who could lend support to the entering wife would probably be missing since it was usually the single male who moved to the city first, and then either found a wife locally or brought one from his own village. When widowed, the woman would no longer have the same extensive support system and family network available to her as in her village. Thus, it may be expected that if changes were occurring, they could first be identified in Tehran, where the population pressure and migration flow were most acute. However, the same processes could have affected the support system in the provinces, where the widow might have been left behind while the sons and other relatives migrated away from their family of orientation.

To be sure, the supports would be there for the widow during the first week of bereavement and perhaps up to the fortieth day, as discussed previously. However, after that the hard realities of everyday life must begin, and the basic problems of managing a household without the husband and breadwinner on whom she had been completely dependent must be faced and many difficulties could arise.

Although, as we shall see, the strict observance of mourning norms has weakened in recent years, it has probably reverted to its traditional state following the revolution, evidenced by the current emphasis on women's dress away from Western styles and away from the use of makeup. After the Islamic revolution in Iran the claim was made that women in the West were appreciated only because of their physical appearance, and the revolution wanted to have women appreciated for other reasons. Inconsistently, while emphasis was placed on the traditional role of the woman as a wife and mother in the home, she was still seen as important to the revolutionary guard—for marching in demonstrations in her black *chador*, a symbol of the new woman participating in political activities as long as it supports the revolution of the Islamic Republic.

By the fall of 1980, if women wished to continue working in government offices, they were required to wear a *hejab* (a covering over their hair but *not* over their face) and a drab uniform that consisted of slacks and a loose jumper, with no makeup. Although this was only required of public employees originally, pressure to adhere to this garb spilled out into the streets. Once the government made an official statement about women's dress, religious fanatics in the streets began demanding women to wear similar dress outside the home or face physical punishment. Threats circulating among the population, and a few actual incidents, were enough to achieve adherence to the dress code in the streets, even among non-Muslims. Nevertheless, women who wore Western dress and makeup before the revolution reverted back to it in the safety of their own homes or at private gatherings.

However, at mourning ceremonies, one would be less likely to do as one wishes. It has even been reported that at wakes for men killed at war the revolutionary guards discourage sorrowful mourning ceremonies. Since the men killed at war have fought for the revolution, they are considered martyrs who go straight to Heaven—their death should be celebrated not mourned. The government is giving the families of those fallen at war some social security, so the loss of the traditional support is being compensated. It is not the same, however, for those killed who opposed the revolution.

To address the issue of to what extent the development process prior to the revolution, which brought urbanization and industrialization to Tehran, was having on adherence to mourning norms and the traditional support systems, a study of widowhood was conducted by the

Comparative Sociology Section of the Institute for Social Studies and Research, University of Tehran. The data were collected in Tehran City in 1976, the year prior to the major upheavals preceding the revolution of 1978–79. Therefore, this study provides a benchmark for measuring the effects of the urbanization and industrialization processes on changing norms and the structure of the family since the whole orientation of the society changed the following year.

Sample and Methods

The universe was based on the 1973 sample survey of the Iranian Statistical Center, which reported 103,800 widows living in Tehran City and 69,200 widows aged 10–64. The age group 65 and over was eliminated because a sample study demonstrated that it was not possible to obtain adequate responses from that age group. Furthermore, women aged 55–64 could be compared to elderly groups in Western societies because of their attitudes after their childbearing years. Women perceive themselves as having entered old age once their reproductive function has terminated. The lower life expectancy in non-Western societies also means that the 55 and over age group can best be compared to other developing societies.

A systematic sample from 3,549 rebuilt statistical areas of the 493 Iranian Statistical Center enumeration districts, containing approximately 200 households each, was chosen, utilizing a random start and cluster sampling in the final stage. A listing was made of the 78 sampled districts in order to construct the cluster sample, and a total of 922 widows were listed. The number of districts was established after the variances were calculated. An attempt was made to contact every widow in the listing up to three returns. The final sample included 482 widows.

The data were collected by means of personal interview using a structured questionnaire with both open-ended and precoded questions. In addition, many similar items to those used in widow studies in other countries were built into the interview schedule so that cross-cultural comparisons could be made. Only female interviewers were used so that refusals were almost nonexistent.

Mourning Norms in Contemporary Tehran

One aspect of this study investigated the extent to which the traditional mourning norms were still being performed. It found that only 8 percent did not wear mourning clothes, which meant wearing black, and more than two-thirds wore black for six months or more. However, the other types of mourning norms affecting one's personal appearance were not followed by a large proportion of the sample. For example, 38 percent reported not refraining from plucking their hair and 31 percent did not refrain from cutting or dyeing their hair. However, those who did refrain abstained from using makeup (see table 6.1).

Concerning adherence to the customs for honoring the dead, only 11 percent reported not visiting the grave after the mourning ceremonies of 40 days, and 11 percent said that they did not give alms to the poor. The widows studied in Tehran were almost equally distributed between those who visited the grave frequently and those who visited infrequently. However, at least 41 percent claimed to have given alms to the poor once a week. The custom of honoring the deceased by having a *majlis yadbod* or *roseh khani* (which are ceremonies in which a

Table 6.1   Mourning Norms Performed by Widows Under
Age 65 Living in Tehran City, 1976 (in percentages)

Length of time performed	Mourning norms			
	Wore mourning clothes (black)	Refrained from plucking hair	Refrained from cutting or dyeing hair	Refrained from using makeup
Total	482	482	482	482
	(100.0)	(100.0)	(100.0)	(100.0)
Did not follow custom	8.1	38.2	30.9	71.4
Did follow–				
Up to 40 days	5.8	2.1	2.3	.8
40 days to 3 months	9.9	1.9	2.9	1.0
3 to 6 months	7.0	4.8	5.2	2.3
6 months to 1 year	38.2	23.2	25.5	11.8
1 year or more	31.0	29.8	33.2	12.7

religious reader recites from the Koran, and a *mullah*—a Muslim priest or minister—preaches and recites prayers at the gathering of family and friends invited to the occasion) was followed by only half of the widows, and the majority of those only claimed to have it once a year or even less frequently. There were some, however, who had the ceremony performed periodically all year long (see table 6.2).

A fifth of the widows did not repay visits after the mourning ceremonies were completed. The major reasons given were that it was not their custom, they were sick and could not do it, they had no family or friends in the city, or that no one visited them. Nevertheless, 80 percent did repay visits, and half of them felt that it was an emotional help to them. A quarter said that it made no difference, and another 25 percent reported that it created problems for them but that they did it to adhere to the customs (see table 6.3).

Finally, when the widows were questioned about remarriage, nearly all said that they would not remarry even if given the opportunity. At least half of them claimed they would not remarry for their children's sake, some expressing a fear that their children's inheritance might be

Table 6.2   Customs for Honoring the Deceased Performed by Widows Under Age 65 Living in Tehran City, 1976 (in percentages)

Length of time performed	Visiting the grave	Alms to the poor	*Majlis yadbod* or *roseh khani**
Total	482	482	482
	(100.0)	(100.0)	(100.0)
Not at All	11.2	11.4	48.1
Once in more than 1 year	13.5	13.3	16.0
Once a year	13.7	7.1	24.4
Every 6 months to 1 year	8.3	3.3	8.3
Every 2 to 6 months	10.0	5.2	8.3
Every 1 to 2 months	19.5	11.0	2.9
Every 8 days to 1 month	9.1	6.4	1.5
Once a week	14.1	41.5	1.0
No answer	.6	8.3	1.4

*Ceremonies where a religious reader will read from the Koran and a *mullah* (religious man) will preach and recite prayers at a gathering of invited family and friends.

Table 6.3   Repayment of Visits to Those Who Attended
Mourning Ceremonies by Widows Under Age 65
Living in Tehran City, 1976 (in percentages)

Did not repay visits: reasons	Percentages	Did repay visits: reaction	Percentages
Total	99	Total	383
	(100.0)		(100.0)
No one visited the widow	15.2	Was emotional help	49.4
Economic reasons	5.0	Made no difference	25.3
Distance	7.1	Created problems	25.3
Not the custom	22.2		
Medical problems	22.2		
Family–no family in Tehran	18.2		
No answer	10.1		

Table 6.4   Desire to Remarry Among Widows Under Age 65
Living in Tehran City, 1976 (in percentages)

If had the chance to remarry, would or not	Percentages	If no, why not?	Percentages
Total	482	Total	446
	(100.0)		(100.0)
Yes	6.9	Customs do not permit	11.0
No	92.5	For sake of children	49.8
		Too old	13.9
		Other	18.9
		Combination of above	6.3
No answer	.6	No reason	.9

affected. Others felt that they were too old or that normative pressure prevented it (see table 6.4).

Living Arrangements

When the living arrangements of the 482 randomly sampled Tehran widows were examined, it was found that 41.3 percent were living with one or more married child, 33.2 percent with all unmarried children, but only 15.4 percent lived with their own relatives, either with or without children. There were only 3.7 percent living with their husband's relatives, and 6.4 percent lived with nonfamily or alone, 6.2 percent with nonfamily, and only .02 percent lived completely alone. These findings are in direct contrast to the widows living in Chicago, who were more likely to be living by themselves.

Even when widows had no children, they tended to live with their own relatives or with nonfamily. As the number of children increased, the more chance there was for the widow to live with one of her married children, most probably her son. At the same time, the probability that she would live with her own family decreased; seldom was there a likelihood that the widow would be living completely alone. This reflects the general orientation of Iranian society toward women living alone, who are often viewed as women of the streets or even prostitutes. Since any value attached to the woman is also a reflection on the family, a widow living alone is usually not tolerated by the family, even if she is an adult whose children are grown and married (see table 6.5).

In the United States as a whole, as in Chicago, the orientation of widows is toward being independent and not being a burden on the family. Children are not socialized to anticipate caring for their widowed mother, and the attitude of daughters-in-law toward having an elderly mother-in-law is different than it is in the Middle East. While it is expected in Iran, it is totally rejected in the United States. Similarly, American parents learn to accept their status and are socialized from youth to be independent and self-reliant. Whether this is fully accomplished or not is another factor.

Support Systems

Another goal of the study was to identify various economic and service needs of the widow beyond living arrangements, to what extent these were fulfilled, and who provided the supports.

Economic Supports

While living with a relative automatically provides some economic support, there were other areas of need expressed by the widows, such as needing money for personal things, rent, or indirect economic

Table 6.5   The Relationship between Number of Living Children
and Living Arrangements of Widows Under Age 65
Living in Tehran City, 1976 (in percentages)

Living arrangement	Total	Number of own living children		
		None	One	Two or more
Total	482	29	43	410
	(100.0)	(100.0)	(100.0)	(100.0)
Lives with nonfamily or alone	6.4	48.3	14.0	2.7
Lives with unmarried children	33.2	—	23.3	36.6
Lives with married children	41.3	—	32.6	45.1
Lives with own relatives with or without children	15.4	51.7	27.9	11.5
Lives with husband's relatives with or without children	3.7	—	2.3	4.1

help for food, clothing, medical expenses, and even for travel. Around
80 percent of the widows studied claimed that they needed money for
personal and medical expenses. Nearly the same proportion needed
help for food and clothing, although a smaller proportion (61 percent)
claimed the wish for vacation money. The least needed support—less
than a third—was help in paying the rent since most widows were
living with their own children or with other family members. In all but
a small proportion (usually ranging from 12–20 percent), the widows
did receive the economic support they needed. In 75–85 percent of
the cases, this support came from children. Sons and their families
played a predominant role in providing economic supports for their
mothers, although there was a sizable proportion, ranging from 20–25
percent, where no distinction was made and the support could have
come from either a son or daughter. Daughters alone were mentioned

as an economic support only occasionally, and the husband's relatives were not active at all in helping the widow economically (see table 6.6).

Physical Service Supports Outside and Inside the Home

The main service support needed outside the home was transportation. The other two areas of need were in doing shopping for the widow or taking her out for some recreation. While not as much a need as general transportation, these supports were still mentioned by two-thirds of the widows. Since it is only recently that women have begun to drive, primarily only mass transportation would be available to most widows, either bus or taxi. While the buses were inexpensive, they were often so full that the experience could be unpleasant for an elderly or sick person. In addition, the buses ran on major lines and not necessarily near the small streets in Tehran. While taxis also were inexpensive, they could only carry a limited number of people and were in such demand that usually five or more were crowded into a small foreign-made car. Similarly, they would normally only drive on the main streets.

Usually, the widows had their needs met in all three items, and in 80–85 percent of the cases it was the widow's own children and their families who provided the support. Sons headed the list, with both sons and daughters fulfilling some of the needs of the widows, and daughters alone helping between 10–13 percent of the time. If support was given by others, it was usually the widow's own family that helped out or, in some cases, nonfamily. However, help from the husband's family was practically nonexistent.

Service supports inside the house followed a similar help pattern to that found for service supports outside the home. However, while 80 percent of the widows claimed that they needed help with repairs, only two-thirds mentioned needing housekeeping help, and only 45 percent needed help with sewing. In the first two areas the pattern of receiving help from sons, their family, or both sons and daughters was the same as for the needs outside the home; with sewing, however, a larger proportion of help came from the widow's own daughter or from nonfamily. Since it is not traditional for men to do mending despite the existence of many male tailors, it may be expected that daughters provide such a service. Similarly, since the cost of dressmakers was comparatively low, the widows may have used their services when necessary (see table 6.7).

Table 6.6   Direct and Indirect Economic Support for Widows
Under Age 65 Living in Tehran City, 1976 (in percentages)

Receipt of supports	Direct economic support			Indirect economic support	
	Given money	Rent paid	Food/ clothes	Medical exp. paid	Vacation/ travel exp. paid
Total	(482)	(482)	(482)	(482)	(482)
	100.0	100.0	100.0	100.0	100.0
Did not want or need support	18.1	69.7	21.4	17.0	39.0
Wanted/needed support	81.7	30.1	78.4	82.8	60.8
Total	(394)	(145)	(378)	(399)	(293)
	100.0	100.0	100.0	100.0	100.0
Did not receive	14.5	21.4	13.5	12.5	19.5
Received	85.5	78.6	86.5	87.5	80.5
Total	(337)	(114)	(327)	(349)	(236)
	100.0	100.0	100.0	100.0	100.0
From children	72.4	85.1	83.8	68.8	85.2
Sons, spouse, child	46.6	57.0	50.8	43.0	53.4
Daughter, spouse, child	5.3	6.1	7.0	5.5	8.1
Both, not specified	20.5	21.9	26.0	20.3	23.7
From others	27.6	14.9	16.2	31.2	14.8
Own family	10.1	4.4	8.0	7.2	6.8
Husband's family	2.4	2.6	2.1	1.4	2.5
Nonfamily	15.1	7.9	6.1	22.6	5.5
No answer	.2	.2	.2	.2	.2

Welfare and Managerial Service Supports

The service support needed by nearly all the widows was care in time of sickness (93 percent) and 86 percent claimed that they received it when necessary. In this case, the proportion of widows helped by only daughters nearly doubled compared to economic and other service

Table 6.7   Physical Service Support Outside and Inside the Home
for Widows Under Age 65 Living in Tehran City, 1976 (in percentages)

Receipt of supports	Outside the house			Inside the house		
	Trans-portation	Shopping	Taking out for recreation	Help with repairs	Help with house-keeping	Help in sewing
Total	(482)	(482)	(482)	(482)	(482)	(482)
	100.0	100.0	100.0	100.0	100.0	100.0
Did not want or need support	15.1	33.4	37.1	19.1	34.0	54.2
Wanted/ needed support	84.7	66.4	62.7	80.7	65.8	45.6
Total	(408)	(320)	(302)	(389)	(317)	(220)
	100.0	100.0	100.0	100.0	100.0	100.0
Did not receive	21.6	29.1	25.0	27.5	30.0	31.8
Received	78.4	70.9	73.5	72.5	70.0	68.2
Total	(320)	(227)	(222)	(282)	(222)	(150)
	100.0	100.0	100.0	100.0	100.0	100.0
From children	80.9	84.6	85.1	85.5	88.3	70.7
Sons, spouse, child	46.2	47.2	47.7	54.3	46.8	29.3
Daughter, spouse, child	13.1	13.2	9.5	9.9	24.8	27.3
Both, not specified	21.6	24.2	27.9	21.3	16.7	14.1
From others	19.1	15.4	14.9	14.5	11.7	29.3
Own family	11.3	8.4	10.8	8.5	6.8	6.0
Husband's family	2.2	1.3	1.4	1.4	1.3	2.7
Nonfamily	5.6	5.7	2.7	4.6	3.6	20.6
No answer	.2	.2	.2	.2	.2	.2

supports. The proportion of widows helped by both daughters and sons also increased.

The area in which help was least needed was in caring for small children. Since most of the widows had older children at the time of widowhood, it was only the young widow who needed such help. It is reasonable that others would provide this service rather than her own children. In this area, the widow's own family helped in one-third of the cases, with the husband's family or nonfamily helping in the rest of the cases. However, it is still important to note that the widow's own children also helped with caring for their siblings.

Even though some widows were young by Western standards, they probably did have some grown children because of their early age at marriage. The legal age at marriage at the time of this study was the completion of 15 years. However, it was possible to marry earlier (13) with the approval of the parents and the examining physician of the court, who must rule that the girl has reached the age of puberty. In fact, girls were often pledged even younger but married once they reached the age of puberty; in such instances the betrothed couple might reside in the homes of their parents until the legal age was reached. Some of the older widows had married at the age of puberty as there was no legal restriction on age at marriage before 1935. Since children are highly valued, the wife would be expected to bear children as soon as possible after marriage, and to begin providing for her future support system.

The final area of service support needed by the widows was in the area of managerial supports. As might be predicted from the previous discussion of the role of the wife, 82 percent felt they needed help in decision making. However, 70 percent claimed they had no need for help in administrative work. The latter may have occurred because most widows were residing with their own children and/or other relatives; thus, any administrative work that may have occurred never filtered down to the widow. In the area of decision making the majority received help from their own children, with sons playing the predominant role. However, in this case the widow's own family played a slightly more active role than in other areas. As discussed earlier, if the father of the widow or her brothers were available, they would often be consulted before making important decisions (see table 6.8).

Table 6.8   Welfare and Managerial Service Supports for Widows
Under Age 65 Living in Tehran City, 1976 (in percentages)

Receipt of supports	Welfare service		Managerial service	
	Care in sickness	Help with children	Help in decision making	Help in administrative work
Total	(482)	(482)	(482)	(482)
	100.0	100.0	100.0	100.0
Did not want or need support	7.1	84.4	17.4	69.7
Wanted/needed support	92.7	15.4	82.4	30.1
Total	(447)	(74)	(397)	(145)
	100.0	100.0	100.0	100.0
Did not receive	14.3	67.6	18.4	33.8
Received	85.7	32.4	81.6	66.2
Total	(383)	(24)	(324)	(96)
	100.0	100.0	100.0	100.0
From children	81.2	41.7	81.2	82.3
Sons, spouse, child	34.5	25.1	40.7	44.8
Daughter, spouse, child	23.7	8.3	12.7	12.5
Both, not specified, specified	23.0	8.3	27.8	25.0
From others	18.8	58.3	18.8	17.7
Own family	12.8	33.3	13.3	12.5
Husband's family	1.3	12.5	3.4	3.1
Nonfamily	4.7	12.5	2.1	2.1
No answer	.2	.2	.2	.2

Conclusions

In general, this contemporary, but prerevolutionary, study showed a lack of support given by the *taiyefeh*, or *khandan*, members who were sometimes not physically available because of the push-pull effects of urbanization. However, it is important to note that the family of procreation was still the major support in all areas, both economic and service.

In Iran, sons were found to be the main providers of support for the widow and daughters in only a few minor areas. In the United States, specifically Chicago, just the opposite was found. Widows felt closer to their daughters and obtained emotional support from them, even if not economic help. In Iran it was the son and his family to whom the widow turned; the son, in turn, was socialized to anticipate providing for his parents, especially his mother. Since the woman in the past had always been dependent on a male—first her father, brothers, and then husband—it follows that she would continue this dependency after widowhood, now on her son.

In Chicago, widows were found living alone in the majority of cases, which is encouraged by the high value that American society places on independence: of children from their parents and vice versa. In Iran it is quite the opposite, for dependence is highly valued —dependence of children on parents, of females on males, and of aged parents on their children. Widowhood may not be considered such a crisis situation in Iran as it is in the West because of the value attached to the status of mother as well as the children's—especially the sons' —continuing feeling of responsibility toward their elders.

The absence of any large-scale formal government organization, such as a social security system that could have replaced the traditional support systems, may in fact have helped to maintain one of the most traditional forms of support, one's own children.

The situation, however, may have changed following this study, for it was soon after that the revolution occurred in Iran. Many of the sons have been and are still being killed, either in the war with Iraq, while on revolutionary guard duty, or have died in the process of opposing the existing regime, thus impacting the urban widow's traditional support system. Parents of children who are martyred for the cause of the revolution (that is, the Islamic revolution) will reap some benefits from the existing government, unless there should be a change in power. Those parents of children killed in opposing the present regime

and the Islamic revolution, however, will have no recourse to government support. This may mean that the extended family will be forced
to take a more active role in the support of some widows in the future.

The situation in rural areas has most probably not changed drastically since the rural population is further removed from political activity than is that in the city. In fact, emigration from rural areas may have
been stayed since little work is to be found in the large urban centers, a
situation caused by the disruption of economic activity before, during,
and after the revolution. Whether there is enough agricultural activity
to support the current youthful population, however, is questionable.
Some of the youth and even children are being taken up by the army to
fight in the war against Iraq and joining the ranks of the martyrs. It
remains to be seen whether the bulwark of the country's very existence,
the strength of the family, will be able to overcome the severe hardships it is facing as a result of the major societal upheavals.

7   Widowhood in Israel

RUTH KATZ AND NITZA BEN-DOR

Israel and Its Women

Israel, located on the Middle East continental bridge between Asia and Africa, is flanked by the Mediterranean Sea on the west, Jordan and Syria on the east, Lebanon on the north, and Egypt on the south. Occupying an area of 20,000 square kilometers, the country has a population of some 4 million, of which 84 percent are Jews and 16 percent non-Jews, mostly Muslim Arabs. The Jews in Israel constitute 22 percent of the total population of Jews in the world. Most (88 percent) of the population of Israel is urban, concentrated in four big cities: the capital, Jerusalem, the holy city of the three great religions; Tel Aviv, the financial center of the country, set midway along the seashore; Haifa, a port city and the largest city in the north; and Beersheba, the urban center of the south, the mainly Negev desert area.

The Jewish settlement of Israel in the modern era began in the latter part of the nineteenth century and coincided with the massive emigration of Jews from Eastern Europe to the United States, the British Commonwealth, and Latin America. Another large wave of Jewish immigration to Israel from Europe occurred with the rise of Nazism in the 1930s. After the establishment of the state in 1948, there were two large sources of immigration: the remnant of the holocaust in Europe and from the Islamic countries (North Africa, Iraq, Syria, Yemen, etc.). The 1960s saw immigration from the West (United States, Canada, England, etc.); and in the 1970s there was relatively large-scale immigration from the Soviet Union. Recently, thousands of immigrants have come from Ethiopia. As a consequence of all these migrations, Israel is a pluralistic society.

In 1980 the women of Israel numbered 1,614,000, and their average age was 31.2.[1] Most women marry in their early twenties, and more than 80 percent of them are married before the age of 29.[2] The proportion who remain single throughout their lives is extremely small—only 2.4 percent. Most (54 percent) Jewish women were born in Israel, 26 percent came from Europe or America, 11 percent from Africa, and 10 percent from Asia. Women aged 45 and over were more apt to have been born abroad (Israel Central Bureau of Statistics, 1980: Table 22/B). The average Israeli woman had ten years of schooling. There is a strong positive correlation between education and participation in the labor force. This involvement stood at 40 percent of all women in 1980, but it was equal to that of men of the same educational background for those with a college education. The impact of rapid modernization is reflected in the significant changes in education and labor-force participation of Israeli women over the last three decades. In recent years this has included mothers, half of whom are now employed (Israel Central Bureau of Statistics, 1983, Section 12). However, this increase in female work for pay has not been accompanied by an expansion into all sectors of employment, since the majority of women are in a few, female-dominated occupations (Ben Porath, 1983). In addition, women's average hourly wage is only 80 percent of that for men.

The fertility rate of Israeli women has been dropping, although it is the highest in the world among industrialized countries. It increases after each war and is highest among the less-educated women. Divorce is lower than in most industrialized countries and occurs primarily in the first years of marriage. There are twice as many divorced women as men, the men being three times as likely to remarry and to choose single women. The children of divorced parents remain with the mother, accounting for an increase in single-parent families headed by women.[3] A committee appointed in 1976 to examine the status of women considered such women as in situations of distress in three spheres (Israel Office of the Prime Minister, 1978). The first is social: Israel is a familial society, and unmarried life, whatever the reasons for this state, is frowned upon. The second is psychological: heads of single-parent families have difficulty adapting to their new roles and identities, which results in isolation and loneliness. The third is economic: income decreases while expenses remain approximately the same or even increase. The situation of widows is similar in these three spheres to that of divorced mothers.

Some special characteristics of Israeli society may help explain its familial nature: frequent wars, tending to increase the birthrate; a demographic structure that includes populations with traditional patterns of behavior; the central position of the Jewish religion, which contributes to the strengthening of the family; and the existence of efficient, close-knit networks of social control (Peres and Katz, 1981). In such a societal setting it is obvious that the single-parent family in general and the widow in particular would encounter hardships.

Mourning Customs and the Status of the Widow

Mourning and Widowhood in Jewish Religious Tradition

The Jewish faith includes a belief in the immortality of the soul and in an afterlife. It sees death as a departure from the material world and transition to the world of eternity. In Ecclesiastes (12:7), it is written:

And the dust returneth to the earth as it was,
And the spirit returneth unto God who gave it.
(*The Holy Scriptures*, 1952)

Jewish tradition encourages the individual to accept the idea that death is the end of all flesh and the inevitable fate of life in its bodily state:

It is better to go to the house of mourning
Than to go to the house of feasting
For that is the end of all men,
And the living will lay it to his heart.
(Ecclesiastes, 7:2)

Mourning customs serve two purposes: to console the bereaved as they take leave of the deceased, and to fortify the spirits of the mourners by deepening their belief in God in order to make it easier for them to face their own eventual deaths. These customs reflect a recognition of the gravity of the emotional experience that the mourner goes through and a perception of mourning as a gradual process. The obligation to observe mourning rites for the deceased falls on the immediate family (children, spouses, siblings, and parents). For one's father or mother the period of mourning extends over a year's time; for other kin, 30 days, with a few additional rites to be observed until a year passes (Leo, 1978:358).

As soon as the funeral is over, a seven-day period of intensive mourning begins, called *shiva* (from the Hebrew word for seven). During this time mourners are supposed to stay at home, sit on the floor or on a low stool, light a memorial candle for the deceased, and abstain from all activities likely to "gladden the heart," such as drinking wine, studying the Torah, washing, changing clothes, or having sexual relations. They are to be relieved from all activity that might interrupt their mourning (e.g., household duties). Relatives and friends may pay condolence calls throughout this week, partly to ensure that there will be a quorum of ten men—*minyan*, the minimum assembly required for public prayer—so that the male mourner will be able to pray at the specified times without leaving the house. (Female mourners have no such obligation to pray.) Attending a funeral and consoling the bereaved are considered to be pure acts, without any utility or profit, since the deceased cannot reciprocate (Leo, 1973:363).

After the *shiva* period is over, the mourners may leave the house and return to work, but they are forbidden to have their hair cut or to shave for a month, and they must abstain from buying or wearing a new article of clothing or going out for amusement for a year. Men are obligated to recite the *kaddish*, the special prayer for the dead, at synagogue services every day for a year. On the thirtieth day, mourners visit the grave of the deceased for a memorial service, which includes prayer and a eulogy. On the first anniversary of the death, mourners pay a visit to the grave and light a memorial candle, a custom that is repeated every year thereafter. Most of these customs are still followed with variations by the general population in Israel. The religious sector follows the tradition much more closely, of course. Variations also exist between Israel and the Jews outside of Israel.

Mourning customs have implications for the ability of the widow to adjust to her new situation. In a study carried out among Israeli war widows in order to determine the variables that promote their adjustment and renewed involvement in society (Amir and Sharon, 1979), it was found that widows of European and American origin made a better adjustment than those of Asian or African origin. The differences were attributed, in part, to the way families of Asian and African origin relate to the rites of mourning and to the widow, who is encouraged to practice prolonged mourning and to play the traditional "role" of the widow. Over time the emotional support she receives turns into social pressure, which isolates the widow and prevents her from leaving the house, breaking with the past, and attempting to build a new life.

Widows and Fatherless Children in Jewish Tradition

Jewish tradition has devoted special concern to widows and fatherless children, which has been expressed in explicit instructions regarding financial, social, and legal aid. The following examples will demonstrate.
Economic provision:

> When thou beatest thine olive tree, thou shalt not go over the boughs again; it shall be for the stranger, for the fatherless, and for the widow.
> (Deuteronomy 24:20)

Social support:

> And thou shalt rejoice before the Lord thy God, thou . . . and thy stranger, and the fatherless, and the widow.
> (Deuteronomy 16:11)

Legal aid:

> Seek justice, relieve the oppressed, judge the fatherless, plead for the widow.
> (Isaiah 1:17)

Although the Bible protected her rights, a widow was placed in the same inferior category as strangers. On the one hand, for example, she was considered an independent person who could inherit her husband's estate and receive custody of her children and their property; on the other hand, if she did not have a male heir, she was supposed to marry her deceased husband's brother, a custom that ensured the preservation of family property. If the brother-in-law refused to marry her, the widow performed a leviratic ceremony, after which she was free to remarry (Deuteronomy 25:5–10).[4]

The Position of Widows in Israel

There are some 143,000 Jewish widows in Israel, nearly three times the number of widowers. The legal status of women in general and widows in particular in Israel is both unique and complex because of the special nature of the legal history of the state. Their status is determined by a combination of highly progressive, modern laws and some of the most ancient customs. As mentioned, the State of Israel delegates authority in matters concerning the personal status of Jews, including questions of marriage and divorce, to the jurisdiction of the rabbinical courts. The biblical-originated custom of levirate, for example, is still in force — and presents two problematic consequences for the widow: first, the deceased's brother may try to profit at her expense and demand payment in return for performing the rite; second (though rare), the brother-in-law may be too young to perform the rite and so the widow has to wait until he reaches the age of 13, when he can do so.

As for property and inheritance rights, the Law of Equal Rights for Women of 1951 guarantees reasonable equality between men and women by stating, in part, that marriage does not adversely affect the status of the property a woman accumulated previous to her marriage. This law changed a situation in which, among certain ethnic groups, the wife's rights to property and inheritance automatically transferred to her husband or his brother (Atzmon, 1980:9–10). A later law (the Law of Inheritance — 1965) stipulates that in the absence of a husband's will, the widow is to receive a considerable portion of his estate. Her share depends on the existence of other beneficiaries. For example, if the deceased husband has offspring from a previous marriage, the widow is to receive one-fourth of the inheritance; if the offspring are from the present marriage only, she receives one-half of the estate. The 1973 Law of Monetary Relations Between Spouses further protects the property a woman possessed before marriage by stipulating that it remains hers in the event of the dissolution of the marriage by divorce or death. It should be mentioned that the legal system also bestows rights on a woman who was not legally married but lived with a man as a common-law wife.

Support Systems for Widows in Israel

The laws that deal with the rights of widows distinguish three categories of widows according to the cause of death of the spouse: (1)
Husband's death was connected with the security of the country,
whether in military service or as a result of hostilities against the
civilian population. (2) Husband died in work accident. (3) Husband's
death was from any other cause (widow termed "survivor"). Widows in
the first category will be referred to as "war widows";[5] those in the last
two categories, "civilian widows."

In accordance with various laws, each of the three categories carries
with it the right to a certain "package" of benefits. The amount, variety,
and quality of these benefits vary according to category: "war widows"
receive the most benefits, "survivors," the least.

Following Lopata (1979), the support systems of widows will be ana-
lyzed along two axes: one involves the kinds of support that the widow
receives; the other, the societal frameworks that impart the different
types of support.

Financial Supports

The principal source of financial support for widows in Israel is social
security.[6] The financial base of the country's social security system
rests on the compulsory deduction by the state of a portion of employee
earnings and a proportional "contribution" by the employer. The system involves allowances and benefits that the state bestows on various
categories of beneficiaries according to law. There are ten different
laws that apply to civilian widows and two to war widows.

Civilian widows. The main laws that apply to civilian widows are the
Social Security Laws, which stipulate compulsory insurance for all
employed persons in Israel, various pension laws, which apply to
some but not all work places, and the Income Maintenance Law. The
circumstances of the husband's death, his type of workplace, and the
duration and continuity of his employment determine the laws under
which the widow is to receive financial aid and other benefits. For
example, widows whose husbands died in work accidents are entitled
to a dependent's pension, linked up to 60 percent of the salary of the
deceased. Widows whose husbands died of illness, road accidents,
and suicide are entitled to a survivor's pension. For such a widow with
two children the sum will be between 24 and 40 percent of the average

salary in Israel. Civilian widows whose husbands' employment history did not enable them to accumulate enough savings to make them eligible for pensions receive an income maintenance allowance, the maximum payment of which is 29 percent of the average income (Social Security Institute, *Statistical Quarterly*, 1984). About 34 percent of the urban widows in Israel live exclusively on one or another type of social security payment—i.e., no supplementary pension or job income (Gordon, 1978).

Civilian widows are entitled to one year of vocational training, but this benefit is subject to the judgment of social security officials that the widow is "amenable to rehabilitation." The cost of her training —including a small stipend—is borne by the Social Security Institute. Civilian widows are not exempt by law or other arrangement from various taxes and fees; 75 percent of the financial benefits is subject to income tax.

War widows. There are two laws dealing with the rights of widows who lost their husbands in hostilities, the Law for Families of Soldiers Lost in Action of 1950 and the Law for Victims of Hostile Acts of 1970. The former assigns responsibility for financial, vocational, emotional, and social aid to the Ministry of Defence; the latter, covering widows of citizens killed by hostile elements either in Israel or abroad, to the Social Security Institute. Both laws fix the monthly allowance for a widow with one child under 21 years of age at 126 percent of the average monthly salary of an average-ranked state employee. For every additional child, there is an increment of 11 percent. The benefit is bestowed regardless of the widow's income and is exempt from income tax. The average allowance is equivalent to the average monthly salary in Israel; if fringe benefits are taken into account, the total income of a war widow exceeds the average net income in the Israeli economy. Additionally, war widows are entitled to exemption from many taxes and fees, as well as to aid in purchasing electrical appliances, a telephone, a car, and an apartment. They are also entitled to a job-training program, which includes university studies and may even involve a period of study abroad. The children of war widows receive free occupational training up to completion of a bachelor's degree, a special grant upon marriage, and other benefits.

There is, then, considerable discrepancy between the financial aid given to war widows and that given to civilian widows. The disparity reflects basic values in the Israeli society. The civilian widow is entitled to a minimal standard of living because widows and fatherless children should not be neglected; the widow whose husband died in a work accident is eligible for additional benefits as a reward for her husband's having been an active laborer in a society in which labor parties and workers' organizations have been very powerful elements in the structure of government; men who died in war are viewed as heroes who sacrificed their lives for their country, and their widows are entitled to lead a comfortable and respectable life.

Excerpts from debates in the Knesset reveal the special attitude toward war widows: "We are not granting (war widows) charity . . . we have to pay them ransom for our own lives . . . it is because of them that we have a free and independent homeland" (Member of Knesset Yalin-Mor, *Knesset Proceedings*, 1950). "The concern for the families of the fallen men . . . also determines . . . the military readiness of the nation" (Member of Knesset Victor Shem-Tov, *Knesset Proceedings*, 1963). The first statement emphasizes the national feeling of debt, the second the concern over the security of the country and the motivation to fight.

A study that examined a sample of war widows found that, two years after being widowed, the women were not worried by either financial or bureaucratic problems (Amir and Sharon, 1979). At about the same time a similar study of civilian widows found that 58 percent of them were in the bottom decile of the Israeli income scale and 75 percent in the bottom three deciles; about 70 percent were very worried about financial problems (Gordon, 1978; 1981).

Personal Resources

A gap exists between war widows and civilian widows also with regard to the personal attributes relevant to the Israeli labor market. Most war widows are younger, more educated, and better integrated into Israeli society than the other widows (Shamgar-Handelman, 1975). Among the civilian widows it was found that 6 percent did not know the Hebrew language, 18 percent had no education whatsoever, 40 percent had a high school education, and only 17 percent had higher education. Sixty percent had no vocation or profession at the time they were widowed (Gordon, 1978); nevertheless, after being widowed, 58 percent of these women worked outside the home, many in low-income jobs (Rotter and Keren-Yaar, 1974). Another study, which examined the work satisfaction of widows, found a positive correlation between work satisfaction and level of education and a negative correlation between this satisfaction and number of children (Gordon, 1978; 1981). The obvious conclusion, of course, is that the lowest level of satisfaction will be found among widows with little education and many children. The women have no choice but to work, but the jobs they are able to obtain are not interesting and provide low remuneration.

Two styles of social adjustment, whereby widows attempted to regain social status for their families, were discerned in a study carried out among war widows three years after the death of their husbands (Shamgar-Handelman, 1983). One style involved an effort to retain the status of "_____'s wife" or to invest in the status of "_____'s widow." In each variation, the basis for status was the dead husband. The second style of adjustment was based on the capabilities of the woman herself; that is, on her attempt to achieve "independent" status through her own talents and achievements in the work place, one of the primary sources of status in Israeli urban society. The widows who adopted this style, however, discovered very quickly that the Israeli job market, especially the higher occupational levels, bestows greater benefits and prestige on male employees than on females (see "Women in the Labor Force" in the first section). In summary, although salaried employment constitutes a source of economic resources, it is more available to widows equipped with education, a vocation or profession, and a certain degree of involvement in society.

Service Support System

Studies dealing with the welfare of widows in Israel have not directly examined service support systems. Nevertheless, these studies do point to a number of patterns. Among civilian widows, 62 percent report that their families are the ones who help them with all kinds of bureaucratic arrangements. In contrast, 29 percent report that they do not receive any help from relatives, friends, or neighbors. Fifty-seven percent of the widows have problems with red tape, but most manage to solve these by themselves. Fifty-two percent encountered legal problems, most of which had not been resolved after two years. Among those who had hired lawyers, a considerable number were dissatisfied with their counsel. Of the 213 widows who responded to offers of assistance made by the Social Security Institute in 1982, 27 percent reported that the Institute had helped them (Gordon, 1981). In contrast, a study of war widows revealed that these women did not experience difficulties with red tape. The researchers attribute this situation to the attention given these widows by the Ministry of Defence (Amir and Sharon, 1979).

It appears then that the family may constitute a source of aid to widows in dealing with the bureaucracy, but that friends and acquaintances rarely provide this kind of support. Not all governmental institutions make it easy for the widow to get through the bureaucratic maze, as some operate more efficiently than others.

It should be mentioned that two voluntary women's organizations, WIZO (International Women's Zionist Organization) and Na'amat (Pioneer Women), offer free legal aid to women, including widows. It is not known what proportion of widows in each category use this service, nor how satisfied are those who do use it.

Social Supports

Most widows suffer from social isolation; 83 percent of a sample in one study expressed agreement with the statement "It is very hard for a woman to get along by herself" (Gordon, 1978). During the first three years of widowhood, it was found, war widows lose much of the social status they enjoyed while their husbands were alive (Shamgar-Handelman, 1983). As for civilian widows, 35 percent have reported that they had no connections with neighbors; 45 percent, that they had no friends or acquaintances. The situation is no different for the widow who succeeds in building a professional career for herself; she and her family are slowly but surely pushed to the edges of their social circle. Widows who do have connections with friends also maintain ties with relatives; they differ from other widows in being younger, more educated, employed, and of European origin (Gordon, 1981).

Some of the same results were found in a study of divorced women in Israel. The sphere that troubled these women the most, and made it difficult for them to adjust, was that of social relations, especially intimate relations. These women felt isolated and rejected by society, a feeling that was not mitigated over the years (Katz and Pesach, 1985). Israel, as mentioned, is a family-oriented society, and only about 2 percent of its population remain single all their lives. The centrality and stability of the family are also manifested in the fact that very few women choose to rear children alone (the divorce rate and the rate of births to single mothers are lower than those in most industrialized countries). In a family-oriented society like Israel it is difficult to adjust socially to any kind of single parenthood.

Voluntary organizations as a source of social supports. Although voluntary organization is not a common source of social support in

Israel, there are two self-help organizations: Yad Labanim ("Memorial for the Fallen Sons"), and the Organization of Survivors. Up to the time of the Six-Day War (1967) Yad Labanim included fatherless children and bereaved parents in addition to widows. For various reasons, parents played the dominant role in this organization, while widows were marginal (Shamgar-Handelman, 1979). After the Six-Day War a group of "fresh" widows formed their own association. It became active, even militant, and mobilized the support of the press and public opinion. In response, the Ministry of Defence raised the level of financial support and the quality of service for war widows. After seven years of activity, this group rejoined the Memorial Organization, this time as a full partner.

In comparison, the Organization of Survivors has made only modest gains. The initiative for its establishment came from employees of the Social Security Institute, who initially selected a number of widows and organized a therapy group (Levy and Mandola, 1979). Over the two years that the group met, the widows were encouraged to organize for two aims: to provide mutual support and to form a pressure group that would seek increased widow's benefits. The Organization of Survivors was formally set up in 1977 in conjunction with WIZO and the Social Security Institute. Despite holding a demonstration in front of the Knesset building and meeting with ministers, members of the Knesset, and other public figures, the organization has been unable to accomplish much. In 1979, only 40 percent of the population of new widows interviewed knew about the organization; only 3 percent were active members, while another 6 percent occasionally took part in its activities. These findings were surprising in view of the fact that most civilian widows had expressed a desire to join such an organization, as well as an interest in participating in meetings with other widows (Gordon, 1981). Compared to war widows, civilian widows seem to lack excess energy, are less homogeneous, and receive less public sympathy for their organization and status.

Remarriage. Remarriage is likely to constitute a source of social support in several ways. The marriage itself is likely to break a widow's isolation and enable her to rejoin the mainstream of Israeli society. Remarriage will give her a provider. Finally, the status that a husband provides is more respectable than any status the widow could attain by herself in Israel. To date, no study has been made of Israeli widows who have remarried; neither their remarriage rate nor the attributes of widows who do remarry are known. What is known is that firstly, widows constitute a notably small proportion of individuals who remarry; secondly, compared with single and divorced women, widows have a stronger tendency to marry widowers than other categories of potential spouses, single or divorced men (Israel Central Bureau of Statistics, *Israel Statistical Yearbook—1983*, Table 8/C).

All the war widows studied by Shamgar-Handelman (1982) three years after the death of their husband perceived remarriage as one of the alternatives for the future, although they expressed different expectations regarding such marriage. It is reasonable to suppose that those war widows who receive considerable financial support would hesitate to forego most of it by a remarriage, and, as Golan indicated (1981:187), "where soldier-husbands are memorialized publicly as heroes, as they often are in Israel, the wife's remarriage may be looked upon by her social networks as disloyalty to the first husband's memory." In contrast with war widows, most survivors did not view remarriage as a viable alternative because of the difficulty in finding a suitable mate and fears concerning the children and shame (Gordon, 1978).[7]

Emotional Supports

A survey of the findings of studies based mainly on therapeutic experience with Israeli widows (Levy and Mandola, 1979; Golan, 1975) reveals several patterns. As in other areas, there are differences in the form and quality of the emotional support that the Ministry of Defence and the Social Security Institute give widows. The ministry sends a representative to the bereaved family during the *shiva* week of intensive mourning. In times of war, when there are many deaths, it operates a network of volunteers for this purpose. The ministry representative also transmits up-to-date information on how to apply for widows' benefits. War widows are attended to by Ministry of Defence social workers, who serve as a source of emotional support and who, if necessary, will refer the widow to other professional counseling.

The Social Security Institute does not initiate contact with a widow. She must submit an application for aid to the nearest branch office of the institute. After receiving a claim, the institute may send a "rehabilitation worker," who will help the widow plan for the future and who may, in certain instances, recommend professional therapy. Both the institute and the Ministry of Defence offer widows group therapy under the guidance of a trained social worker or psychologist.

According to Golan (1981:184), "In Israel, the use of small social groups of war widows, led jointly by a social worker and a widow who had already passed successfully through the mourning process, was found to be very helpful for about a year following the death of the women's husbands. During this time they comforted each other, shared practical advice on how to manage the children, and swapped stories of in-laws' interference."

The family. Most widows mention the family as a source of emotional support, especially in the first period of widowhood. Relatives help the widow observe mourning rites. Even if the family is not religiously observant, it supports the widow and her children during the period following the husband's death. The proximity of their families, however, may burden widows. Some are troubled by the dependent role assigned to them and by their being treated as though sick and weak (Shamgar-Handelman, 1979). Some feel that although the family has drawn closer, it has also begun dictating how the widow should behave. Tensions may emerge between the widow and the husband's family over matters of property, money, the children's education, and the widow's own conduct.

Friends. A good proportion of widows have no friends at all. Like the emotional support given by family, that provided by friends is most intense in the first months of widowhood. After that, among the younger widows a gradual breaking off generally occurs. The more educated generally meet with more success in finding new friends.

Conclusions

Israeli civilian widows resemble the urban widows studied by Lopata (1979) in Chicago in their demographic characteristics, their educational level, and in the fact that the women did not spend their childhood in the same city in which they grew old. Particularly because of this last attribute, older urban widows find it difficult to adjust to the demands of life in a modern city. Another similarity between widows in Chicago and civilian widows in Israel lies in the types and levels of support that they manage to mobilize from the various support systems. One noticeable difference between these two groups of widows stems from mourning customs; Jewish customs give the Israeli widow a kind of moratorium during which she can receive support from both family and friends.

In contrast, Israeli war widows exhibit different demographic characteristics from the Chicago widows. The employment capabilities and the social status of these Israeli women also differ from the Chicagoans. The situation of war widows in Israel, in fact, proves that single-parent families in general, and widows in particular, do not have to suffer a sharp decline in their economic position. The fact that the war widows are relatively better off makes them a reference group for other widows. As one civilian widow, a participant in a group organized by the Social Security Institute, put it, "I didn't have anyone to consult with or anyone I could go to; it was terrible. If he had died a few months before he did, while serving in the Reserves, at least I would have been considered a war widow, and I'd have something to live on and someone to turn to. A year later I fell into a depression and was referred to psychiatric treatment." On the other hand, the treatment of war widows in Israel does show that without public support and without efforts at political organization, the chances for widows to improve their situation are slight.

Finances, however, constitute but one problem. In comparison with the war widows, Israeli civilian widows feel inferior and less respectable, suffering from deprivation beyond that brought on by their financial and social situation. In the words of a bereaved wife: "To be a widow of someone who slipped on a banana peel and didn't die as a martyr is disgraceful and brings you down to the bottom of the hierarchy of widows" (Levy and Mandola, 1979).

In the end, every widow in Israel's family-oriented society has to adjust to living somewhat out of the accepted mainstream. Money, prestige, and even emotional support can help alleviate the agonies of widowhood only to a certain degree. The loss of status arising from the death of a husband is stronger in Israel than in the United States.

8 Support Systems of Elderly Widows in the Philippines

EVANGELINA NOVERO BLUST

This chapter discusses the support systems of a select group of elderly widows in the Philippines, with emphasis on children as resources. The presentation is based chiefly on a study of intergenerational perceptions of filial responsibility conducted by the author.[1]

Support systems and social integration are influenced by society and culture, the community, family, and personal resources (Lopata, 1979). Thus, for a better understanding of the support systems of elderly widows in the Philippines, an overview of the nation, family characteristics, and values and the status and roles of women is in order.

The Philippines

The Philippines, a southeast Asian country of some 7,000 islands lies in the South China Sea. The country has a total land area of 299,404 square kilometers (115,600 square miles), about 91 percent of which is contained in its 11 largest islands and two-thirds in two islands (Lightfoot, 1973). The country is a single unit, containing a variety of peoples; it is divided between Christians, Muslims, and indigenous religious groups, rich and poor, rural and urban, and uplanders and lowlanders. Its population of more than 50 million reflects diversity in racial–ethnic, linguistic, and other backgrounds (Javillonar, 1979; Steinberg, 1982). The majority are of Indonesia-Malayan ancestry, with

Chinese, European (largely Spanish), American, and Japanese blood introduced at different periods in history. There are about 70 languages spoken in the country, 90 percent of the population speaking one of the eight major languages. Widows whose support systems will be discussed here are all Tagalog-speaking Roman Catholics.

The Philippines is still predominantly rural, with two-thirds of the population in such areas (United Nations, 1983), where social services and economic activities are limited (Rojas-Aleta et al., 1977). Similar to other developing countries, the Philippines is plagued with problems of mass poverty, malnutrition, unemployment, and housing. In contrast to developed nations, on the other hand, social welfare services are minimal.

In spite of the significant variations in culture patterns, the Philippine population reveals more similarities than differences (Fox, 1963), especially among the eight language groups. Strong affinities are evident in the family and kinship structure, inheritance, religious beliefs and practices, and economic and political organization throughout the country. The subsequent discussion of the contemporary Filipino family is based on what Fox (1963:345) termed "a generalized Christian Filipino culture and society, which is an abstraction of similarities among Christian Filipinos."

Filipino Family Characteristics

The Filipino family maintains structural features and performs functions to meet the needs of its members throughout their lifetime.

Residential Arrangements

The term family to a Filipino encompasses the family of orientation in which one is born and the family of procreation, both of which extend bilaterally (Castillo, 1977). The bilateral nature of relationships provides for the continuing support and protection to the man and woman by their respective families and kin groups (Fox, 1963).

In most Philippine studies of the family, the household is the operational unit within which relationships among members are observed. A household refers to "a group of persons living together and sharing the same housekeeping, kitchen, and eating arrangement" (Castillo, 1977:365). Castillo's analysis of several studies of the Filipino households over the years shows that there are more nuclear than extended households in the country; that is, most households consist of father, mother, and unmarried children. Those households that include relatives other than parents and unmarried children are minimal. Furthermore, a higher proportion of nuclear households is observed in rural than in urban areas. When age of members of the household is considered, more extended than nuclear households have members aged 65 years or older (Lim cited in Castillo, 1977), an indication that problems of aging parents and grandparents are taken care of by the family.

As would be expected, independent living is uncommon in the Philippines. A 1968 demographic survey showed that single-person household constituted less than 1 percent of the total households (Nartatez cited in Castillo, 1977:385). The proportion increased to 1.4 percent in 1973.

The Filipino Family as a Support Network

In spite of some rapid and fundamental social, political, economic, and religious changes in the country over the past centuries, "the Filipino family has remained remarkably stable" (Javillonar, 1979:347). Social scientists note no significant change in the bilaterally extended kinship relations, in familial roles, or in patterns of parent-child relationship. Steeped in traditions that emphasize mutual obligations and respect, the Filipino family continues to play an important role in the care and support of its members. Javillonar (1979:372) posits that the relative inability of the Philippine social welfare organizations to perform their social service or economic functions because of their limitations contributes in part to the stability of the Filipino family. She concludes, "Forced to its own devices in meeting the needs of daily living, as well as crisis, the family forms a cohesive network of mutual protection and assistance." Indeed, the Filipino family is a dispenser of social welfare, accommodating the jobless and sharing food with all members (Fox, 1963; *New Philippines*, 1974). Despite limited housing conditions, Filipinos share living space with relatives who cannot afford to own or rent. In cases of personal loss, bilateral relations make up an "instant aid society," providing financial help, comfort, and company. As provider of social psychological, physical, and economic support, the Filipino family then is described as "the most able social welfare agency" (*New Philippines*, 1974:4). Patterns of interdependence within the family persist, depending on need, throughout all stages of life. In the ideal sense, its environment is characterized by emotional closeness and security (Bulatao, 1973). As Castillo (1977:362) states:

> To put it succinctly, positively, and perhaps sentimentally, the Filipino family, large and functionally extended as it is, provides social security, old age pension, jobs, scholarship, unemployment benefits, nursery services, credit, land, labor, capital, income redistribution, work sharing, companionship to the unmarried, care for the sick, home for the aged, counsel for the troubled, and most of all love, affection, emotional sustenance, and social stability without which a Filipino's life is meaningless.

Respect within the Family

Interpersonal relationships within the family are partly determined by some social and cultural values. One such value is generational respect, which requires obedience, deference, and respect for the opinions, attitudes, values, and decisions of all persons older than oneself (Fox, 1963). Age rather than sex is the basis of hierarchy of authority (Javillonar, 1979). Older members have considerable power and influence over younger ones. Children are expected to obey their parents as well as their grandparents, other adult relatives, older siblings, and cousins. Among siblings, the greater the age gap, the greater is the respect (Mendez and Jocano, 1974). Respect is shown through forms of kinship address and behavior at all times (Eggan, 1968; Javillonar, 1979). For example, older brothers or sisters have their titles of respect (*New Philippines*, 1974). Disobedience and disrespect are viewed as ingratitude, which invites social sanctions (Javillonar, 1979). It is a widely held belief that a child who is disobedient and disrespectful will encounter misfortune and hardship throughout his or her lifetime. Conversely, accidents or adversities are at times attributed to misbehavior earlier in life.

Children as Old-Age Security

One of the values attached to children in the Philippines reflects the Filipino attitude toward care and support of the elderly. For example, case studies in six rural communities show that children are considered sources of financial, physical, and emotional support in old age

(Castillo, 1977). Kâğitçibaşi's (1982) analysis of the data of the Value of Children Project, a comparative social-psychological study on motivations for childbearing in nine countries, reveals a similar finding. Respondents from less-developed countries like the Philippines, Indonesia, Thailand, Turkey, Taiwan, and Korea are more likely to consider children as sources of security in old age than those from Singapore, the United States, and the Federal Republic of Germany. Apparently societies with low levels of technological development and limited social welfare institutions rely more on the family, especially the adult child, for the care of older people. Moreover, because they work hard and in some cases, sacrifice to give their children a better life, parents expect their children to return the favor by taking care of them in their old age (Mendez and Jocano, 1974). Filial care may be in the form of physical accommodation in the children's home or mere companionship to provide emotional security.

The Value of Utang na Loob

The value of children as security in old age is further strengthened by a form of reciprocity known as *utang na loob* (literally translated, debt inside oneself or debt of gratitude). *Utang na loob* is an awareness of one's indebtedness to others for favors received and willingness to repay when one is capable of doing so (Hollnsteiner, 1973). Hollnsteiner's study of reciprocity in lowland Philippines showed that *utang na loob* operates within the family and the kinship system and extends to relations with nonrelatives as well. Apparently, *utang na loob* assures continuity and maintenance of kinship and other social ties. A Tagalog proverb, which states that "one who does not look back to where he comes from won't be able to reach his destination," implies the importance of *utang na loob* to Filipinos. To be successful in life, one must help those who help him or her, especially one's family.

The parent-child *utang na loob* relationship is complementary rather than reciprocal; parents do not develop *utang na loob* toward their children (Hollnsteiner, 1973). Parental obligation to rear children is complemented by the children's responsibility to respect and obey their parents and to take care of them in their old age. Adult children are expected "to be everlastingly grateful to their parents not only for all the latter have done for them in the process of raising them but more fundamentally for giving life itself." Failure to perform one's obligation "arouses deep bitterness and feeling that a sacred unifying bond has been torn asunder and a family betrayed" (Hollnsteiner, 1973:76). Such an individual will be regarded as *walang utang na loob*, that is, having no sense of gratitude, and *walang hiya*, being shameless or insensitive (Hollnsteiner, 1973; Mendez, 1974; Almirol, 1982). *Hiya* means shame or losing face and must be avoided at all cost (Almirol, 1982). Thus, care and support of elderly parents as obligations of adult children are not questioned and are seldom a topic of inquiry.

Status and Roles of Filipino Women

The socioeconomic situation of Filipino women is limited, to some extent, by their ability to generate resources and create their support systems. The majority of Filipino families are in poverty, living at a predominantly subsistence level. Further, 64 percent of the women are rural, "preoccupied with day to day survival. Most of them are not college-educated; not elites; and not ladies of leisure, either" (Castillo, 1977:483).

Education and Employment

Presently, because of the high priority the country has given to education, the difference in literary rates between male and female has become very minimal (Szanton, 1982). The 1970 census data revealed literacy rates of 84.6 percent for males and 82.2 percent for females. The disparity lies on the literacy of rural and urban residents (Castillo, 1977; Rojas-Aleta et al., 1977). Female urban literacy in 1970 was 91.8 percent, rural literacy, 77.2 percent.

Despite equality with men in education, only one-third of women ten years old and over are in the labor force, and half of them are married (Castillo, 1977; Rojas-Aleta et al., 1977). In general, women need a high level of education to increase their work participation rate. More women from rural than urban areas spend their time in housekeeping (Castillo, 1977). However, rural wives contribute to the family's income more than do urban wives. The majority of rural women who work are in farming; others are engaged in manufacturing and sales (*sari-sari*, or small variety-store owner, market vendor, or street peddler).

Urban females find employment mostly in commerce or trade, domestic service, government, community, business, and recreational services, and in manufacturing.

Domestic Status and Roles

In the Filipino home the husband is traditionally the head and principal breadwinner; the wife takes on the homemaking responsibilities. The predominant roles for men and women are not only culturally prescribed but also reinforced in the law. The Civil Code (n.d.:31–32) provides that "the husband is responsible for the support of the wife and the rest of the family" while "the wife manages the affairs of the household." Furthermore, studies on attitudes toward male–female roles show a strong support for the husband-head-provider and wife-for-the-home role definitions (Illo, 1977; Castillo, 1977). As a rule, the woman is also the person who holds the purse strings and controls the family budget. The husband is expected to turn over his earnings to his wife; in return, he receives an allowance (Mendez and Jocano, 1974). Licuanan and Gonzalez's study (cited in Gonzalez and Hollnsteiner, 1976:62), however, shows that women of low-income families have barely enough money to meet basic family needs and that they are "unable to exercise the power and resource allocation component" of the treasurer role.

That the home is the woman's domain and that a double standard of morality still prevails are reinforced by the attitude that the woman more than the man is responsible for upholding society's moral code (Illo, 1977). In other words, marital harmony is primarily a woman's concern (Castillo, 1977). She is expected to keep her marriage intact and the family close together no matter what the husband-father might do (Bulatao, 1973).

Although the husband is the acknowledged head of the family, the relationship between spouses is considered egalitarian (Mendez and Jocano, 1974; Castillo, 1976; Rojas-Aleta et al., 1977). Studies on household decision making show that husband and wife decide jointly on most family issues and authority patterns are shared (Porio et al., 1975; Castillo, 1977; Illo, 1977). In addition, each spouse has his or her sphere of influence. Women exert more power over matters that concern domestic activities, such as household tasks, child care, and budgeting (Mendez and Jocano, 1974; Montiel and Hollnsteiner, 1976). Men, on the other hand, have more control over livelihood or occupation. Decision making of spouses in their respective areas is further characterized by mutual consultation. Both parents assume responsibility in task allocation and task performance of children in the household (Castillo, 1977). Moreover, husbands participate in household tasks traditionally defined as female's, such as food preparation, doing the laundry, child care, and marketing.

Legal Status

Under the law a Filipino woman's rights include the right to life, liberty, and property; citizenship; education; information; equal work opportunities; organization of associations not contrary to law; right to vote; and liberty of abode. Also under the law, wives suffer certain restrictions. In the Philippines male citizens and unmarried females have more or less the same rights; married women, on the other hand, are delegated to the status of second-class citizens (Castillo, 1976). The rights of the latter are restricted by specific provisions in the Civil Code in the areas of: choice of residence, mixed marriages, parental authority, property rights, right to work, court suits, and legal separation (Montiel and Hollnsteiner, 1976; Rojas-Aleta et al., 1977). In practice, however, these restrictions are not quite evident. As Rojas-Aleta et al. (1977:185) comment, "Filipino women barely know their legal rights. They only become conscious of their rights when in a dilemma, and, generally, would rather leave such matters to the husbands for decision making." Also, Szanton's (1982) hypothesis of stronger legal enforcement of laws among the urban residents and those from the higher socioeconomic level than among the rural and low socioeconomic strata during the early historical period may still hold true at present. The former group easily uses or misuses legal channels while the latter are unfamiliar with laws and regard formal channels as unreliable.

In general, the traditional norms, patterns of behavior, and the law allow considerable autonomy and equality to Filipino women. As shown above, however, it is not primarily women's status against men that needs improvement and development but the lower-income, rural, and married women's situation.

The Empirical Study

As noted before, the material used in this presentation is based on an earlier study on intergenerational perceptions of filial responsibility. The study is essentially a field survey in which 40 elderly widows and their primary care-givers were interviewed. Based on widows' report, the daughter who provides them the most care and support is identified as the primary care-giver.

The study was conducted in Los Baños, a town on Luzon, one of the two largest islands, which lies 62 kilometers (32.4 miles) southeast of Manila, the capital. Los Baños, which is basically an agricultural community, consists of 13 *barangays*. (A *barangay* is the smallest sociopolitical unit in the country.) Sixty-five percent of the total population of 49,523 (Municipal Census Supervisor's Report, 1980) reside in ten *barangays* that are classified as rural.[2] The other 35 percent of the population live in the remaining three urban *barangays*. Los Baños is the site for one of the campuses of the University of the Philippines system and a number of national and international research centers. The urban portions of the town have business and recreational establishments that cater to the university population and to its residents. Furthermore, the university and other institutions are major employers in the southern Tagalog region of the country.

The sample comes from two urban and two rural *barangays* of Los Baños. The two urban *barangays* constitute the town proper or *poblacion*, where the municipal hall is located, with a town church and regular church services, a public market, a health center, a town park near the lake, and commercial and recreational establishments. Except for a *barangay* chapel, all other facilities in the urban *barangays* are absent in the two rural areas. The latter, however, are not more than five miles from the *poblacion* and the other urban *barangay*; hence, resources in the urban areas are physically accessible by jeeps and tricycles, the town's public transport. It might be worth mentioning that relatively few people, especially in the rural areas, have their own transportation. Among the 40 households studied, only five owned a car.

Characteristics of Elderly Widows

The widows in the study are not representative of all widows in Los Baños or in the Philippines. These are widows who have at least one daughter living in the same *barangay*. Between a son and a daughter who are accessible, the latter is assumed to provide more care and support to the widow. Not included in the study are widows who have sons only, or who have daughter(s) in another place but not in the same community. Also excluded are those who do not have any children or relatives. Forty-five percent of the respondents come from the rural *barangays*, the other 55 percent from the urban communities.

Demographic Characteristics

The elderly widows' ages range from 61 to 100 years; the mean age for the group is 69.6 years. Length of widowhood varies from six months to 40 years, with an average of 15.2 years, which indicates that at the time of her husband's death, the respondent was 54.4 years old. Thirty percent have been widows for less than six years. Two of the 40 were widowed twice.

Nearly three-fourths of the women have no more than a fifth-grade education and only one respondent has a college degree. Their education is approximately at the fourth-grade level, an average of 3.93 years. Eleven of the 18 rural widows did not go beyond the first grade. Among urban widows, except for the one who finished college, all have seven or less years of schooling. Their average amount of education (5 years) is higher than those of the rural women (1.2 years).

Annual income ranges from zero to 108,000 pesos ($12,705), with a mean of 16,730 pesos ($1,968).[3] One urban widow reported not receiving any income from any source. Rural–urban difference in income is evident among this group of women. The average annual income of urban widows (25,366 pesos or $2,984) is almost four times as much as that of rural women (6,655 or $783). Two-thirds of urban and one-third of rural respondents have more than one source of income. Children are the most commonly mentioned source of income, with 60 percent of all widows being recipients. One-fifth report children as their only source of income. About four out of ten widows (rural and urban) have a farm that provides seasonal income. These farms, like most farms in the Philippines, are much smaller than farms in the United States. Thirty percent earn money through sales, either as *sari-sari* (small variety) store owner, market vendor, or street peddler. Pension is received by eleven of the forty widows, ten being surviving dependents and one as a retired government employee. Only three women mention rentals, interest, and dividends as income sources.

Urban–rural differential in income of widows may be traced from the socioeconomic status of their families when their husbands were still alive. Sixteen of the 18 rural widows worked as market vendor, street peddler, *sari-sari* store owner, or farmhand. As household treasurer, these women were aware of their financial status; hence, they engaged in income-producing activities to augment their husband's earnings from farming, fishing, or hired labor. To lower-class women, working outside the home is considered an extension of their being a good wife and mother (Licuanan and Gonzalez, cited by Gonzalez and Hollnsteiner, 1976). Nine of those 16 who worked previously continued to earn money through the same activity. In contrast, only nine of the 22 urban widows worked, either as dressmaker, market vendor, or teacher (the college-degree holder) when their husband was alive. The others were full-time homemakers. One of those who worked earlier still has her clothing stall at the marketplace. Another widow, who considered herself a full-time housekeeper before, opened a *sari-sari* store recently; she indicates it primarily gives her something to do. Occupation of most urban husbands included services in government, community and business, and teaching in the university. Four husbands who were with the U.S. Army earned dollars, hence, their relatively higher income in pesos, and subsequently, the higher income of their surviving widows.

Three-fourths of the respondents (18 urban and 12 rural widows) own their place of residence. Twenty-five (62 percent) are in the same house they lived in when their husband was still alive. Ten (25 percent) moved to the homes of their children or other relatives after their husband's death. It must be pointed out here that rural housing is quite different from housing in the urban areas. Many rural homes are small and temporary, usually made of light materials such as nipa, bamboo, and a few pieces of lumber, and in some cases, with concrete walls and ground floor. Urban homes, especially of better-off families, are relatively bigger, more solid, comfortable, and expensive. However, whatever the house structure is, family members tend to share the living space. Half of the respondents belong to a household of five or fewer members. Most of the households (65 percent) consist of three generations: the elderly widow, married child(ren) and spouse(s), and grandchildren. One widow resides with her married grandson's family. Eleven are in two-generation households: ten with unmarried children and one with a grandson. As expected, only two of the 40 widows live alone. However, they have at least one child as next-door neighbor.

Health Status of Widows

Although most widows suffer from arthritis (80 percent), insomnia (50 percent), and blood circulation problems (42 percent), their functional health assessments show that 75 percent are able to walk half a mile, take care of themselves, and do household tasks without help. More than half rate their health as either good or excellent. Other health findings indicate that, in spite of the perceived decline in their health status, the elderly widows consider themselves as healthy as, or healthier than, others of the same age.

Characteristics of Adult Children

Widows in the study have a total of 198 children, an average of five per respondent; the typical filial gender profile is three females and two males. Over half (54 percent) of all offspring are females. Forty-eight percent of all children are of rural mothers, 52 percent of urban mothers. In conformity with the design of the study, all mothers have at least one daughter. Five of these daughters are lone offspring and another five are only daughters in a family with children of both sexes. Twenty-three widows (58 percent) have children who are all married or had been married; three daughters are widows and one is separated. Forty percent have both married and single offspring. Only one mother has children who are all single. This indicates that 42 percent of the widows have at least one child who has never married.

The level of education of adult children, a mean of 9.7 years, is higher than their mother's. Reflective of the national trend, rural–urban differential is evident in the educational attainment of this group. The average years of schooling for urban and rural sons are 12.9 and 7.1 years, respectively. Urban daughters' educational level, an average of 12.9 years, is much higher than that of their rural counterparts at 5.9 years. Moreover, 74 percent of urban children have a college degree compared to only 9 percent of those from the rural areas. The difference in socioeconomic level between urban and rural families may help explain the trend in education of children. It is possible that those from the rural areas are forced to drop out of school early because of financial difficulties. Early marriage, especially of rural daughters, may also have contributed to low educational attainment.

Similar to education, there are marked differences between occupations of rural and urban children. The majority of sons of rural mothers (64 percent) are either farmers, fishermen, or hired laborers. Ten percent belong to the professional-technical group; another 5 percent are unemployed. Among the rural daughters, more than half (52 percent) are either housekeepers or housekeeper-farmers. Thirty-one percent engage in sales (market vendor, *sari-sari* store owner, street peddler, or middlewomen of farm produce). Almost half of urban sons (49 percent) are business proprietors, administrators, or in professional-technical occupations. Fifteen percent have clerical or office jobs, and another 15 percent are unemployed. Most of the urban daughters are in the following occupational groups: professional-technical and administration, 44 percent; full-time homemaking, 31 percent; and clerical, 14 percent.

As mentioned above, the majority of the widows do not live alone. Nine out of ten mothers live with at least one child. Eighty-two percent of urban and 50 percent of rural households have at least one employed son or daughter living with them. There are more urban (39 percent) than rural children (20 percent) who live with their mothers. This may be attributed to the higher proportion of unmarried offspring in the urban communities (32 percent) than in the rural areas (17 percent). In the Philippines it is not uncommon for unmarried children to continue to live with their parents no matter how old they are, especially if they do not have any job or their place of work is in the area of residence of the parents. In some ways this arrangement maintains emotional closeness, security, and interdependence in the family. Thus, mothers who have more unmarried children tend to have more children living with them.

Widows in the study have children not only at home but also nearby. Again, the rural–urban difference is significant here, with 77 percent of rural mothers versus 40 percent of urban women having at least one child in the same community. In addition, more than half, 58 percent, of rural children compared to only 21 percent of sons of urban mothers live in the same *barangay* as their mother or in another community in Los Baños. Apparently, those from the urban areas tend to move outside their place of origin more than do rural children. The trend is evidenced by 40 percent of urban sons and daughters in another town or province, or even abroad, compared to 22 percent of their rural counterparts. The higher educational attainment of children from the urban areas may have opened up job opportunities in other places, hence, their higher rate of migration.

Children's Contributions to Support Systems

The discussion on contributions of adult children to support systems of mothers includes the latter's report on their filial expectations and actual support received from their children. Twenty-five items of filial support are considered here. These items are classified into five types, namely: (a) financial and material aid, (b) personal care, (c) service provision, (d) respect, and (e) warmth and affection. Mean scores of the widows for each type of support represent the amount or frequency of aid they expect or receive from their children.[4]

Financial and Material Aid

This type of support includes money received on a regular and/or occasional basis, financial help in times of crisis, food, and clothing. Financial items are expressed in terms of quantity (large or small amount), while frequency of provision is used to measure food and clothing support. In general, widows expect very little financial and material aid from their children (table 8.1). A comparison between expectations and support provision by children shows that widows receive more assistance in this category than they expect. This trend may be attributed to the fact that almost all of them reside with at least one child. In living together, resources are usually shared with minimal or no formal arrangement. Two mothers, for example, say they do not have to expect any money from their children because they live and eat together. Three indicate their children volunteer to give money, hence, there is no need to expect it. Similar to the speculations offered by Streib (1958), Shanas (1962), and Lopata (1973) in their study of the elderly and widows, women in the present study might have felt that expecting financial support would threaten their affectional ties with their children. It must also be remembered that a widow might just expect assistance from one offspring and not from others, hence, their low overall score for expectation. Further, those who have sufficient income might have thought they do not need any economic assistance from their children.

Three items of economic support are commonly received by mothers either in small or large amounts from more than half of the children: occasional monetary help, financial aid in crisis, and food assistance (table 8.2). It must be noted that all widows receive financial aid from at least one of their children in one form or another. One mother might also get financial assistance from more than one adult child. Between sons and daughters, mothers expect and receive more economic support from the latter (table 8.1). The difference is evident in items of food, financial help in times of crisis, and clothing. Seventy-eight percent of all daughters versus 56 percent of sons extend food assistance to the widows. Also, in times of crisis more daughters (64 percent) are able to help financially than sons (43 percent). More females (60 percent) than males (27 percent) pay for clothing for their mother.

Urban and rural children differ in their provision of financial and material aid. More urban (31 percent) than rural daughters (4 percent) give their mother money regularly. These urban women, who might be employed and living with their mother, turn over part of their salary to her, not as financial help, but to be used for the whole household. In such a case the mother continues to perform her household manager-treasurer role. On the other hand, more rural (85 percent) than urban

Table 8.1   Amounts of Support Widows Expect and Receive from Children, the Philippines

Type of support	Mean amount expected[a]			Mean amount received[a]		
	All children[b]	Sons[c]	Daughters[b]	All children[b]	Sons[c]	Daughters[a]
Financial and material aid	1.34	1.22	1.42	1.70	1.57	1.80
Personal care	1.31	1.11	1.42	1.39	1.13	1.48
Service provision	1.39	1.05	1.54	1.59	1.21	1.79
Respect	2.64	2.60	2.68	2.67	2.61	2.71
Warmth and affection	1.57	1.54	1.58	2.15	2.10	2.22

[a] Range = 1–3; 1 = none or never, 2 = little or some, and 3 = much or frequently.
[b] Number of widows = 40.
[c] Number of widows with son(s) = 34.

Table 8.2   Percentages of Children Providing Various Types of Support to Their Mothers, the Philippines

	Amount provided		
Type of support	None or never	Little or some, occasionally	Much, frequently
Financial and material aid			
Regular monetary support	82	7	10
Money in crisis	46	27	27
Occasional money	43	44	13
Clothing	55	36	8
Food	32	34	34
Personal care[a]			
Grooming	89	9	2
Dressing	90	9	1
Bathing	91	9	1
Sick care	30	26	44
Eating	93	7	
Service provision[a]			
Laundry	79	14	7
Food preparation	65	20	15
Shopping	67	18	15
Cleaning	79	14	6
Escorting	46	31	23
Respect[a]			
Action	2	25	74
Speech	2	12	85
Family socials	5	42	53
Consulting	10	48	42
Listening	3	19	78
Warmth and affection[a]			
Gift-giving	24	29	47
Visiting	6	34	60
Pasalubong[b]	16	32	53
Recreational materials	86	10	4
Touch and hug	26	25	48

[a] Percentages are based on number of children for which widows have responses.

[b] Item (different from a gift) that is brought to the widow by a child who comes from a trip, shopping, or when visiting, if from another town or province.

daughters (71 percent) are food givers. It is possible that with lower income and some farm produce, rural women would be more able to share food than money. One widow, for example, reports receiving a supply of rice from one of her daughters in another province. Sons of rural mothers tend to give more food and financial assistance during crisis than their urban counterparts. Because more rural children live within the same community as their mother, it might be easier for them to extend food and financial assistance, especially during emergencies.

Personal Care

This category assesses the frequency of direct aid for the physical care of the widow. Items included are help in grooming, dressing, bathing, eating, and sick care. Elderly widows expect and receive very little assistance from their children in the area of personal care, especially from sons (table 8.1). Their expectations and actual support received from sons and daughters are notably different, with the latter favored as provider. The most frequent help received by mothers is care during illness (table 8.2). Ninety-one percent of daughters who are accessible (within Los Baños or nearby places) take care of their mother when she is sick. The difference between the proportions of rural and urban daughters (94 percent and 88 percent, respectively) who provide sick care is minimal—an indication that both groups of daughters make themselves available when their mother is ill. Only a few daughters (9–17 percent) and no sons help their mother with grooming, dressing, bathing, and eating.

Less assistance provided by children in personal care may be attributed to the health status of the mothers. These women are physically healthy, hence, are able to take care of their own physical needs. Also, there are other family members who may be providing the widows assistance in personal care. Ten widows, for example, mentioned that their granddaughters help them with grooming (cutting nails and combing hair) and bathing.

Service Provision

The items included in this type of support are considered instrumental to the widow's comfort and convenience; they are food preparation, shopping, cleaning, doing the laundry, and escorting. Similar to their reports on personal care, widows express low expectation and receive little assistance from children in this support category (table 8.1). Overall, however, the amount of service provided by children is significantly higher than the amount mothers expect. Also, there is a significant difference in expectations for service provision between sons and daughters. The same is true for amount of service received from both sexes. Mothers expect and receive more service from daughters than from sons. This does not come as a surprise because four of the five service items (food preparation, shopping, cleaning, and laundry) are traditionally defined as female tasks. Lopata's (1979) findings also point out the importance of daughters in the widows' service-support system, especially in the female-activity areas.

Escorting is the only service item that most children (30 percent of sons and 68 percent of daughters who are accessible) provide to their mother (table 8.2). The proportion of daughters living within Los Baños who render the other services to the widows are as follows: 53 percent in food preparation, 50 percent in shopping, 36 percent in cleaning, and 33 percent in laundry. As in other types of support, a widow might receive help from just one daughter for all items or she might have two or more children doing the tasks for her. It is also possible that she does not get any assistance in some of the service items.

As mentioned earlier, widows in general are in good health and are physically active. They can do things for themselves, do household tasks, and can move around town with ease using public transportation; hence, they are able to continue performing their housekeeping role. Twenty-three (58 percent) report taking care of their grandchildren or great grandchildren almost every day. Twenty-two (55 percent) prepare food daily for the whole household. The same number do some house-cleaning regularly. Eighteen (45 percent) do their own laundry. Sixteen (40 percent) go to the public market almost every day, not only to shop but to socialize as well.

The division of labor in some urban households reflects interdependence between the mother and daughters rather than assistance to the former. For example, five mothers who live with employed daughters act as manager of the household. Their responsibility includes shopping, budgeting household finances, care of grandchildren (if there are any), and doing menial household tasks. If there is a live-in paid help (usually female), she does almost all the activities in the house. All in all, there are one rural and eight urban households with at least one live-in paid help. The daughter, on the other hand, provides money for

food, bills, and household maintenance and helps with some light
tasks when she gets home from work. Possibly, other households have
similar task allocations to members.

Respect

Respect as a support category involves children's show of regard and
deference, recognition of the widow's experience and knowledge, and
recognition of her presence. The items included here are respect
through actions and speech, inclusion of the widow in family conversation and family social events, consulting by the children when having
problems or making important decisions, and listening. Of all support
categories, respect is expected and received most by mothers from
their children (table 8.1). No significant difference is found between
expectations and provisions in this area. Also, mothers perceive no
difference in respect shown by sons and daughters. These findings
show relatively high demand for respect by widows. Specific items that
are given special attention by the children are show of respect through
speech, actions, and listening (table 8.2). Among children who are
accessible, 23 percent of urban sons do not consult with their mothers
about their problems or in decision making. Mothers, however, consider such action more a sign of independence than disrespect. One
widow comments, "He is already of age so he knows what he is doing."

As mentioned before, generational respect is strongly valued in Philippine culture. This is further emphasized by some respondents when
asked about their expectations for warmth and affection. One widow
said, "My children do not have to hug me or kiss me or give me
presents. What is important is for them to respect me, listen to me, talk
to me in a nice way, and treat me as a human being." In the same vein,
another commented, "What is hugging or kissing if they don't respect
you?" Furthermore, two mothers feel that touching (hugging and
kissing) is flirting with the children, which makes them disrespectful.

In spite of the report of high respect shown by children, some
mothers express displeasure about their relationship with at least one
child. Three mothers report that their daughter always answers back.
One widow is not on speaking terms with her two sons and considers
both very disrespectful. It is possible that other mothers feel the same
way about some of their children but because of the social desirability
of the topic, they gave favorable responses.

Warmth and Affection

This type of support refers to special concern and love received by the widows from their children through thoughtfulness and kindness, recognition of the widow's best interests, and physical touch. The items assess the frequency of gift-giving, visiting, provision of *pasalubong* and recreational materials, and touching and hugging. *Pasalubong* is an item or items different from a gift that is brought to the widow by an adult child who comes from a trip, or shopping, or when visiting (if from another town or province).

Warmth and affection rank second to respect in terms of expectation and support received from children by the widows. The amount of support provided by children for this category exceeds the amount expected (table 8.1). No significant difference is found between sons and daughters in this area. This observation and the above finding on respect are contrary to Lopata's (1979) findings, which indicate the domination of daughters in the emotional support system of the widows; apparently, mothers in the present study view both sons and daughters as sources of affective support. The contradiction, however, may be attributed to the different measures used in the two studies.

Warmth and affection are expressed by the majority of the children through visits, *pasalubong*, gifts, and touch and hugs (table 8.2). Giving recreational materials, apparently, is not considered by most children as a gesture of warmth and affection. It is only the urban children who give their mother some items of recreation, usually reading materials. One difference noted among children is in gift-giving. The fact that more daughters (85 percent) than sons (66 percent) give presents to their mothers may be indicative of expressiveness and thoughtfulness of the former. Urban daughters (92 percent) tend to be more into gift-giving than women from the rural *barangays* (74 percent). Presumably, those from the urban areas have more financial resources such that most of them are able to give presents to their mothers.

Summary and Implications

As shown above, three major trends characterize the provision of support by children to the widows. First, mothers receive more financial and material aid, service, and warmth and affection than they expect from their children. Expectations for respect and personal care from their offspring are congruent with the amounts of support provided to them in those areas. These findings indicate that mothers perceive their children as meeting their expectations in all support categories, indeed, exceeding expectations in three areas of support. In that the Filipino widows do not wish to be a burden, it is possible that having low expectations is an indirect form of aid to the children. That is, modest demands may free up material and psychological resources of children, allowing these to be directed toward the multiple responsibilities to their own families and jobs. Also, lower expectations bring fewer disappointments, hence, receiving more support than one expects may enhance satisfaction. Widows who expect less and receive more would "take more pleasure in their children's care, love, and attention" (Castillo, 1977:347).

Second, sex differential in the provision of support to mothers is evident in the study. Mothers expect and receive more financial and material aid, personal care, and service from daughters than from sons. This observation supports the importance of the care-giving role of daughters in the life of aged parents in the Philippines. Studies in Western cultures have revealed similar findings (Townsend, 1957; Adams, 1968; Lopata, 1973, 1979; Shanas, 1979). Adult daughters, more than sons, are involved in parental care and support. In the present study, however, both male and female children are sources of affective support for mothers.

Lastly, provision of support by children from rural and urban barangays diverges in some categories. The differences, particularly in financial and material aid, reflect the resources available to them and their mothers. Because women and children in the rural areas have relatively lower incomes than those from the urban areas, food instead of money becomes an important support item. Likewise, the proximity of many rural children has made it easier for them to provide food assistance and financial help in crisis. Urban children, especially daughters who live with their mother and are employed, are more apt to give money regularly and retain the mother in her treasurer-homemaker role. Further, urban widows who are relatively well-off are able to solve their financial problems, hence, they do not need any help from their children. It is interesting to note that, overall, children from both urban and rural areas show considerable respect and warmth and affection to their mothers.

All in all, the study suggests that the Filipino widows, unlike their counterparts in developed countries, do not live independently, but in interdependence with their families. This arrangement is primarily attributed to the cultural values Filipino families uphold and to the socioeconomic situations of families. A Filipino widow, then, has a special place in the home like any other family member, not only because of her homemaking skills and other resources but also because she is a mother (and/or grandmother), respected and loved. However, she and her family are not without problems. With the worsening of the Philippine economy, one can only guess the fate of widows and their families, especially those from the rural and low-income groups in the country.

Although this research has focused primarily upon filial support, children are not the sole contributors to the widows' support systems. Similar to Lopata's (1979) study, a clearer understanding of the dynamics of support of elderly Filipino widows, or older people in general, might emerge from research examining other sources of support. These might include, for instance, neighbors, friends, other relatives, and community resources. Moreover, the results of the present study pertain to a small purposive sample of widows. Research utilizing larger, more representative samples of elderly Filipino parents might enhance the reliability and generalizability of these data. In the absence of such research, the present results remain suggestive.

9 Widowed Women in Melbourne, Australia

LINDA ROSENMAN AND ARTHUR D. SHULMAN

This chapter focuses on the needs and the support systems of widowed women in Australia, specifically of women in Melbourne, one of the country's major cities. The report is based on the findings of an in-depth, structured interview with widowed people—both women and men—that was carried out in 1980.[1]

The Australian Setting

Australia is a country of fifteen million people. Although its population is small relative to its land mass, it is also one of the most urbanized countries in the world. Over one-third of the population lives in two cities—Sydney and Melbourne. The majority of the population, 70 percent, lives in the coastal capital cities and in a small number of regional cities along the coast and inland. Outside of the cities, population density is extremely low.

Although geographically situated in the Western Pacific Basin and close to Southeast Asia, the population is mainly of European, particularly of British descent. In 1981, 21 percent of the population was foreign-born. Language, customs, and heritage are British, although immigration policy since the end of World War II has brought in a large non-English-speaking population. Originally migrants were drawn from southern and Eastern Europe; more recently they have come from Southeast Asia.

While rates of immigration are high, rates of internal migration are relatively low. In 1980, 16 percent of the population aged over 15 changed residence, but of these only 10 percent were interstate moves; 50 percent stayed in the same capital city, and 40 percent in the same state. There is, however, some evidence of the beginning of retirement migration of older people from the south to the warmer coastal areas of the northeast. This particularly affects Melbourne, which has one of the colder winters in Australia.

The patterns of migration have important implications for social policy and practice relating to widowhood. Approximately 22 percent of the widowed females and 24 percent of the widowed males are foreign-born. Of these, close to 40 percent of the widowed women and one-third of the men are from countries other than the United Kingdom or Ireland. This implies, first, that many of the widowed who are migrants may not have a functioning family support network available to them, and, second, that there will be social and ethnic differences and cultural prescriptions about widowhood that are often not understood by the larger society. While members of many migrant groups, especially Italians and Greeks, may have been living in Australia for many years, it is not uncommon for the women, in particular, to have learned very little English and to have relied upon husbands and/or children for communication with the larger English-speaking society. Such women face major difficulties on the death of a spouse. In addition, for the widow, conflicts may occur between the cultural prescriptions relating to mourning in her society of origin and the expectations of Australian society, and often of her Australianized children. Some of the conflicts were made clear in interviews with a subsample of Greek-speaking widows, as will be discussed.

Age, Sex, and Marital Patterns

There are approximately equal numbers of women and men in Australia. At early ages the number of men slightly exceeds the number of women; beyond age 50 the "masculinity ratio" declines, due to higher male mortality rates. At ages 65 and above, there are approximately 72 men to every 100 women. As the population ages, it becomes increasingly female and is increasingly likely to be widowed. Women in Australia tend to marry men older than themselves, and since mortality is greater for males at every age, women are likely to spend some proportion of their later years as widows. In 1982 life expectancy at birth was 71.2 years for males and 78.2 years for females.

Rates of marriage are high for both women and men. In 1982 the median age at first marriage was 24.6 years for males and 22.4 for women. Among the majority of Australians, selection of a marital partner follows a similar pattern to that of North America and Western Europe; i.e., men and women make their own decision about marriage and parental consent is not required by the state unless either partner is under 18. Arranged marriages are still practiced among some of the migrant groups, particularly the Arab minorities. Divorce, since 1975, has been relatively easy to obtain on the sole ground of irretrievable breakdown of marriage. Prior to 1975 there were many different grounds, requiring the attribution of fault, and long waiting periods. Perhaps for this reason, there were several women in our sample who admitted that their marriages had been unhappy but that divorce had been either unacceptable or unattainable; consequently, widowhood had not been altogether unwelcome. Widowhood still is the major cause of marital termination for both women and men. In 1981, 11 percent of the female population aged over 15 was widowed, with the incidence of widowhood increasing with age (see table 9.1).

Table 9.1   Percentage of Female Population Widowed, and Percentage of Total Female Population by Age, Melbourne, Australia

Age (years)	Female	Women widowed
15–19	48.9	.02
20–29	49.4	.26
30–39	49.4	1.03
40–49	48.9	3.77
50–59	49.4	11.62
60–69	52.8	25.31
70 and older	58.0	60.36

Source: Australian Bureau of Statistics, 1981 Census of Population and Housing.

The Research Setting

Melbourne, with a population in 1980 of 2.8 million, is the second largest city in Australia. It is situated on the southern coast of the mainland of Australia. The city and suburbs are built around a large port and harbor—Port Phillip Bay—but as do most Australian cities, it covers a large area with suburban development sprawling north and east into the mountains, and in the west almost into the neighboring city of Geelong. Despite its large area, public transport is relatively good, accessible, efficient, and cheap, but it tends to be designed for moving people into and out of the central business district. Public transportation between suburbs or across the country is relatively poor.

Economically, Melbourne was originally the manufacturing and financial center of Australia. In recent years the nationwide decline in manufacturing has led to large-scale loss of employment in many of the industries in which women were employed, particularly in garment manufacturing and other light industries that were centered in Melbourne.

Melbourne was traditionally seen as the most "English" of Australian cities, but ethnically it is now extremely mixed, with large Chinese, Greek, and Italian populations, the largest Jewish population in Australia, and a recent influx of Vietnamese immigrants. The Chinese, Greek, Italian, and Jewish communities are well-established, with their own cultural, welfare, and educational programs, newspapers, and community centers. While the original migrants still tend to live in the inner city and adjacent suburbs, their more-affluent children have tended to move to the outer suburbs. As in many cities, members of ethnic groups have tended to settle in geographical proximity to one another, leading to concentrations of ethnic clubs, restaurants, and other facilities within certain areas.

The climate is not as extreme as that of American cities such as Chicago or St. Louis. Accordingly, it is less likely to limit the ability to get around.

Research Design and Procedure

The research on which this report is based collected comprehensive data on widowed women and men in Melbourne in 1977 and 1980. Information was collected on the social, economic, health, and employment-related situations of the widowed, as well as psychological, emotional, and mental health needs. Data were also elicited on the personal, family, and community resources used to deal with such problems and their usefulness. Parallel data have also been collected on widowed women in St. Louis, Missouri, in the United States, enabling cross-national comparisons to be made (Rosen, Shulman, and Cartwright, 1981).

The research was carried out in two phases. The initial study was carried out from June–August 1977 and was aimed at collecting background information on widowed women in Australia. Based on the results of an open-ended pilot interview phase, a structured interview schedule was developed. This was administered to a sample of 298 widowed women who were obtained from a pool of five hundred, most of whom volunteered to be interviewed (See Penman, Rosenman, and Shulman, 1981). Then, in 1980, the major study of widowed women was carried out in Melbourne; this paralleled the study being carried out in the United States. The interview schedule developed in the United States was adapted for Australian conditions, taking into account the results of the earlier Australian study (Rosenman, 1982).

The sampling procedure drew a stratified random sample of widowed women and men. The sample pool was obtained from records kept by five Melbourne funeral directors, whose clientele ranged across the socioeconomic spectrum. The sample was stratified by five age categories—under 39; 40–49; 50–59; 60–69; and 70 and over. Length of widowhood was similarly stratified into three time periods since the death of the spouse—6–18 months, 19–36 months, and 37–60 months. Once selected, widows and widowers were sent a letter describing the project and enclosing a paid reply card on which they could indicate their willingness to participate in the interview. The interviews were carried out predominantly in the widow's home by trained interviewers. Most of the women were interviewed between June and August 1980. During this phase, 243 widowed women and 131 widowed men were interviewed. For the purposes of this chapter the discussion will be mainly limited to the findings on the widows from the 1980 study.

Respondents were required to speak English well enough to be able to be interviewed; of the 20 percent of the sample that was foreign-born, half came from a non-English-speaking country. In addition, a smaller study of 30 Greek widows was carried out, with a version of the interview schedule translated into Greek and adapted to Greek-Australian conditions. These women were selected from records of

Greek funeral directors in Melbourne and the Greek Welfare Society. The interviews were carried out in Greek by a Greek-speaking member of the project staff (Kobatsiari, 1981).

Needs and Difficulties Brought Up By the Widowed

The research uncovered many difficulties and problems that the widowed saw themselves as experiencing. Most of these data were gathered by giving respondents a list of areas of need that had been generated from the initial studies. They were asked whether or not they had been experiencing any difficulties in those areas, and, if so, to discuss in more detail the nature of the difficulties, and what, if any, they perceived as ways of dealing with them. The respondents were asked to discuss personal, family, and societal resources that they had drawn on to meet these needs and to give an evaluation of how useful these resources had been. The resources used, and their assessed usefulness in helping to deal with problems, are indicative of the availability of social supports and the accessibility and knowledge about social resources within the community.

While in most cases significant differences in needs and resources did not exist in terms of how long a person had been widowed, retrospective information suggests that most people saw the few months immediately after the spouse's death as having been the most stressful time and of having generated a wide range of needs and problems. Those whose spouses had gone through a period of terminal illness or declining health prior to the death also saw this "forewarning" period as having been extremely difficult and as having placed major stresses on the family's financial, as well as social and emotional, resources, particularly upon the children.

Ethnic differences are somewhat harder to assess since we interviewed only a small sample of Greek widows. However, in general, their difficulties, especially those related to financial management and emotional readjustment and health, were particularly severe.

In relatively few cases did women see their difficulties as having existed before they were widowed—with the exception of those who had had spouses with a terminal illness. Many of the difficulties associated with widowhood, then, arose from adjusting to living as a single person in a larger society organized by, for, and around marriage and

family existence. In addition, they were related to age and stage of the
life span. Younger widowed women expressed significantly more difficulties than older women, with the exception of health and transportation, which were particularly likely to be seen as problems for
widowed women in their sixties and beyond (see table 9.2).

The six most frequently mentioned areas of concern—loneliness,
home maintenance, health, psychological and emotional problems,
financial concerns, and planning for the future—are closely linked
to the availability and accessibility of resources and support systems.

Table 9.2   Areas of Difficulty or Concern at the Time of the Interview,
Melbourne, Australia (ordered by percentages reporting need)

	Unremarried widowed women $N = 239$	
Rank	Concern	Percent
1	Loneliness	51.1
2	Home maintenance/household matters	32.2
3	Health	31.4
4	Psychological/emotional problems	23.9
5	Financial matters	23.0
6	Planning for future	23.0
7	Children	20.9
8	Self-betterment	20.1
9	Transportation	18.0
10	Employment	15.5
11	Family (other than children)	15.5
12	Independence	15.1
13	Personal safety	15.1
14	Keeping busy/things to do	14.2
15	More free time	13.0
16	Opposite sex friends	11.7
17	Legal matters	8.4
18	Sexual matters	8.4
19	Privacy	7.5
20	Getting on with people	7.1
21	Issues related to spouse's death	7.1
22	Same sex friends	6.0
23	Funeral matters	0.78

Support Systems of Widowed Women

The support systems available to widowed women in Melbourne can be categorized into economic, service, and social supports. While the economic and service systems are potentially the same for most women, the extent to which women know about them, see them as being available, and utilize them varies considerably. The responses, in terms of resources used to meet needs, give some indication of the extent to which available resources were utilized.

The Economic Support System

Economic difficulties were directly mentioned by over a quarter of the sample. In addition, close to half of the women (48.6 percent) saw their economic status as having deteriorated since their spouse's death. This usually resulted from the loss of the spouse's earnings or pension. None of the women had been the major breadwinner in the family, so the death of the husband usually meant the loss of the family's major income source. Women in their forties and fifties were particularly likely to see their economic situation as having deteriorated. Before their husband's death, many of these families had begun to achieve some level of financial security—the husband having reached an acceptable level of income in his employment, and the costs associated with raising children having begun to abate. This relative economic comfort was usually lost at the husband's death. On the other hand, younger widowed women (49 percent of those aged under 40) were likely to see their income as being inadequate to meet their needs.

There are several possible sources of economic support for women in widowhood. One is dependence upon the income and assets left by the former husband. A second is for the widowed woman to rely upon herself in terms of her own income-generating capacity either through employment or service provision, e.g., renting rooms. A third is to receive economic assistance from the state in the form of publicly provided income-maintenance programs, and a fourth is receipt of economic assistance from family and friends.

The late spouse as an economic resource. In Australia, as in America, it is the responsibility of a husband to ensure financial security for his family after his death. Life insurance, disability, and retirement income schemes are available in the private sector for those with the resources and inclination to take advantage of them. Contributory pension schemes (known as "superannuation") are also available through some jobs, predominantly those in the public sector. Most occupational super-annuation schemes pay a widow's benefit in the event of the death of the plan participant while employed. Since most covered workers take their superannuation benefit as a lump sum payment at retirement, there is no provision made for a woman widowed after her husband has retired (Rosenman and Leeds, 1984).

In our sample the majority of men had done some planning for their families after their death. Most had made wills, but 17 percent of the men died intestate. Two-thirds of the women said that their spouse had organized his financial affairs before his death; however, thirty-three of the widowed women said that their lives would be easier now had their husbands made better arrangements while they were living for the financial security of their wives and families. Some of the most frequently mentioned comments were that the husband should have taken out life insurance, that he should have saved or invested more money for the family during his lifetime, or that he should have gone over financial matters with his wife before his death.

As can be seen from table 9.3, relatively few of the women reported receiving income from the husband's superannuation or life-insurance policies, but a majority were receiving income from investments or savings that had, in the majority of cases, been accumulated by, or jointly with, the husband. There is a definite age pattern in this. Women in their forties and fifties were more likely to be receiving some income from a husband's superannuation plan than were younger and older widows. The reasons for this are related to the employment and income levels attained by men in that age group, who are more likely to have access to and be fully vested in occupational superannuation schemes than are younger men or those past retirement. A higher proportion of younger widowed women, however, were receiving some income from life insurance policies, which men were more likely to have taken out when their families were young and ceased as their children grew up. Only a small proportion of women were receiving life insurance payments, and the amounts on average were fairly small. Older women, on the other hand, were likely to have some income from interest or dividends. Presumably men at retirement had made investments or saved money to supplement their pensions. This income would then be available to the widow.

There was a fairly high degree of correlation in terms of each of these income sources. Women whose husbands had superannuation coverage were also likely to have some life insurance income and to report higher amounts of dividends or interest income. Those women whose husbands had worked in low-paying jobs without fringe benefits were correspondingly less likely to have been able to rely on income left to her at his death.

The great majority (over 87 percent) of the widowed women in our sample owned their own homes. Rates of home ownership in Australia are high, and the women and their husbands usually owned, or were paying off, their own home. While this meant that the difficulties and costs associated with renting were less likely to be present, many of the women were experiencing physical and financial difficulties in maintaining their homes.

The income security system as an economic resource. The Australian Income Security System has a category of benefit specifically for widowed women. The Widows Pension established in 1942 is a non-contributory cash benefit designed to cover women against the loss of a spouse whether through death, divorce, or separation. It is contingent upon the woman having care of a dependent child (aged under 16) or herself being over the age of 50. Pension receipt is subject to a means test of income and assets.

The means test is tapered in such a way as to allow some other income to be earned and some pension benefits to be retained. At the time that these interviews were carried out (1980), pensioners who had less than $40 of other income a week also received free medical and hospital treatment as well as other fringe benefits. Consequently, it paid women to keep earned income low enough to continue to qualify for the Pensioner Health Benefits Card. Nearly two-thirds of the sample were receiving a pension.

Self as an economic resource. In Australia, as in other Western countries, employment is increasingly becoming accepted as the norm for women as well as for men. In 1983, 44.8 percent of all women between 15 and 60 years of age and 42.6 percent of married women were in the labor force. The labor-force participation of women has been increasing rapidly during the past decade, especially among younger women and those whose children have entered school. It tends to be expected that women with young children will stay at home; nevertheless, government-subsidized child care is provided for children from six weeks of age, although demand far outstrips availability. The younger widowed women were more likely to have been employed

Table 9.3   Percentage of Sample Receiving Income
from Different Income Sources by Age Category,
Melbourne, Australia

Age	Own earnings	Pension	Superan- nuation	Insurance
Under 40	65.9	48.8	26.8	14.6
40–49	51.9	44.4	44.4	17.8
50–59	55.9	54.2	30.5	8.5
60–69	9.4	77.4	28.3	5.7
70+	4.4	97.8	15.6	8.9
	37.3	65.1	29.5	10.9

at the time of the husband's death; older women, those widowed in
their fifties and sixties, were unlikely to have been employed since the
time of their marriage and were less likely to see working as a way of
dealing with financial problems. Retirement age for women in Australia is lower than for men. Sixty is the accepted retirement age for
women (compared with 65 for men), and many firms allow (and often
expect) women to retire at 55.

Among widowed women, labor-force participation is closely linked
to social welfare policy—particularly to income-maintenance policies.
The design of the pension systems in Australia is such as to limit
income from other sources—particularly through employment. The
availability of pensions provides an alternative to labor-force participation for those who fall into the categories covered by the pension
scheme. For widowed women in particular, employment is an alternative to full reliance on the pension.

One-third of the widows in our sample were employed. Slightly over
half (55 percent) of the employed women were working full time, the
remainder part time. Labor-force participation rates declined as age
increased. Close to two-thirds of the younger women were employed,
approximately half part time and half full time.

Widowed women had extremely varied reasons for working or not
working. The most frequent reasons given for working were, first,
financial need, second, companionship and keeping busy, and, third,
because the woman was "bored at home." It appears, then, that for
widowed women, work to some extent fulfills psychological and social
as well as purely financial needs.

Despite the increase in the incidence of paid employment for women

Interest dividends	Rental income/ Board	Help from social agencies	Regular help from family/friends	Other	W (%)
56.1	7.3	2.4	7.3	24.4	41
55.6	37.8	2.2	0	26.7	45
50.8	35.6	0	0	8.5	59
71.7	11.3	0	3.8	5.7	53
71.1	4.4	0	2.2	2.2	43
61.4	20.3	.8	2.4	12.7	241

in Australia, it is still socially accepted that women, particularly those with young children, should not work. It was not necessarily the case, however, that decisions on whether or not to work were completely dependent on whether or not the widow had dependent children. Multiple regression analysis indicated that the best predictors of whether a widowed woman would be working were her educational level and her prior work history. These are indicative of her earnings potential and her degree of career commitment.

Once these factors—i.e., education and previous work history—were controlled for, having young children at home reduced the probability that a woman would be working but was not statistically significant. It appears that having young children had a greater impact on whether the women decided to work part time rather than full time. Among women in particular, there is evidence of a cohort rather than strictly an age effect on employment. Younger women—whether or not they had dependent children—were more likely than middle-aged women to be working or feel a need to work. It is likely that younger women in general are more "career" or "work-committed" as a result of changing social mores and are probably likely to retain this attitude as they age. Women of working age—i.e., under 60—who did not work gave a combination of reasons for this decision, including poor health and fear of losing their Widow's Pension.

Sixteen percent of the women mentioned experiencing employment-related problems. They talked about the difficulties they were experiencing in finding employment or actually getting a job. For many, this was closely related to lack of skills or work experience and the need for additional education and job-related training.

The vast majority of the sample (86 percent) had a high-school education or less. Associated with enhancing employability or improving employment status was the desire expressed by over one-third of the women to take training or further education, but only ten of the women were actually pursuing training at the time of the interview, and most of these were experiencing at least some difficulties. These included time pressures (particularly if children were present) and lack of confidence in their own abilities. The reasons given for not taking training or education despite an interest in doing so were related to a fairly pervasive lack of self-confidence, which was expressed in terms of questioning their own ability to reenter education usually after many years away, and to practical problems associated with lack of information about available or appropriate programs, child care, transportation, and money issues.

Women who were working were particularly likely to see themselves as being under extreme stress and complain about needing more time. Since the majority had dependent children and were trying to juggle these responsibilities with home care and job, it was not surprising that most were so stressed. Nineteen of the 85 women who were employed had entered the labor force since their husbands' deaths, and they seemed to be having particular difficulties in adjusting to the stress of so many new demands being made upon their time.

Services that might help to make employment more feasible for widowed women, such as home help or a housekeeper who could provide after-school care, are provided by publicly funded services and by some local governments, but are usually short-term, and are rarely available to nonaged women. Given the low incomes of such women, such services are prohibitively expensive when purchased privately; only 4 percent of the women had hired a housekeeper. Those who did have a housekeeper enjoyed the benefit of a small percentage of the wages paid being rebatable through the income-tax system.

Family and friends as an economic resource. In Australia there is no social or legal expectation or obligation upon family or in-laws to financially support a widowed member. Consequently, family was much less likely to be viewed or used as a resource for dealing with economic problems. There were two potential means of help from family and friends. It tends to be expected in Australian families —particularly in those with low-to-moderate incomes—that working children pay a regular weekly amount for room and board. (This is listed as rental income or board in table 9.3.) Apart from this, regular help from friends or family was rarely reported, with the exception of the youngest women (i.e., under 40), several of whom were receiving regular income from a male friend. Several women, however, mentioned that in an emergency they could probably obtain some financial help from their families.

The income of widowed women. In general, widowed women in our sample were likely to report lower incomes than the men, and this is reflected in their complaints of financial need. There were two aspects of financial difficulties that were often, but not always, brought up in conjunction with one another. First was the difficulty of coping with limited resources and of making ends meet. A second general area of financial need (for women in particular) was the difficulties they were experiencing in having to manage finances and take the initiative in obtaining money—e.g., insurance or pension money to which they believed they were entitled.

The sources of income for these widowed women were varied. The majority of women had more than one source of income (table 9.3). Income sources also varied by age. Women under 40 were likely to be receiving some income from a variety of different sources—through their own employment, the government, the widow's pension, interest and dividends, and some superannuation from the deceased spouse. Widows in their forties were less likely to be receiving income from the widow's pension since they were less likely to have dependent children at home and were not eligible for the pension. A much higher percentage, however, were receiving payments from their spouse's superannuation. As age increased, the percentage of women receiving some pension income also increased.

The Service Support System

Most of the women perceived the need for services to provide help with home maintenance, health problems, and transportation.

Home maintenance. Maintenance of the home was one of the most frequently mentioned problem areas for widowed women of all ages. Two things that came up frequently were, first, the difficulty that many experienced in carrying out routine maintenance tasks around the home. The other was finding reliable tradesmen for major maintenance tasks. The problems that women faced arose partly from lack of financial resources to pay tradesmen and partly from lack of knowledge and experience with home maintenance tasks, which had usually been carried out by the husbands.

Home ownership rates in Australia are high, and Australians prefer to purchase a freestanding house on its own piece of land. Consequently, routine maintenance and yard work is a continual demand. In the majority of marriages such responsibilities were usually allocated to the husband. Over two-thirds of the women (68 percent) reported that home maintenance had been their husband's responsibility when he was alive. After his death, resources for dealing with home maintenance problems varied. The majority (80 percent) said they took major responsibility for it themselves, 10 percent said they relied on family or children, and a further 8 percent relied on hired help. In addition, over one-third of the women reported receiving some household help, including home maintenance, from their children.

Some municipal governments in Melbourne offered assistance with small-scale home-maintenance tasks to older people and widows living within the municipality. Either the local council had a handyman on staff, or the municipal social worker kept a list of reliable local tradesmen, which was available upon request.

Home maintenance was the major area in which a large number of widowed women said that they were not coping very well (43 percent of the women rated their effectiveness in handling home maintenance as poor or marginally adequate). Some women were contemplating selling their home and moving into an apartment because of the cost and difficulty of routine home maintenance.

Transportation. Getting around was a particular difficulty for the older women (60 and over). Many of these problems arose because women had relied on their husbands for transportation, had never obtained a driver's license, felt they were too old to learn how to drive, and that they could not manage to maintain a car in any case. The rate of car ownership declined with age. Ninety-seven percent of widows under 40 owned a car in comparison with only 33 percent of those over 70. Those who owned cars found the cost of car maintenance, and the difficulty of dealing with mechanics, something of a challenge. In the vast majority of families car maintenance had been the responsibility of the husband.

The major resource for getting around among those who did not own a car was public transportation, which in Melbourne is efficient, safe, reasonably priced, and those on pensions obtain fare concessions.

However, poor health and, to some extent, concern with physical safety were given as reasons for not using public transport, particularly at night. Difficulty with transportation was likely to influence decisions on where to live, ability to participate in social activities, the nature of such activities, and social contacts. In particular, it exacerbated the sense of isolation and loneliness and lack of independence that many of the widowed reported following the death of a spouse.

Adult children and teenage sons were also relied on for help with car maintenance by those who did own a car, and for chauffeuring by those who did not. About 10 percent of those older women who did not own a car relied on children (often adult daughters) to get them around.

Health. A relatively large number of women reported concerns about their health. This agrees with findings from other research carried out both in Australia and in the United States, which suggests that bereavement tends to be linked to a deterioration in physical and emotional health (Clayton, 1976; Maddison and Viola, 1968; Raphael, 1975). Maddison found marked differences between his samples of Australian and American widows in terms of reported medical conditions and utilization of prescription drugs. We found similar patterns.

The Australian sample reported more health problems, rated their health as worse, and reported almost double the number of physician visits compared with our sample of St. Louis widows. It is possible that the Australian widows were, in fact, much less healthy than the American—something that only objective medical ratings could have assessed. However, the fact that over 30 percent of the Australian women reported their physician as a resource, compared with only 17 percent of the American women, suggests that there may be other factors underlying the relatively high rates of physician usage. Our earlier study of widows in Melbourne showed that after friends and family, the doctor was the third most frequently mentioned resource for dealing with problems (Rosenman et al., 1981).

The widows in this study were likely to mention using their physician as a resource for dealing with a wide range of problems in addition to medical care, including emotional support and guidance, emotional and health problems with children, and with family problems in general. Three major interacting societal factors seem likely as explanations for this pattern. One is the structure of medical practice, the second the financing of health care, and the third the relative availability of other, nonmedical, professionals. In Australia, medical practice is still based on the family doctor as the primary source of medical care. Health care is less likely to be carried out by specialists, and general practitioners are based in the community, usually practicing from a storefront, small clinic, or private home rather than from a medical complex. They are likely to know all members of a family and to be acquainted with the personal and social situation of the patient as well as with her/his medical problems.

Other research in Australia (McCaughey et al., 1977) has found that the general practitioner is usually the professional to whom problems are taken in the first instance. In Australia there are also relatively smaller numbers of counselors or other helping professionals. Counseling professionals (psychiatrists, psychologists, social workers) were rarely mentioned by the widows as resources for helping to deal with problems. Slightly more than 4 percent of the sample mentioned using a professional counselor as a resource, compared with the over 30 percent who reported using a medical practitioner.

The structure of medical practice in Australia contributes to the physician being seen as a general helper who is usually familiar with the widowed's family, will usually have known the deceased spouse, and provided continuous care throughout the illness and period of bereavement. In the United States, by comparison, medical care tends to be highly specialized—rarely does the entire family see the same physician, and focus in physician visits tends to be on medical problems. Other helping professions—social work, clinical psychology—exist to fill the void in psychological and social care.

A second major area of difference is in the funding of health care in the two societies. In Australia at the time the study was carried out (1980), a combination of federally subsidized health insurance and direct government payments to physicians meant that most of the cost of physician visits were not paid out-of-pocket by the patient. Widows who were recipients of the Commonwealth Widows or Aged Pension were able to visit their own family doctor free of charge, the cost being reimbursed to the physician through the Pensioner Medical Scheme. In the United States, in contrast, medical visits are not subsidized. If they are not covered by insurance, Medicaid, or Medicare, the cost must be paid by the patient. One of the concerns of many of the American widows was that their health-insurance coverage usually died with their husband, leaving many of them without coverage and unable to obtain it. The funding and structure of medical care means that the better-off have a private physician, and the less-well-off utilize hospital-based clinics, where they rarely see the same doctor regularly.

The result of differences in the structure and financing of medical care leads to a lower overall utilization of physicians by the widowed in the United States than in Australia, and to the physician being less likely to be viewed as a resource for anything but medical or health-related problems.

Social Support System

Despite the practical challenges and financial difficulties that widowed women faced, loneliness was the most frequently mentioned problem. There was a relationship between age and the frequency with which loneliness was reported, with a smaller percentage of the youngest age groups (who were likely to have children at home) and of the oldest women reporting loneliness than those aged between forty and sixty-five. The reason for this pattern seems to be related to the fact that women in their forties and fifties are in the stage of the family life course when children are leaving or have left home, thereby losing one major source of companionship. They are also in that age group in which they are likely to be somewhat socially isolated in a couple-oriented society.

"Loneliness" is an idiosyncratic phenomenon that has a different meaning for each individual. For some it means a lack of companionship, for others the absence of some one person who cares about them, and to others it is missing the dead spouse. Reflecting this, many of the women had trouble knowing what it would take to deal with their loneliness. Almost 20 percent saw reestablishing a male relationship as the way out; about 15 percent mentioned remarriage or a "permanent" male relationship as the key. Others mentioned companionship—"someone to talk to"—and good female friends as ways they tried to deal with loneliness. In addition, nearly one-quarter of the sample expressed a need for emotional or psychological support. In relation to this, women frequently said that "someone to talk to" (32 percent), a permanent relationship (7 percent), or support from the family (7 percent) were goals for dealing with loneliness.

The social supports that women had were important in helping, if not completely resolving, the sense of loneliness. Almost none of the widows in our sample were totally socially isolated; however, their sources of support varied depending in part on age, as is shown in table 9.4. Younger women were more likely to mention family members

—parents, siblings, and friends. Among older women (those 50 and above), the relative importance of family (particularly parents, who were likely to be deceased) as confidants declined, but an increasing number mentioned adult children as a resource.

Children. Children can be an important source of companionship and emotional support. In Australia the low rates of internal mobility mean that adult children are likely to be living in the same city. The push for children to move away from the family home when they reach late adolescence is not nearly as strong as it is in the United States; consequently, the majority of widowed women with children were likely to either have them at home or living nearby.

Nearly two-thirds of the women (66 percent) said that they were at least somewhat dependent upon children for emotional support, which included companionship. This was more than double the number who said they had been dependent on children prior to the husband's death. The nature of the social support offered by children was clearly

Table 9.4   Resources for Discussing Problems by Age,
Melbourne, Australia (in percentages)

Resource	<40	40−49	50−59	60−69	70+	Total
Family						
Parent(s)	29.27	2.2	1.69	—	—	5.8
Brother	14.63	8.9	5.08	5.66	4.55	7.44
Sister	14.63	15.56	5.08	15.09	4.55	10.7
Relatives/ in-laws	—	2.22	3.39	3.77	2.27	2.48
Children						
Son/son-in-law	2.44	13.33	34.5	37.5	43.1	27.69
Daughter/ daughter- in-law	—	17.78	34.5	39.5	31.8	26.5
Children (nonspecific)	4.88	2.22	8.47	3.77	2.27	4.55
Friends						
Male	12.2	13.3	3.39	3.7	2.27	6.6
Female	29.27	33.3	23.7	22.6	15.9	24.8
Non-sex- specific friends	19.5	13.3	22.03	18.87	N.A.	16.62
Neighbors	2.44	8.89	1.69	13.21	2.27	5.77

related to their ages. Those with young children had company in the house, but were lonely for another adult. Women with adolescent children who could have provided some emotional and intellectual support found themselves alone more as children established their own lives.

Children, however, give a less-tangible form of emotional support. They give a purpose to life, as one of our respondents said, "a reason to keep going when there seemed to be no other purpose to live for" (Rosenman et al., 1984). The fact of their dependency—despite the many demands that they made and the resultant stress—meant that there was someone who needed them, an antidote for the sense that no one cares, which was at the base of much of the loneliness reported by the widowed. Adult children who no longer lived at home were likely to be mentioned as resources for emotional support, but not for companionship. Adult children were the resources most frequently mentioned by older women.

Friends as social support. Friends, particularly female friends, were clearly an important part of the social support system of widows. A small percentage of the younger women also mentioned male friends as a source of emotional support. Younger widows in particular perceived major changes in their social status and social network since their husband's death. Two-thirds of those under 50 said they felt like a fifth wheel around married couples, that married friends had stopped contacting them, and that they were now excluded—or had gradually excluded themselves from the married-couple social network. Since the incidence of marriage is so high for women in Australia, despite the rise in divorce rates during the past decade, the removal of married couples from the social network can leave a widow with few friends her own age. In self-defense, a group of widowed women living in the outer suburbs started a network of young-widows groups for social support.

Remarriage and male relationships. Establishing a male relationship was a frequently mentioned goal for dealing with problems, including loneliness. The larger number (14 percent) saw establishing a stable relationship with a man as the goal, while 6 percent said male companionship, but not necessarily a long-term relationship, was the goal. In contrast, our sample of American widows was more likely to express a nonspecific goal of companionship (25 percent) and male companionship (17 percent), but only 8 percent saw a stable male relationship as the goal.

In response to questions about interest in remarriage, one-third of the Australian women said they had some interest in remarrying in the future, while two-thirds expressed little or no interest in the idea of remarriage. Strength of interest in remarriage was inversely related to age—being less frequently expressed by older than younger women. The major reason given for interest in remarriage was for companionship. On the other hand, the most common reason for not wanting to remarry among the younger women was that they liked being unmarried.

Given the high marriage rate in Australia, the extent to which women's lives are defined by marriage, the perceived negative changes in their lives and reductions in their social support following their husbands' deaths, it is surprising that only one-third of the sample expressed an interest in remarriage. This is particularly so given the responses of the widowers to the same question. Fifty-two percent of the men expressed interest in remarriage, giving as reasons their needs for companionship, to have the children cared for, and because they "just liked being married." It would appear from this that Australian marriage may be much more congruent with the needs of men than with the needs of women. This is also suggested by their views on the perceived advantages of widowhood.

Over one-third of the women said that, despite all the disadvantages, they saw as an advantage of widowhood a sense of independence and of expanded horizons. By comparison, widowers were much less likely than widows to see any advantages to widowhood. These responses tend to suggest that the typical Australian marriage sets many more limitations on women than on men. The slow acceptance of married women being employed, much less having a career, and the expectation that a married woman should place her husband's and children's needs above her own, meant that with widowhood a woman was free to live her own life and make her own decisions—often for the first time.

The same proportion (i.e., 32.9 percent) of American widows as Australian mentioned independence and expanded horizons as among the advantages of widowhood. On the other hand, 8 percent of Australian women saw as an advantage the fact that widowhood was a socially acceptable end to a bad marriage—this compares with less than 2 percent of the St. Louis women, and tends to suggest that among Australian women, particularly the older ones, divorce is still a socially unacceptable option.

Australian Widows Compared with Widows
in the United States

There are few other studies of the needs and support systems of widowed women in Australia to either corroborate or dispute our findings. In the United States, however, there are several studies of widowhood. In particular, our own study of widowed women in St. Louis was designed in part to collect data comparative with Australia. Both samples were similarly stratified by age and length of widowhood and responded to essentially the same interview schedule. The results of the St. Louis survey are generally in concordance to those of Lopata (1979) in Chicago. We will therefore compare both of these to the Australian findings.

A comparison of the concerns, resources, and social supports of Australian widowed women with those of widowed women in the United States suggests some general differences between the experience of widowhood in the two societies and differences in the roles, expectations, and status of women.

While Australia is now being affected by the revolution in women's roles and expectations that has been occurring during the past 20 years, the changes have progressed neither as far nor as quickly as they have in the United States. The Australian widows were unlikely to view employment as a way of resolving their financial difficulties, their social network limitations, or as playing a role in their future plans. This was less likely to be the case among younger widows (i.e., up to about age 45) than among older widows, many of whom had not been employed at all outside the home during their married lives.

In comparison, the widows in St. Louis and in Chicago were much more likely to be employed, or to be taking steps toward employment, such as being enrolled in training programs or further education. Reflecting the relative societal value placed on education, particularly for women, the Australian widows had lower levels of formal education (an average of 9.9 years compared with 11.7 years in the St. Louis sample) and were less likely to be planning to improve their situations by taking job-related training. This is reflected in our widowed sample in both their employment and their employability; it is also reflected in Australian income-security policies. The noncontributory widow's pension was established so that it would not be necessary for a widowed woman to go to work. There has never been any challenge to this concept.

Until fairly recently in Australia, the expected "career" for a woman was that of wife and mother. This may partially explain the much stronger tendency among the Australian than the American widows to mention a "permanent male relationship" as being the possible solution to their problems of loneliness, emotional stress, finances, and child rearing. Reflecting social changes, however, the younger Australian widows were much more likely to be self-initiating and more oriented toward establishing their own independence (including employment) than were the older age cohorts.

In terms of social supports, the patterns of reliance upon family —particularly children—and friends for practical help and emotional support were fairly similar between the two societies. Unlike the Chicago widows, among the Melbourne widows there was not such a strong degree of sex stereotyping in the assistance provided by children. While in general sons were relied upon for assistance with home maintenance and financial problems, emotional support and companionship was obtained from whichever child was available, and, in the case of younger women, old enough to be depended upon.

The effects of recent immigration into Australia were evident in the absence of parents, siblings, or extended family from the support systems of those widowed women who were foreign-born. Among the Chicago widows, 19 percent had a foreign-born parent, among the Melbourne widows, 20 percent had been born outside Australia. In addition, the sample of Greek widows revealed the stresses associated with language problems, cultural prescriptions, and lack of family supports potentially experienced by the large numbers of recent immigrants to Australia.

There are other societal differences that impinge upon social support. A major one is the role of religious participation in Australia compared with the United States. Among St. Louis widows, particularly among black women, religious faith was a major source of emotional support, and church participation was a major factor in social life. Over one-third of the St. Louis widows belonged to a religious organization that played an important part in their lives, and 71 percent described themselves as very religious. In comparison, less than 10 percent of Melbourne women were church members, and only one-third said that they were very religious. Such differences were evident also in the frequency with which ministers and church membership were mentioned as contributors to the support systems. In Australia they were not mentioned at all.

Professional helpers—psychologists, psychiatrists, and counselors —were rarely mentioned by either the American or the Australian widows, with one major exception, namely, the frequent use of the family doctor by Australian widows as a resource for all sorts of personal and emotional problems. This is encouraged by the structure of medical practice and the financing of medical care in Australia, which makes doctors much more accessible than in the United States.

There is one other area in which there was a difference between Australian and American widows—concerns specifically about personal safety. This was a much more frequent worry of American than of Australian widows. In fact, it was mentioned as a reason for being interested in remarriage by 11.5 percent of the St. Louis widows—but by none of the Melbourne widows. Many of the Melbourne widows interpreted the question about safety in terms of fear of falling or hurting themselves while alone at home rather than in terms of crime. Even though many of the issues faced by widows in urban areas in the United States and Australia are similar, the awareness and fear of violent crime was much higher in the United States.

Although there are differences between the American and the Australian widows, the similarities are greater than the differences. This is not really surprising. Both countries have a common heritage in Western Europe, particularly England, speak a common language (English), and have been shaped by (predominantly) European immigration. Research was conducted in urban areas of both countries. In the case of our studies, the widows of St. Louis and Melbourne are living in metropolitan centers of approximately the same size (2.8 million). Marriage and family relationships are generally built on a similar nuclear family tradition. Last, but not least, the interview schedules were very similar, the research in each site paralleled in time, and each was influenced by the other. The conceptual framework of both studies was influenced by the earlier work of Lopata in Chicago. We cannot discount the possibility that some of the similarities derive from the conceptual framework and research techniques of the researchers in addition to similarities in societal patterns.

10 Wives and Widows in China

DENISE R. BARNES

The lives of Chinese women have always been shrouded in a bit of mysticism. The limited ability of social scientists to separate the real from the ideal regarding these women is perhaps due, in part, to the restrictions placed on foreigners in gathering information about China, and to China's own rather tumultuous history of revolution and change on many social fronts. The purpose of this chapter is to discuss support systems of Chinese wives and widows. A work of such brevity cannot be considered an exhaustive representation of wives and widows in China but can serve to stimulate a closer, empirically based evaluation.[1]

China and Its History

One of the most striking characteristics of the People's Republic of China is the sheer number of people. Masses of people are everywhere: walking or biking along the streets; shopping in stores (although they are restricted from the Friendship Stores reserved for foreigners); quietly gathering around some unsuspecting traveler changing camera film on Shanghai's Bund; climbing the Great Wall at Badaling, a few miles outside Beijing; tending their crops in the fields and working in factories. Most of the adults wear green, blue, or tan unisex jacket and pants outfits, with women wearing little or no cosmetics or jewelry. It is the children, dressed in brightly colored clothes and ribbons, who catch the eye in a broad sea of faces.

The People's Republic of China (3.7 million square miles) is slightly larger than the United States and is the third largest country in the world, following the Soviet Union and Canada. China's population is 1.3 billion, with an annual growth rate of 1.5 percent (People's Republic of China, State Council and State Statistical Bureau, 1982). One out of every four people in the world lives in China.

China's ability to curve the mortality rate and offer basic public health care has increased the life expectancy from 35 before 1949 to 69 by 1980. Eighty million people age 65 and over accounted for 8 percent of China's population in 1980. It is projected that that number will rise to 130 million (11 percent) by the year 2000 and 280 million (20 percent) by 2025 (Yao, 1983). Women (life expectancy of 69.5) tend to outlive men (66.9 years). Life expectancy is highest in urban areas. As it is, the proportion aged 65 and over, as well as the gap between the expectancy of men and women, is lower than in the United States (Lopata, 1979) and reflects the recentness of change in China.

The government began a concerted effort to institute birth control in the early 1950s. This thrust waned in the late fifties but has been reinstituted more vigorously since 1962. Smaller families (ideally a mother, father, and one child) is the Chinese government's answer to its struggle to feed its people and increase their overall standard of living. The merits of the one-child family are frequently discussed in socialist lectures, portrayed on billboards, and reinforced through governmental/social policies. For example, one-child families receive educational and medical care free of charge. If the plan to curtail the birthrate meets its goal, there will be a zero population growth by the year 2000. An examination of this major movement's impact on the support systems of wives and widows will be presented later.

Ninety percent of China's people live on one-sixth of the land, and only 200 million of China's billion people live in urban areas. The largest ethnic group (94 percent) is the Han Chinese and Mandarin who speak a Beijing dialect, which is considered standard Chinese and is spoken by 70 percent of the Chinese-speaking population. There are several minority nationalities.

Beijing, the capital, with a population of 8.5 million, is located in the northeast and is richly endowed with monuments and cultural relics from the Imperial Era, such as the Forbidden City. Half of its population resides in annexed suburban areas. Like other cities in China, Beijing is technologically simple compared to cities in Western countries. Rural people come to the city to sell produce and many goods are still manufactured by hand.

Eighty percent of China's population lives from the land, much of which was owned in the past by landlords. Prior to 1949, 70 percent of the land was owned by 4 percent of the population (Lewis, 1982); in that year Mao Tse-tung established the People's Republic of China. The question of land reform was a central issue in this agrarian, peasant-oriented society. First, the roles of landlords and landless peasants who tilled the soil reversed as the land was divided. Later, the establishment of communes (part of Mao's "Great Leap Forward" in 1958) had a major and direct influence on the lives of the Chinese people. Collective ownership and property use, as well as strong internal governmental powers, have characterized the commune system in China (Buchanan, 1970). The production team, composed of several hundred people, is the smallest social unit in the commune, save the family. Several production teams combine to form a brigade—one commune could consist of ten to 30 production brigades (Bong-ho Mok, 1983). When the commune flourishes so do individuals. A widow could not only depend on her family but also on other sources for food, shelter, and medical attention. Wives were expected to produce healthy males to strengthen production teams. In turn, they would reap the benefits of collective labor. Communes brought a broader and stronger base of social supports for wives and widows.

The Great Proletarian Cultural Revolution began in 1966 and lasted until 1971. This political movement involved the partial closing of China's schools and the redistribution of its intellectuals and urban youth to rural areas to work with and learn from the peasants. Families were disbanded, and some women were left to fend for themselves, hoping to continue to gain necessary supports from communal living. This was an anti-intellectual, antiforeign movement.

The current regime is headed by twice-deposed Deng Xiaoping. China is changing. It is seriously considering the relationship and mutual benefits between collective and individual enterprise. China's chief goal is to raise its standard of living through modernization. Social groups characteristic of China's experience, such as the clan and the peasant work force, will be affected. An example of China's willingness to try new ways of upgrading the lives of its people is the introduction of the policy concerning family-owned farms rather than commune-owned farms. This fragmentation of communes, while increasing a family's financial stability, may limit social support systems of wives and widows to family members or close neighbors. The interdependence of support systems brought on by communal living may diminish. Some strides can also be seen in the direction of individually owned small businesses on the streets of the rural communes and urban communities. Decision making concerning the law is being shifted from higher governmental levels to more local, grass-roots levels.

It is hoped that this historical background will enable the reader to understand the past transitions and future developments that face the Chinese people. These transitions have forced a reconsideration of the Confucian ethical system. The Chinese people are moving toward more egalitarian relationships among generations. Ideals regarding reverence for the old have been meshed with more practical economic security for all. Shifts have also been seen in intrafamilial relationships, where husbands and wives can now share household duties. The strained relationship between a daughter-in-law and her mother-in-law is changing, taking on new meaning. All of these developments have a direct link to the revolutionary experiences of this country and play a major role in determining the stability of support systems of wives and widows.

Support Systems of Wives and Widows

China's traditional marriage practices included child betrothal, polygyny, and concubinage. Marriage was considered a business arrangement whereby a husband and his mother acquired a virtual "slave." In some areas women worked long and hard hours in the fields, only to come home to be responsible for caring for the household as well. The wife did not expect to receive love and affection for her trouble. Sometimes royal families bound the girl's feet so that she might be a more pleasing and attractive wife. This excruciatingly painful process, however, restricted the wife's mobility and kept her dependent upon the family. A wife was the property of a clan, a bearer of sons, a daughter-in-law. Her relationship with her husband was not private nor considered to be of much importance. She was there to serve all members of an extended family. When her husband died, her loyalty and servitude to his family, and to her widowed mother-in-law in particular, remained.

There has always been much controversy and contradiction about the status of the widow in China. The widow's tenuous position in the Chinese culture was probably augmented by the fact that she was female and that a subservient role was already cast for her by Confucian doctrine. The absence of a husband to dominate the widow only complicated her uncertain position in society. As a widow she was destined to obey her oldest son. The condition of a widow was closely tied to the dynasty in which she lived. Before 208 B.C. widows could remarry without much concern or public ridicule for doing so. The daughter-in-law of Confucius, for example, remarried after her husband's death (Li, 1978). Women's social status began to decline dramatically after the Han Dynasty (202 B.C. to A.D. 220). Social roles became more rigid to the extent that a monastery was built during the North Dynasty (around A.D. 480) for childless widows, who were forbidden to remarry (Ch'en, 1977). During the succeeding dynasty, the Sui Dynasty (A.D. 589–685), an emperor ordered that widows whose husbands were distinguished with a particular official position could not remarry (Ch'en, 1977). It was now law that widows were to be virtuous and remain faithful to their dead spouses. The three hundred years following the Han Dynasty were characterized by many social upheavals and revolutionary changes, and women seemed to be caught in the middle. Should a beautiful wife lose her husband in battle, given her previous isolation and subsequent inability to function independently outside the home, she was often forced into home prostitution to feed herself and her children. The Sung Dynasty (A.D. 960–1280) ushered in forced female chastity as tribute to a dead husband. If a young woman's fiancé died before they were married, she was obligated to move into the house of her husband's parents and maintain her widow status throughout her life (Tung, 1937). As women's position in society began to deteriorate, they began to make sacrifices for chastity, such as self-mutilation and suicide (Sung, A.D. 960–1280 and Yuan, A.D. 1280–1368 dynasties). These self-abuses tended to earn the families of these widows fame and a definite place in recorded history. Amputated arms, noses, fingers, and ears deterred prospective suitors. Governmental policy applauded such practices (Tung, 1937). In 1367 the law to exempt families of sacrificed widows from governmental service was introduced. Officials erected monuments and shrines to these self-sacrificing women. Such attention encouraged widows and their families to practice and engage in more creative ways of demonstrating the worthlessness of women's lives. The more brutal the sacrifice the more certain a family could be that they and the women would be noted in historical records. Women who remarried during the Sung Dynasty were discussed as "the reopening of an old store" (Tung, 1937:145–148). Given the horrors of these times, Chinese widows continued to cope with these atrocities and survived. At the end of the Ming Dynasty (1368–1643) *Wen Mu Hsun* (*Mother's Admonition*) was one of the first works published that suggested varied life-styles if widows chose to remarry or not. The author, in attempting not to stray too far from social norms, suggested that widows who desired to remain unwed should keep very busy at home (Ch'en, 1977). A childless widow could secure her position in her husband's family by adopting her husband's nephew, younger brother, or cousin with permission of other family members. If she remarried, the widow could not sell her husband's joint property or take it with her (Waltner, 1981).

This historical backdrop for wives and widows offers a foundation on which to base a study of the support systems of contemporary Chinese widows and permits a comparison to other widows. Lopata (1979) investigated the support systems of Chicago-area widows. Support systems were determined to be (a) economic supports (income received from and given to a variety of sources); (b) service supports (services received and given, such as transportation, household repairs, help with housekeeping, shopping, child care, car care, health); (c) social supports (activities that people can do with others); and, (d) emotional supports (dealing with relationships and feelings). Each of these supports will be discussed as they relate to Chinese widows.

Economic Supports

The majority of Chicago widows report that the bulk of their income comes from present or past work by the widows themselves or from their late husbands' social security pensions (Lopata, 1979). Affluent widows describe themselves as givers of economic support to their children and significant others. Urban Chinese widows live their lives in stark economic contrast to Chicago widows. Since the prices of daily necessities are low and stable, pension incomes (from a deceased husband) that otherwise look like pocket money to Westerners can be stretched. Rent, water, and electricity cost about 4–5 percent of the average pension (Lewis, 1982:92).

While most Chinese widows, like the Chicago widows, are poor, it is not because their economic situation changed so drastically after their husband's death. Most intact families earn meager wages and, because of this, everyone who works contributes to the family income. A young widow continues to support her late husband's family while she resides in their home, and she in return receives certain benefits of that arrangement. An older widow has no fear of a drastically reduced income after the death of her husband because it is a law that her sons and daughters-in-law continue to support her economically. If there are no children, a widow may "adopt" a son (usually a nephew or cousin of her late husband so that she can maintain connections with his family) and that individual is charged with the responsibility of economic support. In the absence of relatives or if family members live at a distance, the commune is responsible for supplying economic support to help meet the widow's basic needs.

Eight million retired workers and staff are now collecting pensions in China, with men receiving the bulk of these benefits. A number of older women have never been employed but this will not be true of their daughters; all women aged under 40 have been required to work since 1958 (Lewis, 1982). Pensions are a percentage of salary that is calculated by length of time on the job, work performance, and service to the country. Typically, women are paid at a lower rate than men, so a widow's pension would be limited by what she earned before retirement. Male workers and staff members (managers, directors, office workers, service employees, college professors) retire at sixty. Female workers retire at age 50 and become "housewives" for younger working women. Female staff retire at age 55. Most retirees receive free medical care in addition to their pensions. A retired widow can reenter the work force after retirement to supplement her pension benefits and receive 100 percent of her previous earnings, meager though they might have been. Some changes in the pension system in China have involved a recognition that the needs of older people should and could be met by the community and the state. Such changes are occurring simultaneously with more and more women entering the work force. While the Chinese have moved from a no-pension system to one that offers up to 90 percent of the original salary, these changes are closely tied to service to the state. Widowers tend to benefit more than widows since women have shorter work histories and smaller preretirement salaries than their male counterparts.

Because of the compensation now offered to workers and staff, Chinese widows are coming to slowly accept the one-child family policy that, given China's population growth, requires young couples to have only one child. Older widows did not readily accept this policy because it was traditional practice for sons to be responsible ultimately for their elders, and the more children there were the more productive and prosperous a family unit could be. With the coming of the pension system, a widow can contribute to the collective funds of the family unit through her own retirement funds or those of the deceased husband (as determined by the brigade). A 1982 issue of *Women of China* described how a young widow and her widowed mother-in-law resolved economic and social-support issues. The young woman intended to remarry and, fearing reprisals and condemnation from her mother-in-law, left their home without telling anyone, taking the family funds, and leaving her children. The older widow charged that she had a right to property and took her case to the local people's court. After the young widow's husband died, the pension she might have received if she were not healthy or able to work went to her mother-in-law and children. The widowed mother-in-law had a right to the family property for as long as she lived. When the young remarried widow moved to her new husband's family's home, it was agreed that she take some property and leave her oldest daughter with her mother-in-law (Jin Mao, 1982:34–35).

Older rural widows lack the benefits of the pension system because many of them work well past the designated retirement age of widows in urban areas. Rural women, out of necessity, continue to work until they are no longer able. Older rural retirees and widows are protected by the "Five Guarantees," a law instituted in 1950, although it is difficult to discern how rigorously it is practiced and upheld. The Five Guarantees are generally reserved for older adults who do not have children or whose children have been sent to another part of China to work and are thus unable to provide economic support for older parents. Widows are provided for in five areas: food (including fuel, cooking utensils, pocket money), clothing (including bedding), housing (including furniture and home repairs), medical treatment, and a decent burial. Most of the costs for these services are paid for by local communes and brigades, but poorer areas receive assistance from the state. In Old China, sons were the only means of livelihood for retired people and widows and this obligation often led to neglect and abuse. If there was no son in the family, then a nephew or younger male was "adopted" for social security. In New China, filial care is law. Daughters as well as sons are responsible for the financial support of a widowed mother, and there are defined consequences to abuse of these laws.[2]

A widow's source of income could be affected by the type and amount of education she had. Traditionally, the predominant attitude in China was that educating girls was not a profitable venture because girls only grew up to be wives and then widows. This attitude is captured in the old Chinese saying: "To educate a daughter is like watering another man's garden." Families knew that the customary practice of marrying off a daughter could hardly benefit the family, and even an educated wife had very few options in occupational pursuits. Reading and writing meant that she might be encouraged to engage in composing prose or entertaining the men in the family by reading stories to them. These skills, however, did not enhance the family's economic status. Taking time off to go to school meant sacrificing work time when every able body was needed. A valuable wife was one who could work the fields and offer sons to the family.

Data from the third national census show that 605,932,447 people in China have an education at or above the primary-school level. This accounts for 60 percent of China's population (State Council and State Statistical Bureau, 1982). College or university graduates compose 1 percent of that population and 40 percent have a senior or junior middle-school education. There was a 16 percent illiteracy rate for urban populations and a 35 percent rate for rural populations. The national educational average is 440 college or graduate students per 100,000 people. Beijing (3,578 per 100,000) and Shanghai (2,411 per 100,000) populations tend to be more educated than China's total population on average. One in every 3.14 people is illiterate or semiliterate (people age 12 and over who knew less than 1,500 Chinese characters and cannot read simple material). The number of characters (presently reduced to 10,000 from a possible 40–50,000), complexity, and pronunciation variations make learning Chinese no small task. The majority of older wives and widows rely on children to read or write for them. Age by educational level data reveal that of those people between the ages of 12 and 34 years, 16 percent were either illiterate or semiliterate, with the rates of those between 34 and 54 years old at 44 percent, and of those 55 and older at 76 percent. Nationally, the illiteracy rate was higher for women (45 percent) than for men (19 percent). Women of ancient China had been bound to the saying, "Ignorance is a woman's virtue." It seems as though the impact of this adage lingers.

While there has been a general decline in illiteracy rates since the second national survey in 1964, where 53.4 percent of the population age 13 or older was illiterate, it seems as though the amelioration of this condition continues to be disproportionate between men and women. Certainly this could have implications for wives and widows in attaining the "four modernizations" (enhancements in industry, agriculture, national defense, and science and technology) and for playing a role at various occupational levels. As China becomes more technologically advanced, wives and widows will make up the bulk of workers in the lower-paying, unskilled or semiskilled positions. The life of the Chinese wife and widow will be complicated by the fact that the breakup of the communal system will require that they rely on other forms of economic support. Without an education behind her, a wife considering a job other than factory or peasant work will be limited in bringing in additional funds for her family. Without the flexibility that an education can offer, wives and widows will continue to be dependent upon family members for economic supports. An educated wife considering divorce may have more vocational options than would an uneducated woman. With a pension, an educated widow may be able to afford to pay for the service supports she usually received from her family. The educating of Chinese wives and widows will certainly modify support systems traditionally offered by the family and commune.

Service Supports

Lopata (1979) found that most Chicago widows were not involved in extensive service supports. She concludes that this is so because (a) the widows or their associates do not need specified types of help; (b) there is a traditional sex-segregated nature to everyday American life (widows tend to get rid of their cars after their husband's death); (c) the frequency of exchange of services decreases outside one's own household; and, (d) aid is only secured in extraordinary or unusual circumstances. There is much giving and taking among the households of widows in China. Although they live apart, women in kin relationships continue to help each other (Croll, 1983). Community youth may offer services, and the widow may take care of her sons as well as other commune children after school. She also tends to be a vital part of the community, perhaps sweeping streets or organizing after-school study groups. Reciprocity of services is the norm. The young are encouraged to teach the old and vice versa. At the same time, self-reliance is likely rooted in necessity in a poor country such as China. Self-reliance is particularly important for widows, who are

encouraged to stay integrated in society and to seek out ways in which
the services they receive will be least disrupted after the death of a
spouse. Although her husband has died, the widow is encouraged to
continue to lead a full, productive life. Serving the people has deep
roots in socialist principles and practices in China. Reciprocity of
services is not limited to kin relationships and is described in an
article in *Women of China* (Nai Xin, 1982:35) about two widows living in
a Beijing courtyard:

> Tie Guangya, 72, lives in the courtyard of No. 103. After her hus-
> band died, she made a living by doing handiwork and making
> cardboard boxes at the neighborhood factory. She received govern-
> ment relief only after she became ill in later years.
>
> On a recent visit to her home, Tie was peeling apples. A girl and
> boy, two Young Pioneers from the nearby primary school, were
> helping her to clear the window and fill the water vat. The place
> looked clean. After the children finished their chores, Tie offered
> them the peeled apples but the children cheerfully said, "See you
> next week, Grannie!" and ran off.
>
> Tie Guangya said that the children take turns to come and help
> her after class. They do such things as clean the stove and empty
> the garbage, and even brighten up her room with wall decorations.
>
> "Though I'm old and have no family, I have dear ones every-
> where!" said Tie Guangyu. She then explained how cadres respon-
> sible for civic affairs in the subdistrict office and members of the
> neighborhood committee often came to see her and ask what she
> needed. Over the years Tie has received from them money to buy
> a new quilt, a new stovepipe that replaced a leaking one and, on
> festivals and New Year, visits from the subdistrict leaders with gifts.
>
> Dai Quingrong, 86, who lives at No. 16 courtyard, returned from
> the hospital recently.
>
> She explained that one night she suddenly had an acute stom-
> ach ache and felt nauseous. A young man, her neighbor, ushered
> her to the emergency ward on his bike. The doctor diagnosed the
> case as severe deterioration of the gallbladder and she had to be
> hospitalized. The doctors hesitated about an operation. When the
> subdistrict cadre responsible for civic affairs heard this, he assured
> the doctors that he would give the consent and the neighborhood
> office would assume all medical expenses.

The pension system seems to benefit urban widows more than rural widows. Because urban widows can still receive some benefits after retirement, they are free to play a major role in running community life since younger adults are working or going to school. Retired women have organized themselves into volunteer work groups to help with the daily functions of the community and to offer each other emotional support. Women typically retire earlier than men and have already begun a second career by the time their husbands retire five or ten years later or at the time of their husband's death. Retired widows, like other retirees, have several defined roles to fill (Lewis, 1982): (a) mentors (responsible for organizing neighborhood study groups concerning socialist doctrines and after-school tutoring); (b) dispute-settlement counselors (regarding meddling mothers-in-law, husbands who do not fulfill familial responsibilities, or complaints from older citizens who feel they are not being cared for properly by their families); (c) street cleaners (for which they receive a meager salary); (d) child care; (e) "red medical workers" (direct traffic, escort young and disabled children, inspect homes for the aged); and, (f) informal welcomers and monitors of visitors to the commune.

Croll (1983:65) described the life of a retired grandmother, the duties of whom could be determined as considerable should she become a widow. It is not unlikely that a widow performs vital functions for her son's family, with whom she may share a home.

> The present generation of grandmothers have spent much of their lives in domestic servicing. As daughters-in-law they were called on to service their husband's parents and no doubt looked forward to becoming time-honoured members of the older generation, and now as grandmothers they are called on to serve their daughter-in-law. Indeed perhaps no relationship as much as that between mother-in-law and daughter-in-law has been so redefined in the last 30 years. Now it is the daughter-in-law who goes out to work and the mother-in-law who is required to undertake the majority of the domestic services. The question arises whether future generations of grandmothers will be quite so ready to undertake the child care and domestic labour after a life-time in production.

Urban widows are beginning to consider the benefits of living apart from their sons' nuclear families so that they will not be burdened with the cooking, cleaning, and child care of two or more nuclear families. They argue that not enough time is spent on civic responsibilities. They are also aware that even without performing these functions for the family their right to be taken care of is now governed by law.

The government also offers service supports to widows. There are "Respect Homes" for rural retired adults who have no relatives to care for them. For example, three widows may share rooms and offer assistance to one another. They are responsible for washing their own clothes and pay a monthly food fee. Food may be grown by the residents and supplied by a local commune. Should a widow become ill, her roommates become her care-givers. While the Chinese have made great strides in offering medical care to the population, rural widows have difficulty in accessing more sophisticated medical services when their medical needs cannot be met at the local level. Traditional medicine includes acupuncture, herbal medicine, and massage. Retired experts in these areas come to the Respect Home to offer medical services.

The University of the Aged in Jinan (Shandong Province) was recently opened by the government to educate retired male and female cadres, or governmental employees, in good health in order that they might continue to work for a socialist modernization. The curriculum offers two years of instruction in health care (including geriatrics and child psychology), nutrition, physical exercise geared to the needs of the elderly, gardening, painting, calligraphy, photography, music, literature, history, geography, philosophy, and modern technology. All educational expenses are paid. Widows who may stay closer to home to care for grandchildren or offer community services can learn by radio or television (if they are fortunate enough to have these appliances). Wives working during the day may attend night school, receive on-the-job training, attend study groups, or choose correspondence colleges. While the educational options for wives and widows seem to be effective and practical ways for getting an education, they often compete with traditional familial expectations of what services are to be rendered by females. A wife is expected to take care of her family first, before considering any individualistic opportunity to enhance herself. Widows may feel particularly threatened by a daughter-in-law's wish to attend school when family obligations are numerous; her ability to dominate and secure services from the daughter-in-law would diminish considerably.

Social Supports

Lopata's social-support category includes "going to public places such as movie houses, visiting, entertaining, going out to lunch or eating lunch with someone, going to church, engaging in sports, cards, and games, traveling out of town, celebrating holidays and doing anything else that the respondent wished to mention" (Lopata, 1979:85). Her data show that most Chicago widows are involved in celebrating holidays, visiting, and attending church, while over one-half never go to public places. Unlike the Chicago widows, Chinese widows tend to be atheists (by government order). However, Christianity and variations of Chinese religions (Confucianism and ancestor worship) do exist, offering social supports to the widows involved.

One of the most obvious, regular, and striking group activities that Chinese widows can be involved in is tai chi. Around 5:30 or 6:00 A.M., groups of older adults gather in the streets, parks, or courtyards to perform the slow, rhythmic exercise designed to limber muscles and joints and offer a kind of calm over the body to ready the individual for the day. This is a time when widows can gather to engage in other types of manipulative therapies such as massage or deep-breathing exercises.

Chinese widows participate in holidays (like May Day), which involves interaction with family and commune members. However, there are two major events that have a powerful effect on the social role of the Chinese woman: marriage within her family and the death of her spouse. Traditions and practices regarding these social events will be reviewed.

Marriage and divorce. Although social change regarding women's rights had taken place some years earlier, as documented in China's Civil Code, Mao Ze-dong declared that the Communist Party was responsible for granting women their freedom from social bondage in the Constitution of 1954. The Marriage Law was born. One of the major thrusts of this law was to eliminate obligatory or arbitrary marriages. In the past, many women committed suicide or were killed in order to avoid the fate of an arranged and unacceptable union. The Marriage Law states, "Marriage is based on the free choice of the partners, on monogamy and equal rights for the sexes," that "Family planning is practiced," and "Marriage upon arbitrary decision by any third party, mercenary marriage, the exaction of money or gifts, or any other acts of interference in the freedom of marriage are prohibited."

In a rather radical break with tradition, cities like Beijing and Shanghai offer matchmaking services for their youth. These are nonprofit organizations set up by a youth league in collaboration with a woman's association. It costs about 65 cents (U.S.) to participate. These services are aimed at the needs of young adults who may have in their earlier years devoted themselves to intellectual and educational pursuits while neglecting their social lives. Some men and women have been isolated from each other because of work conditions. For example, the textile industry is predominantly staffed by women and maritime transport by men. Matchmaking services offer these two groups a chance to get together. This is done by offering social activities and then helping with marriage arrangements and the like. Because arranged marriages by parents or other third parties have been outlawed, a son's use of these services may ease the mind of many widows who want to reap the benefits of an extended family. Couples register to marry in a local marriage registration office, where a marriage certificate is issued.

In Old China the marriage ceremony was elaborate, lavish, and cast many a daughter's father into debt. Huge dowries from the bride's parents were required, and the girl's parents solicited gifts from the groom's family. A wedding was a major financial transaction between two clans. The matrimonial tides of gift-giving have swelled, ebbed, and swelled again in accordance with China's political winds. While there have been periods when all exchanges of gifts were banned, the practice is gaining momentum in modern-day China, although it is frowned upon by the government. Contemporary Chinese enjoy material goods and large and festive wedding ceremonies. It is not uncommon for there to be an exchange of televisions, radios, and watches, with the future mother-in-law playing a major role. She is to be catered to in order to ease her daughter-in-law's transition into the family. Because of the expense involved, many young couples start their lives together working to pay off the premarital debt incurred by the wedding. For example, in some areas the groom is supposed to hire a car (since individual citizens do not own cars) in which to escort his bride. This is an expensive endeavor. Many urban areas now offer an inexpensive alternative to elaborate weddings. For example, in Beijing, group weddings, sponsored jointly by governmental organizations like the Women's Federation, have relieved some of the financial burden of the wedding from young couples. Couples pay a moderate fee and invite friends and family members to a government building where the bride and groom, along with forty or so other couples, are wed simultaneously.

The ceremony is simple, dignified, involves the family, and is relatively inexpensive compared to customary practices.

Recent political changes have influenced rules regarding the marital status of women. A revised marriage law introduced at the Third Session of China's Fifth National People's Congress in 1980 became effective in January 1981. It stipulates that Chinese women must be 20 and men 22 years old before they can marry, and later marriages and childbirths are encouraged. This is, in part, China's way of handling population control and every potential mother-in-law's source of frustration. The previous minimum age to marry was 18 for women and 20 for men. In Old China a girl child could be wed to an infant boy if her parents so wished. There is a critical housing shortage, so a couple often has to delay marriage, especially in urban areas, until adequate housing for the family can be obtained. Such a disadvantage for the young couple can mean social advantages for the widow. The couple is welcomed in her home and enhances her social status. Any increase in the number and quality of daughters-in-law increases the widow's position in the family and commune. Widows often meet socially to pass along gossip about daughters-in-law or to praise their ability to meet a widow's need. The relationship between daughter-in-law and mother-in-law has always been strained among Chinese women. The widow, herself a daughter-in-law, got firsthand experience from her mother-in-law regarding the rules of interaction. The widow might remember her own feelings of being constrained and dominated by her mother-in-law and intends to deliver the same treatment to her son's wife. Mother-in-law jokes abound in China. They mock the seemingly absurd and unfair treatment of young wives. As the wife struggles to focus on her new family, she also knows that her mother-in-law's generation expects reverence as well. A wife remains subservient on many levels, and more contemporary wives are seeking divorce in an attempt to gain control over their lives.

It was not until the 1950s that the kinship system came under strong attack. The marriage law passed in 1950 gave women the right to divorce. In Old China, a woman had no right to divorce, and couples tended to stay together although their lives may have been miserable. Before 208 B.C., in the spring and autumn, men could "discharge" their wives for any of the following reasons set down by Confucius: disobedience to her parents-in-law, barrenness, adultery, jealousy, disease, stealing, and gossiping (Lang, 1968:400). There were four circumstances, however, under which a woman could maintain her social role of wife: an empress, although barren, could not be discharged; a wife of deceased parents who had no other means of social support could not be ousted; a wife who was liked by her in-laws but not by her husband remained in the household; and, a wife who shared the burdens and responsibilities of increasing the household prosperity could not be abandoned (Lang, 1968:41).

By law, divorce is granted when both spouses desire it. If one spouse wants a divorce and the other does not, the marriage is dissolved only after mediation by the district's people's government. The process of obtaining a divorce is long and laborious. Officials visit both sides of the couple's family to solicit means of reconciliation. A widow may be asked for her opinion about the root of the problems between the couple and how she might assist them in maintaining their marriage. Divorce has always been frowned upon in China because the mutuality between socialist ideals and family practices is strong. Strong, intact families mean a strong, intact society and government. It is expected in Chinese society that one should marry and remain married throughout life.

There are special considerations given to women regarding divorce. For example, a husband is not allowed to apply for divorce when his wife is pregnant or before the child reaches his or her first birthday. Exceptions are made if it is the wife who is applying for divorce or if attention to the husband's case is absolutely imperative. If agreement cannot be reached regarding the disposal of the property after the divorce, the people's court steps in to consider the condition and kind of property and typically considers the needs of the wife and children. Also, if it is determined that a divorcée cannot maintain her children, the exhusband is required to provide financial assistance.

Death of a spouse. Most urban Chinese wives become widows because their husbands have succumbed to diseases correlated with old age — coronary disease and cancer. Rural males still tend to suffer from respiratory and infectious diseases. Since land is needed to grow crops, the government has declared cremation the official means of disposing of bodies. This practice has not been readily accepted by widows. They believe that the traditional elaborate funeral service is the only way in which a family can show respect and that their husbands can leave this world with dignity. Because burials near urban areas are frowned upon, a body may be sent off to other family members, who will bury the husband on a steep, uncultivated, and barren hillside. Funeral services cost about 55 dollars and are paid for by the family. If there is no family, or a widow cannot afford the service, expenses are met by the local commune or brigade from a collective fund.

Urban funeral services are relatively simple rituals. A family prepares for the funeral immediately upon the death. Although there are variations on this ritual, urban family members take three days off from work, with pay, and can extend this furlough without pay. This is a time to support the widow in her grief. The body is transferred to a crematorium and lies hidden behind a curtain. Memorial services are held in the presence of a picture of the deceased, and a local dignitary may offer tribute. Family members view the body after a period of silence. The body is cremated and the ashes are either left at the crematorium for disposal or the family may bury them. The widow wears a black band for one-to-three years, while other relatives wear the band for several weeks (Lewis, 1982).

Chance (1984:139–140) describes a much more elaborate ritual in Half Moon, a Beijing commune:

On the morning of the funeral, a day or so after the death, relatives gather outside the home of the deceased, wearing different clothes depending on their relationship to the departed. Close kin wear mourning robes of white. Women may also place a few white ribbons in their hair. Differing shapes of caps and shoes designate to outside observers the relationship of more distant kin to the deceased. Before the ceremony begins, the family members and relatives may talk and even laugh. But on hearing the sound of a bowl breaking as it is thrown to the ground—the signal for the ceremony to start—all talking stops. Straightening themselves up, the participants utter a unified wail as they line up for the procession to the grave site.

The eldest son, wearing white sack garments, carrying white-colored paper money, and holding a soul-calling flag, stands at the head, and a band playing mourning melodies brings up the rear. Others carry a paper horse (for a deceased man) or a paper cow (for a woman) and more paper money, which are to be burned at the grave site for the deceased to use in the trip to the underworld. As the procession passes through the village, several more bowls, jars, or mirrors are thrown against the ground and broken. Beyond the edge of the village lies the local burial ground,

its location easily distinguished by mounds of raised earth scat-
tered in a haphazard fashion—a puzzle to present-day observers
unfamiliar with the ancient practice of geomancy, a custom that
assures proper placement of the grave.

On arriving at the site, the coffin is lowered into the freshly dug
grave. The lagers stand respectfully while the coffin is covered
over, perhaps joining in with the family of the deceased as they
softly repeat a common lament in a sing-song manner. After the
grave is covered, offerings of eggs, cakes, and white paper money
cut in an ancient shape are placed on top, and the money burned.
The procession then returns to the village to participate in a large
meal hosted by the family of the deceased. After partaking of
elaborate dishes of dumplings, cakes, and other special foods, the
mourners disband and return to their own homes. In April of
each following year, at the time of the qingming festival, family
members return to the grave site, add some new earth, weed or
clean the area, and perhaps burn a little paper money and incense,
thereby illustrating one more continuity in the life cycle of the
village.

The Chinese government encourages widows to remarry. Some widows are still bound by feudal concepts of a widow's chastity and
faithfulness to her husband until she dies. This reluctance to remarry
is found more frequently in rural than in urban areas. An urban widow,
perhaps affected by Western influences, may not receive social stigma-
tization upon remarriage as would the rural widow. Remarriage fills a
social gap left by adult children who may have moved away and the
lack of social security offered by communal living. Remarriage increases
the widow's chance of securing more daughters-in-law.

Family as social support. The family is the basis of Chinese society.
Yao (1983) recognizes six kinship relationships that have changed
according to China's social climate: husband and wife; husband and
children; brother; children of brothers; the brother's grandchildren;
and, the brother's great-great-grandchildren. An extended family consists of the first four relationships, while the addition of the last two
constitutes a clan. Throughout much of Chinese history the lineage or
clan has been noteworthy as one of the few institutions able to give
social support to widows and their families. Social interaction by the
clan even cuts across class lines. Because of the mobility of young
persons of marriage age in many middle- and upper-class families,

some widows complain that their sons are geographically far removed and may only return home periodically—maybe once a year—for a visit. An expression of social support may be that a grandchild is left for the widow to raise. This gesture symbolizes her continued connection with her son. The patriarchal nature of the old Chinese kinship within the family may change, but respect of the elderly is mandated by law.

The nuclear family has come to take a stronger, more defined place in Chinese society. Much more attention is being given to the relationship between husband, wife, and child. The Marriage Law maintains that property acquired during the marriage is under joint ownership unless stipulated otherwise. A widow, then, does not have sole rights to her son's property. Recognition of this fact can put more constraints on the relationship between a widow and her daughter-in-law. Parents must raise, educate, and discipline their children. Children are responsible for the care of their parents, regardless of the sex of the child. Children can take either parent's name, and if they have been injurious to the state or the collective, parents must recompense. Children born out of wedlock enjoy the same privileges as legitimate children and lawful adoption is sanctioned. China's Marriage Law serves to equalize the role of husband and wife in the home. It intends to make it commonplace for both husband and wife in urban areas to be wage earners, share household and child-rearing responsibilities, and support elders in the home.

In ancient China it was not uncommon to find four or five generations living under the same roof. A widow would have a considerably larger hierarchy to rule and by which she was ruled. The number of such arrangements in present-day China has plummeted for three main reasons. First, because of the restriction on the number of children a family may have, the size of the extended family has diminished considerably in urban areas. A widow's social sphere will diminish not only because of a decrease in the number of daughters-in-law but of grandchildren as well. Second, the government has assigned family members to different and remote areas of the country in order to enhance its chances of attaining the "four modernizations." Third, the growth of China's cities is some testimony to the dilution of extended families because many young married couples seek city life for jobs, and older peasant family members choose to stay behind in more rural areas with traditional and familiar surroundings. A widow's household will be diminished because of this migration. A widow in this situation will most likely be involved in communal activities (e.g., after-school care or sweeping the streets) with other women. A familiar sight is that of two or three widows strolling the streets of the commune. Their status as widow, mother-in-law, and commune resident binds them. Since transportation is limited in China, it is imperative that widows create social-support systems within their communes. Yet, in order to maintain familial relationships, some new high-rise apartment buildings in Beijing have suites so that a widow can live with her son and daughter-in-law.

It is Chinese law that individuals are to serve the state, and faithful service will eventually filter down to brigades, communes, and families. The "Five Goods" are moral dictums to which all Chinese families are encouraged to aspire: respect the aged and cherish the young people in the family; maintain harmony in the home; practice planned parenthood and raise children properly; run the household frugally and industriously; and, work hard to become prosperous (*China Today*, 1982). The social relationships of widows are molded, in part, by the government's mandates.

Emotional Supports

Chicago widows indicated that their husbands had been the primary source of emotional support before widowhood. When the husband died, the widow's focus shifted onto the children. Drawing conclusions regarding the emotional support systems of Chinese widows is tricky. Traditionally, the Chinese wife was not to expect much support from her husband because his dedication was directed to his mother and father. It is suspected that, in turn, the wife gained most of her support from her sons, as they were much more valuable additions to the family than were daughters. Today, the Marriage Law has shifted emotional supports within the family. Yao (1983:179) explains:

> With the drastically diminishing authority of mothers-in-law, a young wife has more power in decision making, particularly if, as is very common, she works. The historical resentment and bitterness between the daughter-in-law and the mother-in-law are vanishing. The daughter-in-law is no longer the target of the mother-in-law's anger against traditional suppression. A woman's role in the family is no more specifically to serve and please her in-laws. Instead it is geared to her husband and her children. As a

result, the marital relationship between husband and wife in a small family becomes more intimate than in the large family headed by the oldest family member, either grandfather or grandmother. Parents and children are also closer than in an extended family, where more siblings and other cousins lived under one roof.

Wives can now receive emotional support from their husbands, daughters, and sons. These supports can enhance her self-esteem because they decrease the possibility of repercussions from a mother-in-law. Girl children are now socialized to believe that they are just as special to the family as are boy children. While mothers and daughters tended to be close emotionally, it seems as though this bond will be strengthened. Mothers will come to take pride in their daughters' accomplishments at work and at home. Wives gain emotional support from each other by forming groups to monitor the treatment of women in communes, thereby gaining positive emotional momentum through their sense of collective independence.

A fascinating function of the older widow is the practice of "speaking bitterness," a type of cathartic experience. Widows can tell of the role her deceased husband might have played regarding social change in China. Speaking bitterness involves lecturing to the young about the bitter days of Old China, when people were dying from starvation, suffering from physical abuse, and all of the other injustices New China wishes to overcome. Widows gain a sense of having survived some very hard times while considering how to adjust previous coping strategies to meet the needs of their role as widows. They are filled with pride by telling others how they survived while China was going through political growing pains. Widows can often share the details of the lives of their mothers or aunts concerning their social status change from wives to widows. Self-mutilation and suicide are practices not easily forgotten. The widows provide emotional support to married women, with the hope that reminiscing about such tragedies will prevent them from ever occurring in China's history again.

Widows can also receive emotional support from officials within a commune. If a widow should complain that she is not being treated fairly by her family, communal supervisors will investigate in order to lend her emotional and legal support to rectify her situation.

Conclusions

The previous review of Chinese widows' economic, service, social, and emotional support systems offers a picture of a rich and integrated support system. Economically, a widow can depend on funds from her extended family and the commune. Widows who work can expect support from their pension funds or from their deceased husbands' funds. While the widow can reap many services from communal living she is also invested in offering her services. She may take care of children after school, sweep the streets, and greet visitors to the commune. There are strategies in living that the widow can share with young adults in the commune while they, in turn, organize into volunteer teams to help her with shopping and household chores. China is a poor country, and perhaps this condition has led to the ideal and practice that everyone should contribute and be supported by everyone else.

The extended family was the basis for most of the widow's social supports. It is suspected that the widow's status is most likely due to the nature of Chinese tradition. Respect for elders (although the position of women has been tenuous) and the importance of the family buffers many of the hardships widows would experience if not for these beliefs. Traditionally, there has been very little emotional support for wives, except for their relationship with their own mothers. The tension between mothers-in-law and daughters-in-law is well documented. It is evident, however, that some of the Confucian ideals are giving way to more Western ways of thinking. Wives are gaining more independence from their mothers-in-law and more control over their own families. In the past these women tended to be engulfed by the rules and regulations of the clan and could not enjoy much emotional support.

The communal way of life has been important in support systems of widows, who know they can rely on people outside the family for economic, social, service, and emotional supports. Present-day China's dismantling of the commune will have an impact on widows. Emphasis now is being placed on the nuclear family, consisting of mother, father, and child. There is a slow de-emphasis on the proximity and necessity of the extended family. The development and stability of more intimate relationships brought on by the nuclear family in China will perhaps cause the Chinese widow to more closely resemble Lopata's Chicago widows.

11 Widowhood and Social Change

HELENA ZNANIECKA LOPATA

A Common Focus

We have now examined in greater detail the personal resources, support systems, and life-styles of widows in nine societies of the world. The common focus of the chapters has been on these three aspects of life frameworks, identified originally for a study of widows in Chicago, and replicated in Korea and Iran. Parts of the interview schedule were also used by several other authors in studies of widows in their own countries. Results of surveys were included in chapters on Israel, the Philippines, and Australia. Mainly secondary sources were drawn upon by the social scientists writing on widows in India, Turkey, and China. The authors have, in addition, extensive personal knowledge of these societies. Malu, Vanuatu, was studied by Rubinstein, an anthropologist who spent considerable time immersed in the life and culture of its residents.

All of these studies of widows point to the importance of knowing the social structure and life of the society and of the community in which the widow is located, as well as her personal resources. The concept of community is used loosely to include class and caste subunits of the larger group. What is now needed is an overview, tying together these immensely divergent situations of the widowed women. This chapter aims to do this.

Societal Change and the Situation of Women

Human societies have provided many resources out of which their members can draw together support networks that provide support systems and weave varied life-styles. These resources have changed over time, rapidly in recent decades. Each society contains a culture and subcultures that define categories of members and make available, or unavailable, social roles and the means by which one can prepare for and enter these roles. It regulates life and social interaction, more or less rigidly through norms of behavior. The life frameworks (support systems, social relations, and social roles) of its members spread across religious, economic, political, family, educational, and recreational institutions. What the political state does affects the lives of its members, as in the case of wars in Israel or the revolution in China. Most societies of the world have organized work into jobs for which people must be trained and from which they obtain money to buy goods and services. Some of these jobs have diminished the opportunities for informal economic support and have been closed to certain members of the society. In a money economy, people must be able either to work for pay or obtain an income in other ways, through the work of others, or the support by persons or groups responsible for them. The question always remains: who is responsible for the economic, service, social, and emotional supports of any one category of member? What happens if supporters of the past no longer feel responsible to continue their support? These questions are particularly appropriate when we look at the life frameworks of widows, especially in patriarchal societies in which women are not economically independent.

The authors of these chapters repeatedly point to changes in the societies in which they are located, contrasting new patterns to those of "traditional" ones, located often in rural areas or pockets within cities. Societal changes have drawn the attention of many social scientists who have attempted global analyses of transformations in human life and relationships. Theorists of modernization often contrast small-scale, kin-centered, and face-to-face traditional communities with modern industrial and capitalist societies that have allegedly succeeded them in world history. These draw on Max Weber's (1904/1958) ideas of change, attributing its rapidity in Western Europe and America to the Protestant Ethic, the process of increasing rationalization, and to the triumph of secular, calculating attitudes. Weber's view of bureaucratiza-tion and rationalization was a pessimistic one. By the 1950s approaches to social change in the Third World were based on an optimistic ideology. For example, Lerner (1958) looked forward to the coming of scientific, secular, and bureaucratic ideology and social organization. Inkeles (1983; Inkeles and Smith, 1974) worked out a complex set of indexes of "individual modernity."

Often, however, these were not theories of change, but polarized ideal types: traditional *versus* modern societies. One form of modernization theory can be found in *Political Modernization in Japan and Turkey* by Ward and Rustow (1964). According to these authors, the modern polity contains the following characteristics: a differentiated and functionally specific and integrated system of government, secular and rational procedures for decision making, national identification, achievement rather than ascription of social roles, and an impersonal system of law. Huntington (1978:34–37) summarizes some of the basic tenets of the "Grand Process of Modernization," including that it is irreversible, progressive, and consists of phases. This list of characteristics has been criticized with great vigor, and our authors give support to most of these criticisms. Gusfield (1967; 1976) is especially critical of the model that assumes progress and replacement of traditional culture by "modern" culture. The artificial dichotomy between the traditional and modern rests, according to him, on several fallacies, such as:

1. Developing societies have been static societies
2. Traditional culture is a consistent body of norms and values
3. Traditional society is a homogeneous social structure
4. Old traditions are displaced by new changes
5. Traditional and modern forms are always in conflict
6. Tradition and modernity are mutually exclusive systems
7. Modernizing processes weaken traditions (Gusfield, 1967: 353–57).

One particularly important critique of the Inkeles (1983; Inkeles and Smith, 1974) indexes of individual modernity is that they completely ignore how the processes change women (Papanek, 1978). In recent research on social change in the Third World, modernization theory has been replaced by theories of development. However, these theories continue some of the assumptions underpinning modernization theory, including that changes in the economic institutions of a society are the most fundamental forms of change and inevitably produce changes in the rest of its life, after a cultural lag (Ogburn, 1922). These theories see the Western European and American societies as models of a "developed system." It is obvious that, from the vantage point of the twenty-fifth century, twentieth-century America is not likely to be considered as already "modernized" or "developed," so that the ethnocentrism of these concepts is apparent.

Observers of social change the world over have shown its dramatic rate in recent decades and how various areas of human life have been affected. Sanitation and medical advances have reduced the death rate even before the reduction of the birthrate, leading to rapid overpopulation in certain countries. People still want children when they are an economic asset rather than a drain, to help them in old age and for religious reasons. On the other hand, mass education has been introduced in many places to prepare a new labor force for modernizing industries and for employment by state bureaucracies, as well as for active citizenship. Years spent in school reduce the economic advantage of having children, who are also then able to earn their own economic support. Laws have codified much of human interaction. Much work has been organized into occupational roles in large social units. Urbanization and urban culture have expanded dramatically, spurred on by industrialization and the need for mass transportation and concentrated financial and governmental centers. The mass media have entered many communities with a unifying central culture. Rural-to-urban mobility and migration across national boundaries have been speeded up. New social roles are created and freed from ascribed into achieved entrance throughout the life course (Cowgill and Holmes, 1972; Koo, 1981; Touba and Afghahi, 1978). Religions are receding as a major influence on the lives of many people. More "rational" and calculative decision making and flexibility of social roles within the longer life span have led to a more complex, less-bounded social life space (Giele, 1977; Hareven, 1976; Lopata, 1972; Rogers, 1980).

The future toward which development appears to be moving seems to be a relatively androgynous achievement of social roles and development of both male and female abilities. Life-space opportunities would be available to all, regardless of social class or power (Rohrlich-Leavitt, 1976; Smock, 1977). The women in the most "developed" societies would have the same personal resources and options as men to be involved in a multidimensional role cluster in several institutions of an urban center in a highly educated, industrialized society.

By these standards, no society is as yet developed!

The support systems and life-styles of women in the least-developed communities embed them in social roles and relational rules, supported by strong religions that offer few choices throughout the life course and from which they do not have the personal resources, or even the inclination in some instances, to escape. Such women are unable to live independently, being part of an encompassing interdependent unit, or moving from one to another upon marriage. Given the patriarchal nature of most societies of the past and present, such women live in gender-segregated environments under the control of the father, the husband, and, later, the son. If the religious or family institution is very concerned with the sexual behavior of women and with the fatherhood of the children to which they give birth, they may be heavily controlled between puberty and menopause. However, such societies provide continuous support systems, clearly defined roles and relations, and clear behavior norms, as evident in the care-giving rules of Malo, Vanuatu. And, once women are no longer able to bear children, they are often allowed greater individuality and "blossoming" (Lee, 1985:33) rather than experiencing the contraction of life typical of many women in modern America. Women who have adult offspring but are not yet "frail and dependent" are (1) freed from bothersome restrictions they had to observe when younger; (2) expected to exert authority over specified younger kin . . . exact labor . . . make important decisions; or, (3) made eligible for special statuses . . . recognition beyond the confines of the household (Brown, 1985:2–3). The type of freedom or constriction available to women depends to a great extent on the cultural conceptions of their and men's sexuality (Vatuk, 1985). In cultures in which men are assumed not to be able to control their sexuality, and family line purity is idealized, higher class or caste women can be "protected" with purdah rules from contact with nonkin men, which can be quite confining (Papanek and Minault, 1982).

Feminist critics of economic development argue that the situation of women often deteriorates as their society modernizes rather than being improved by the changes. Boserup (1970) was the first to document the negative consequences of such development. European colonialists, who controlled 67 percent of the world's land surface by 1887 (Magdoff, 1982:17) imposed their version of sex segregation on the native labor force, denying, for example, women agriculturalists the right to grow cash crops. By pushing women into the narrower slots in social production that their Western model of the sexual division of labor imposed, they destroyed much of their economic self-sufficiency, providing resources only to men. Agricultural agents trained only men into new forms of technology and supplied only them with needed products (Tadasse, 1982). "As the cash spheres becomes ever more significant, so the position of the majority of women inevitably declines" (Lambek, 1985:74).

Davidson (1982:11) states, in his introduction to Pamela D'Onofrio-Flores and Sheila Pfafflin's *Scientific-Technological Change and the Role of Women in Development*:

> The chapters in this volume show that in introducing technology in the form of agricultural modernization into rural areas of developing countries, women lose control of their cashearning positions, their hours of labour are increased and their role in the family and in society diminishes. It has also been found that as automation increases, the employment of women is the first to decrease. As urbanized work is introduced, young and physically attractive women become employed and middle-aged women, even when efficient, are ignored.

Women's ability to support themselves in predominantly agricultural areas is highly related to their "access to resources, such as land, farm produce, farm inputs, credits and cooperative membership" (Tadesse, 1982:85). Unfortunately, the introduction of private property of the type developed in Europe and patrilineal inheritance often deprived women of the use of communal land and even of the products of men's work.

Goode's (1963) *World Revolution and Family Patterns* documents the effect of changes the world over upon the family, and we can certainly see the differences of women in family roles between Malo, Vanuatu, and middle-class Chicago. Although some social scientists are trying to offset extremes of generalizations as to families in traditional societies, as does Vatuk (1972) in stating that urbanization did not necessarily change the Indian family structure, historians such as Hareven (1976) support Goode's claim to certain overall modifications. Hareven (1976:193) is critical of much of modernization literature, and focuses on five characteristics of the more "modern" family:

> (1) individually (or couple) controlled rather than socially controlled fertility; that is, the practice of conscious family limitation by couples making "rational" joint decisions about birth control, rather than following the rules imposed by elders, churches, etc.;
> (2) simple and noncomplex family and household structures;

(3) separation between the family of orientation and the family of procreation—that is, the establishment of independent families by adult sons and daughters, which entails economic and social independence from their parents;

(4) nonauthoritarian intrafamilial relationships that lead to a decline in parental authority; and,

(5) low integration with kin, which generally implies the autonomy of individuals or the nuclear family from kin control over individual careers, choice of spouses, the timing of marriage, and child rearing (Hareven, 1976:193).

According to Rohrlich-Leavitt (1975:626), cross-cultural ethnohistorical data clearly show that the nuclear family is the family form imposed by capitalism and that it differs radically from previous family systems in isolating the family from the community and in isolating women from one another. In this type of family, men are made responsible for the support of all family members, thereby locking them into their jobs, and women and children are made dependent upon men, thereby perpetuating male supremacy.

A major factor in the relation between societal members and the society itself is the political system and its activities. As mentioned before, wars disrupt families, as do rural or urban emigration and immigration. Laws give people rights or take them away. Programs and policies help people in trouble or ignore them. The allocation of responsibility and the programs by which this responsibility is met depend on the societal definition of what is and what is not a social problem (Lopata and Brehm, 1986). The government of Vanuatu appears to be of relatively little influence on the lives of residents of Malo, while government is an important factor in the lives of the Chinese.

It is now time to narrow down our focus upon the effects of the social transformations of recent decades upon the lives of widows. What better source of information and theoretical analysis than in the chapters of this book, which should help move development theory to new areas of concern. They provide a unique source of knowledge about a neglected area of research, an area that is, however, symbolic of societal lives.

Widowhood and Societal Change

A major contribution to macrosociological theory being made by the authors of this book is the documentation of the inadequacy of any theory that pictures economic development as a "seamless web" (Higgins, 1977) or as a systemic, homogenizing, irreversible, and progressive process (Huntington, 1978). No matter how "modernized" American society, the life frameworks and self-concepts of many widows, even in the urban areas, are far from displaying the kinds of characteristics, behavior patterns, self-concepts, attitudes, and relationships that Inkeles (1983) labeled as modern. Of course, for the most part widows have not worked in factories, which he considers to be an important experience moving people away from traditionalism. However, they do have some education and have functioned, albeit often minimally, in a very complex social system. Throughout the chapters in this book we are reminded that most of the world is still rural and agricultural and that the direction of change for women may not lie in the same path as it does for men. Tradition certainly influences the lives of the women studied by Rubinstein, in spite of the fact that American and other soldiers were stationed in Malo, Vanuatu, during World War II, public schools and cash cropping have been introduced, and health improved. Underutilization of formal societal resources exists all over the world, with only relatively upper-class people knowing how to benefit from these resources.

The complexity of the situation of widows in several countries has led our authors to reexamine modernization theory. Gujral found that the changes experienced by them have had a mixed effect. Transition in India of recent centuries was imposed from the outside, by forced "Westernization," and the importation of values and standards that undermine many of the traditional family norms. For example, although education has increased the ability of many young people to support themselves and, in the case of men, a family of procreation, it has reversed the flow of wealth. The more "modernized" families no longer send it up to parents; children become an economic liability. The early transitional family relations often benefit parents in societies such as India, Turkey, and Iran, since part of the income earned by children away from home is sent back as remittances, increasing the standard of living of the nonmigrants. However, over time the economic independence of the children can decrease the feelings of obligation for all the women in the extended family, including the widows.

In the case of India the combination of the weakening of felt duties by sons with the traditional lack of obligations by the daughter can result in lack of supports when they are needed. Parents in India, Iran, and Turkey worry about this possibility.

Several contributors to this book stress the dramatic consequences on the life framework of widows arising from the weakening of the power and supports of the patrilineal family. This weakening has accompanied several trends of development: the creation of a money economy and jobs for pay, as well as mass education removed from the kinship system. This has been accompanied by a shift in ideology that defines childhood as a time for learning and play—not for economic contribution to the sustenance of the family. Thus, the child is legally and culturally free to prepare for adult roles outside of the family of orientation, and to create his/her own interdependent unit of the family of procreation. Neither the husband's nor the wife's families have rights of decision, nor is the new unit dependent upon inheritance for support. In this situation, the woman cannot count on economic supports from either line when her husband dies. He must either insure that support, she must earn it herself, or the society must take over. Adult children no longer have the obligation to live in the ancestral home, to bring the widow to their household, or to support her economically. Chicago and Australian widows, as well as those of similar societies seldom receive economic support from their relatives, including children.

Freedom from the male line allows couples, and then the widows, to live where and in what style they wish that is within their reach. Grandchildren are no longer automatically filiated with the husband's family, their names can even be changed if they are young enough and the widow remarries. There are no guarantees of grandparenting, and in-laws seldom appear in the support systems of Chicago widows. At the same time, it frees both generations from the frequently unpleasant mother-in-law/daughter-in-law dependencies, which have been so traumatic in traditional China, Iran, Turkey, India, and so forth. Blumberg (1985) found that one of the important factors influencing the lives of widows the world over is the presence of daughters-in-law who can either provide services that the older woman needs only to supervise or who compete for the affection of the man, with negative results for the mother when she has no control over resources nor a powerful culture and community to protect her rights.

As mentioned in chapter 1, one of the secondary effects of social development that has weakened the power of the male line, where it previously existed, is the increased importance of the daughter. Of course, some of the literature stressing the importance of the patriarchal system has underestimated the closeness of the mother-daughter tie. For example, although the daughter in India has no obligation to her family of orientation once she marries, she often comes back to visit and to have her babies, and often remains for extended periods of time (Gujral). In most of the more-developed societies we have studied, the sons still provide some form of support, usually of a gender-segregated nature, as I found true of Chicago widows. Daughters become the main providers of service, social, and emotional supports when they are no longer obligated to support only the husband's family and can help decide the location of residence and the distribution of their time and work. Brody (1985), in a study of the supportive activities of daughters, found many overburdened by demands of three or even four generations of kinfolk.

The effects of modernization or social development upon the lives of widows are often indirect, affecting first the younger members of their families and the community structure. If the women themselves are older, they do not directly participate in social changes. The forefront of change hits mainly the male, middle-class, and more-educated members of each society, who benefit more from capitalism, new technology, and the world system. The poorer, less-educated, peripheral members often lose more at first than they gain. Traditional means of supporting themselves and relating to others are gradually withdrawn, and the people are not resocialized to function in the new system. Pelman (1985) and the California team studying the supports of poor minority widows found that it was much more beneficial to these women to offer them direct help in the form of money than to spend time, effort, and considerable cost in trying to reeducate them into taking advantage of existing community resources. On the other hand, the formal economic system often does not wipe out the informal one, and women accustomed to finding peripheral ways of supporting themselves economically and also socially in that economy can continue to do so. A very important feature of self-support in such situations is access to the market, which is part of the traditional culture in some areas of the world (Blust, this volume; Raybeck, 1985; Touba, 1980). Thus, deprived of avenues to resources such as education or training in the new technology provided by men, women continue to use more traditional means of self-support. Handicapped by the male-dominated nature of much of the economic development in their societies, they operate at the subsistence level in the old manner, or develop new entrepreneurial activity.

Yet the changes are opening some doors. Women in Turkish towns, according to Heisel, now have jobs and retain their women's network. They are increasingly free to move and to develop their independence as the men move away from the local involvement. Most who have migrated would not return to the village and the combined control-support of their male relatives. Some women are finding greater companionship in relations with their husbands, so that sex segregation appears to be breaking down in the larger communities. The Filipino widows appear quite satisfied with the supports they receive, not only from children but also from friends and neighbors.

In fact, expanded mobility and size of the interacting group affords widows greater flexibility in roles and relations and in behavioral norms throughout the life course. Some societies, such as the American, really do not have a social role of "widow," and so that part of a woman's identity can be virtually ignored in most of her social roles. Social change multiplies options for many people, if they can take advantage of it.

Yet, regardless of the complexity of societal development, measured by whichever set of characteristics or scales, the pattern is neither consistent nor, as Gusfield (1967) pointed out, homogeneous. Traditional and more modern aspects of life frameworks coexist on all levels, and, with some tragic displacement, most people are able to interweave them into their own lives. The chapters in this volume demonstrate how uneven are the resources available to widows. Australia has federally subsidized health insurance, with payments directly to physicians for office visits, something the other societies, including the United States, have not instituted. China has organized many community services for its elderly and widows of all ages, through the commune system, although some of that may be changing under the new rulers. The Chinese system appears to have provided the greatest number and complexity of resources. The Israeli kibbutz is also a community with guaranteed economic, service, and social supports. The retirement community in Florida (see volume 2) draws people from a great distance who voluntarily enter its formal and informal supports. Companionship is easily available with people of the same, or neighboring, cohorts and ethnic backgrounds. Hochschild's (1973) book *The Unexpected Community* describes a community that emerged without planning. There has been a rapid increase of retirement hotels in northern urban America that provide many service and social resources, contact with others being guaranteed without leaving the confines of the building. Voluntary associations, including churches and related groups, offer social and emotional supports to those willing and able to join, and are available in developing and more developed societies, proliferating in the latter.

The great heterogeneity among widows of the world arises not only from the wide range of societies and communities in which they are located but also from the ways they are lodged in them or combine and build the support systems, life-styles, and self-concepts. Some widows are relatively passive, accepting changes produced by the death of the husband. Some, of course, have little choice. Others acquire personal abilities and characteristics that draw upon elements of traditional and more-developed cultures and social structures to lead satisfactory lives in any size of social life space. In fact, some women bloom in widowhood. Some stay in pockets of high tradition, surrounded by, but almost oblivious to, changes around them. Others eagerly seek new resources and social roles. The societies vary not only in the resources but also in the degree to which they seek out people whose lives have been disorganized through crisis in order to provide new lines of engagement. The initiative does not necessarily come only from the woman who must organize a life framework, although it is increasingly up to her to do so, with more or less direct supports from traditional sources or from the newly developed societal resources. Among the traditional ones are the family, neighbors, and friends. Expansion of horizons enables the making of friendships with people of similar interests even if they do not live nearby. While geographical mobility can disperse families, modern transportation and communication can provide continued supports.

Obviously, what is needed now is further research, more comparative than was possible the first time around. We need to know more about the economic supports of different types of widows, their daily life and support networks in the other three support systems — service, social, and emotional. The impact of social change on widows in different segments of societies must be studied in greater depth. What is the difference between change experienced directly, and that met by changes in the lives of people upon whom the widow is dependent or those dependent upon her? There is much yet to learn about societal change and the life frameworks of women in marriage and in widowhood. The life frameworks of widows are highly symbolic of the change in a society itself and its various communities.

We now turn to North America—Canada and the United States—to examine the life frameworks and especially the support systems of widows in various localities of these allegedly highly developed societies. Volume 2 awaits us.

About Our Contributors

Denise R. Barnes, Ph.D., is an assistant professor in the Clinical Division of the Department of Psychology at the University of North Carolina at Chapel Hill. She teaches courses in adult development and aging and mental health aging. She is currently involved in research dealing with cross-cultural perspectives in aging, coping strategies of black middle-age daughters and their mothers, and incontinence in elderly adults. Some of the information for this chapter was gathered during a trip to China in the spring of 1984.

Nitza Ben-Dor, M.A., is a social worker specializing in child therapy. She is a teacher in the School of Social Work at the University of Haifa at the Tel-Hai College and is a field supervisor for social work students.

Evangelina Novero Blust was an instructor of family and society and human development at the College of Human Ecology, University of the Philippines at Los Baños, for nine years. She received her B.S. degree in home technology and M.S. degree in family resource management from the same university. She attended Kansas State University for her Ph.D. degree in home economics (life span human development) under the Republic of the Philippines-International Bank for Reconstruction and Development (RP–IBRD) fellowship grant. Currently, she is assistant professor of gerontology at Green Mountain College, Poultney, Vermont.

Jaya Sarma Gujral, a graduate student in the department of sociology, the University of Chicago, since 1982, is completing her requirements toward the Ph.D. Her areas of interest include social change in comparative and historical perspectives, aging and migrant populations, and the fertility of older women. She is working on a project that is evaluating the outcome of bilingual education on Hispanic students in a two-year college in the Chicago area. She has a master's degree in the social sciences from Ruhr-Universität, Bochum, West Germany, and a master's degree in public health from the University of Texas at Houston.

Marsel A. Heisel, Ph.D., is a member of the faculty of the School of Social Work, Rutgers University, where she teaches methods of social research and gerontology. Currently at work on aging in Turkey, she has written a number of professional articles on the black aged in the United States and on aging in developing countries. She is originally from Turkey and holds degrees from the universities of Istanbul and Wisconsin as well as a doctorate from Rutgers, the State University of New Jersey.

Ruth Katz, Ph.D., is a lecturer at the School of Social Work and the department of sociology and anthropology at the University of Haifa. Her interest is marriage and family relationships. She is currently conducting a comprehensive study of one-parent families in Israel.

Jasoon Koo obtained her Ph.D. in sociology at the University of Missouri–Columbia. Her dissertation concentrated on the support systems of widows, replicating in part the Chicago study. It compared rural to urban widows undergoing the process of modernization or social development. She then went to the Institute of Women in Development, founded by the Korean government, the director holding cabinet rank. At present she is in the department of sociology, Hanyang University, Seoul, Korea.

Linda Rosenman, Ph.D., is an Australian who is currently associate dean of arts and sciences and associate professor of social work at the University of Missouri, St. Louis. She has done considerable cross-national research and publication on older women in Australia and the United States. The research on which this chapter is based was partly funded by the National Institute on Aging and was carried out while she was on the social work faculty at Latrobe University in Melbourne, and subsequently as a visiting fellow at the Social Welfare Research Centre in Sydney. This chapter was coauthored with her husband.

Robert L. Rubinstein is a cultural anthropologist in the behavioral research department of the Philadelphia Geriatric Center. He has made two field trips to Malo (Natamambo), Vanuatu. In addition, he has done research on older men and on the home environments of older people in the United States.

Arthur D. Shulman, Ph.D., is an associate professor of psychology at Washington University in St. Louis. His research was carried out jointly while he was the Inaugural Ashworth Fellow at the University of Melbourne. This research was part of a larger research project funded by the National Institute of Aging on Widowed Women in St. Louis and in Melbourne.

Jacquiline Rudolph Touba received her Ph.D. from Purdue University and a diploma in comprehensive planning from the International Institute for Social Studies and Research in The Hague. She taught at the University of Delaware before going to Iran in 1967, where she first worked with the Iranian Statistical Center. In 1970 she joined the University of Tehran, where she was associate professor of sociology and the head of the comparative sociology section of the Institute for Social Studies and Research until nine months after the "hostage crisis" of 1980 and until the university system was closed in June 1980. After returning to the United States, she settled in upper New York state with her husband and daughter. She went into private business and was a visiting professor at Skidmore College. Presently she is the general director of an educational and arts organization called The International Arts and Culture Association, which serves upper New York state and aims to broaden the scope of rural communities about other cultures and countries. She has turned her research interests to Morocco, where she is working on women and work and especially their role in handicrafts.

Notes and References

1 Widowhood: World Perspectives on Support Systems

References

Bennett, Amanda. 1983. Population Lid: China Cajoles Families and Offers Incentives to Reduce Birth Rate. *Wall Street Journal* 6:1, 16.

Cumming, E., and W. E. Henry. 1961. *Growing Old: The Process of Disengagement*. New York: Basic Books.

Felton, Monica. 1966. *A Child Widow's Story*. New York: Harcourt, Brace and World.

Fry, Christine. 1984. *Dimensions: Aging, Culture and Health*. South Hadley, Mass.: Bergin and Garvey.

Inkeles, Alex. 1983. *Exploring Individual Modernity*. New York: Columbia University Press.

Inkeles, A., and D. H. Smith. 1974. *Becoming Modern: Individual Change in Six Developing Countries*. Cambridge, Mass.: Harvard University Press.

Lopata, Helena Z. 1971. *Occupation Housewife*. New York: Oxford University Press.

———. 1973. The Effect of Schooling on Social Contacts of Urban Women. *American Journal of Sociology* 79:604–19.

———. 1976. *Polish Americans: Status Competition in an Ethnic Community*. Englewood Cliffs, N.J.: Prentice-Hall.

———. 1979. *Women as Widows: Support Systems*. New York: Elsevier.

Lopata, H. Z., and H. Brehm. 1986. *Dependent Wives and Widows: From Social Problem to Federal Policy*. New York: Praeger.

Miller, Barbara D. 1981. *The Endangered Sex: Neglect of Female Children in Rural North India*. Ithaca, N.Y.: Cornell University Press.

Mosher, Steven W. 1983. Why Are Baby Girls Being Killed in China? *Wall Street Journal* (July 25):9.

National Committee on the Status of Women. 1975. *Status of Women in India*. New Delhi: Indian Council of Social Science Research.

Papanek, H., and G. Minault, eds. 1982. *Separate Worlds: Studies of Purdah in South Asia.* Delhi: Chanakya Publications.

Ramusack, Barbara N. 1981. Women's Organizations and Social Change: The Age-of-Marriage Issue in India. Pp. 198–216 in N. Black and A. B. Contress, eds., *Women and World Change: Equity Issues in Development.* Beverly Hills: Sage.

Ross, Arlene. 1961. *The Hindu Family in Its Urban Setting.* Toronto: University of Toronto Press.

Stacey, Judith. 1983. *Patriarchy and Socialist Revolution in China.* Berkeley: University of California Press.

Weber, Max. 1958. *From Max Weber: Essays in Sociology.* (H. H. Gerth, and C. Wright Mills, trans. and eds.) New York: Oxford University Press.

———. 1956/1964. *The Theory of Social and Economic Organization.* (A. M. Henderson, and T. Parsons, trans.) New York: Free Press.

2   Women as Widows on Malo (Natamambo), Vanuatu (South Pacific)

1   Fieldwork during which the data presented in this chapter were gathered took place from June 1975 to November 1976 and was funded by the National Science Foundation and Bryn Mawr College; research in July and August 1983 was funded by the National Science Foundation. The support of these organizations and of the Philadelphia Geriatric Center is gratefully acknowledged.

2   This discussion is part of a complex line of thought that I have greatly simplified here. For a more complete discussion, see Rubinstein, 1978.

References

Brody, E. 1981. "Women in the Middle" and Help to Older People. *Gerontologist* 21:471–80.

Chowning, A. 1973. *An Introduction to the Peoples and Cultures of Melanesia.* Addison Wesley Modules in Anthropology, no. 38. Menlo Park, Calif.: Cummings.

Lopata, H. Z. 1979. *Women as Widows: Support Systems.* New York: Elsevier.

New Hebrides Government. 1979. *Provisional Results of the General Population Census, 15–16 January 1979.* Port Vila.

Nydegger, C. 1983. Family Ties of the Aged in Cross-cultural Perspective. *Gerontologist* 23:26–32.

Rosow, I. 1967. *Social Integration of the Aged.* New York: Free Press.

Rubinstein, R. L. 1978. Placing the Self on Malo: An Account of the Culture of Malo Island, New Hebrides. Ph.D. dissertation, Bryn Mawr College.

———. 1981. Knowledge and Political Process on Malo. In M. Allen, ed., *Vanuatu: Politics, Economics and Ritual in Island Melanesia.* New York: Academic Press.

———. 1984. Old Age and the Aging Process on Malo, Vanuatu. Report submitted to the National Science Foundation, Washington, D.C.

Rubinstein, R. L., and P. T. Johnsen. 1984. Toward a Comparative Perspective on Filial Response to Aging Populations. *Studies in Third World Societies,* publication 22.

Shanas, E. 1981a. Social Myth as Hypothesis: The Case of the Family Relations of Older People. *Gerontologist* 19:9–15.

————. 1981b. The Family as a Social Support System in Old Age. *Gerontologist* 19: 169–74.

Strathern, A. 1981. Death as Exchange: Two Melanesian Cases. In S. C. Humphreys and H. King, eds., *Mortality and Immortality: The Anthropology and Archaeology of Death.* New York: Academic Press.

Weiner, A. B. 1980. Reproduction: A Replacement for Reciprocity. *American Ethnologist* 7: 71–85.

3   Widowhood in India

Agarwala, S. N. 1967. Widow Remarriages in Some Rural Areas of Northern India. *Demography* 4 (i):126–34.

————. 1973. *Some Problems of India's Population.* 2d ed. Bombay: Vora.

Bose, A. 1973. *Studies in India's Urbanization, 1901–1971.* New Delhi: Tata McGraw-Hill.

Boserup, Ester. 1970. *Women's Role in Economic Development.* London: George Allen and Unwin.

Caldwell, J. C. 1982. *Theory of Fertility Decline.* New York: Academic Press.

Dandekar, Kumudini. 1962. Widow Remarriages in Six Rural Communities in Western India. *Medical Digest* 5: 30(2).

Goode, William J. 1963. *World Revolution and Family Patterns.* London: Free Press of Glencoe.

Gopalan, C. 1985. The Mother and Child in India. *Economic and Political Weekly* 20(4, January):159–66. Bombay.

Government of India: *Census of India, 1971.* New Delhi.

————. 1974. *Towards Equality: Report of the Committee on the Status of Women in India.* New Delhi: Department of Social Welfare, Ministry of Education and Social Welfare.

————. 1978. *Women in India: A Statistical Profile.* New Delhi: Department of Social Welfare, Ministry of Education and Social Welfare.

————. 1982. *National Account Statistics 1970–71 to 1979–80.* New Delhi: Central Statistics Organization.

Gupte, S. V., and Divekar, G. M. 1963. *Hindu Law of Succession,* esp. "The Hindu Succession Act, 1956," pp. 412, 426, 436. N. M. Tripathi Private Ltd., Law Publishers.

Hajnal, J. 1965. European Marriage Patterns in Perspective. Pp. 101–43 in D. V. Glass and D. E. C. Eversley, eds., *Population in History.* London: Edward Arnold.

Hyman, Herbert H. 1983. *Of Time and Widowhood: Nationwide Studies of Enduring Effects.* Durham, N.C.: Duke University Press.

Inkeles, A., and D. H. Smith. 1974. *Becoming Modern.* Cambridge, Mass.: Harvard University Press.

Kapadia, K. M. 1966. *Marriage and Family in India.* 3d ed. London: Oxford University Press.

Kohli, K. L. 1977. *Mortality in India: A State-Wide Study.* New Delhi: Sterling.

Lopata, H. Z. 1979. *Women as Widows: Support Systems.* New York: Elsevier.

Miller, Barbara, 1981. *The Endangered Sex: Neglect of Female Children in Rural North India.* Ithaca, N.Y.: Cornell University Press.

Rosen, George, 1967. *Democracy and Economic Change in India.* Berkeley: University of California Press.

Saha, A. N. 1965. *The Hindu Marriage Act: Act No. 25 of 1955.* Calcutta: S. C. Sarkar and Sons.

Srinivas, M. N. 1967. *Social Change in Modern India.* Berkeley: University of California Press.

Vatuk, S. 1980. Withdrawal and Disengagement as a Cultural Response to Aging in India. Pp. 126–48 in C. L. Fry, ed., *Aging in Culture and Society.* New York: Praeger.

————. 1982. Old Age in India. Pp. 70–103 in Peter N. Stearns, ed., *Old Age in Preindustrial Society.* New York: Holmes and Meier.

Willis, Robert J. 1982. The Direction of Intergenerational Transfers and Demographic Transition: The Caldwell Hypothesis Reexamined. Pp. 207–34 in Yoram Ben-Porath, ed., *Income Distribution and the Family.* Supplement to *Population and Development Review.*

4   Widows in Seoul, Korea

1   The data reported here were collected as part of a doctoral dissertation completed by the author under the supervision of Donald O. Cowgill at the University of Missouri—Columbia.

2   Money problems are especially acute in the rural areas. Many Korean village farmers own their land, but the holdings are not generous. The average size of a farm is 2.63 acres. Lack of capital prevents farmers from buying medical services or modern conveniences or paying educational fees for their children. Families sacrifice to send boys to schools in cities. Capital is also transferred out of the village to educate sons or to help them set up small businesses. The economic system in rural areas still can be described as "agrarian" and economic exchanges take place in kind, not in cash. As the nation modernizes, rural people acquire the need for cash all the more, and this makes them relatively poor. Seoul widows had a median income three times higher than that of the rural widows.

3   In the Chicago study the question was stated differently, accounting for part of the variation. Lopata (1979) asked whether the respondent engaged in a variety of social activities, such as going to public places, visiting, entertaining, eating lunch, traveling, spending holidays, and so forth. If she replied "yes," she was asked with whom she shared this activity.

References

Amundsen, Kirsten. 1971. *The Silenced Majority: Women and American Democracy.* Englewood Cliffs, N.J.: Prentice-Hall.

Cho, Hyoung. 1975. The Kin Network of the Urban Middle Class Family in Korea. *Korea Journal* 15 (June):22–33.

Choe, Jae-sok. 1963. Process of Change in Korean Family Life. *Korea Journal* 3 (October):10–15.

Choi, Syn-duk. 1975. Social Change and the Korean Family. *Korea Journal* 15 (November): 4–13.

Chosun Ilbo. 1976. (Seoul, Korea), 11 December.

Chung, Pom-mo. 1971. *Psychological Perspectives: Family Planning in Korea.* Seoul: Korean Institute of Behavioral Science.

Cowgill, D. O., and L. D. Holmes, eds. 1972. *Aging and Modernization*. New York: Appleton-Century-Crofts.

Dongah Ilbo. 1976. (Seoul, Korea), 11 December.

Goode, William. 1963. *World Revolution and Family Patterns*. New York: Free Press.

Hahbdong Tongshinsha. 1980. *Korea Annual*. Seoul.

Ju, Nak-won. 1963. Social Function of the Family. *Korea Journal* 3:28–36.

Kim, Chu-su. 1976. The Marriage System in Korea. *Korea Journal* 16:17–29.

Koo, Jasoon. 1981. *Korean Women in Widowhood*. Ph.D. dissertation. University of Missouri—Columbia.

Korean Economic Planning Board. 1966. *Population and Housing Census Report*, vol. 1. Seoul.

————. 1978. *Census Report*, vol. 1. Seoul.

Lopata, Helena. 1979. *Women as Widows: Support Systems*. New York: Elsevier.

Marris, Peter. 1958. *Widows and Their Families*. London: Routledge and Kegan Paul.

Nuckols, R. C. 1973. Widows Study. *Journal Supplement Abstract Service Catalog of Selected Documents in Psychology* 3:9.

Roh, Chang-shub. 1972. Recent Changes in Korean Family Life Patterns. *Journal of Comparative Family Studies* 3:217–27.

Townsend, Peter. 1967. *The Family Life of Old People*. London: Routledge and Kegan Paul.

Young, M., and P. Willmott. 1957. *Family and Kinship in East London*. London: Routledge and Kegan Paul.

5 Women and Widows in Turkey: Support Systems

Abadan-Unat, N. 1974. Turkish External Migration and Social Mobility. Pp. 362–402 in P. Benedict, E. Tumerkin, and F. Mansur, eds., *Turkey: Geographic and Social Perspectives*. Leiden: E. J. Brill.

————. 1976. Turkish Migration to Europe (1960–1975): A Balance Sheet of Achievements and Failures. Pp. 1–44 in N. Abadan-Unat et al., *Turkish Workers in Europe, 1960–1975*. Leiden: E. J. Brill.

————, ed. 1981. *Women in Turkish Society*. Leiden: E. J. Brill.

Afetinan, A. 1962. *The Emancipation of the Turkish Woman*. Paris: UNESCO.

Aswad, B. C. 1974. Visiting Patterns Among Women of the Elite in a Small Turkish City. *Anthropological Quarterly* 47:9–27.

Benedict, P. 1974. The Kabul Günü: Structured Visiting in an Anatolian Provincial Town. *Anthropological Quarterly* 47:28–48.

Census of Population. 1975. Social and Economic Characteristics of Population. Prime Ministry State Institute of Statistics, Turkey.

————. 1980. Social and Economic Characteristics of Population, 1% Sample Results. Prime Ministry State Institute of Statistics, Turkey.

Çillov, H. 1974. The Structure of the Turkish Population. Pp. 57–84 in F. Karaday et al., eds., *The Population of Turkey*. Ankara: Institute of Population Studies, Hacitepe University.

Coşar, F. M. 1978. Women in Turkish Society. Pp. 124–41 in L. Beck and N. Keddie, eds., *Women in the Muslim World*. Cambridge, Mass.: Harvard University Press.

Duben, A. 1984. 19. ve 20. yuzyil aile ve hane yapilari. Pp. 91–113 in N. Erder et al., eds.,

Türkiyede Ailenin Değişimi: Toplumbilimsel Incelemeler. Ankara: Türk Sosyal Bilimler Derneği.

Ekşioğlu, Kâni. 1984. *Sosyal Sigortalar Yasasi.* Istanbul: Yasa Yayinlari.

Erder, L. 1981. Women of Turkey: A Demographic Overview. Pp. 41–58 in N. Abadan-Unat, ed., *Women in Turkish Society.* Leiden: E. J. Brill.

Eren, N. 1963. *Turkey Today—and Tomorrow: An Experiment in Westernization.* New York: Praeger.

Fallers, L. A., and M. C. Fallers. 1976. Sex Roles in Edremit. Pp. 243–63 in J. G. Peristiany, ed., *Mediterranean Family Structures.* London: Cambridge University Press.

Fişek, H. 1984. Türkiyede Ailenin Değisimi—Yasal Acidan Incelemeler. Pp. 261–71 in N. Erder et al., eds., *Türkiyede Ailenin Değişimi: Toplumbilimsel Incelemeler.* Ankara: Türk Sosyal Bilimler Derneği.

Hinderink, J., and M. B. Kiray. 1970. *Social Stratification as an Obstacle to Development: A Study of Four Turkish Villages.* New York: Praeger.

Kâğitçibaşi, C., ed. 1982a. *Sex Roles, Family and Community in Turkey.* Indiana University Turkish Studies. Bloomington: Indiana University Press.

———. 1982b. *The Changing Value of Children in Turkey.* Honolulu: East-West Center Population Institute.

———. 1982c. Old Age Security Value of Children: Cross-national Socioeconomic Evidence. *Journal of Cross-Cultural Psychology* 13:29–42.

Kandiyoti, D. 1977. Sex Roles and Social Change: A Comparative Appraisal of Turkey's Women. *Signs* 3:57–73.

———. 1981. Dimensions of Psycho-Social Change in Women: An Intergenerational Comparison. Pp. 233–58 in N. Abadan-Unat, ed., *Women in Turkish Society.* Leiden: E. J. Brill.

———. 1982. Urban Change and Women's Roles in Turkey: An Overview and Evaluation. Pp. 101–21 in C. Kâğitçibaşi, ed., *Sex Roles, Family and Community in Turkey.* Indiana University Turkish Studies. Bloomington: Indiana University Press.

Karadayi, F., et al. 1974. *The Population of Turkey.* Ankara: Institute of Population Studies, Hacitepe University.

Karpat, K. H. 1976. *The Gecekondu: Rural Migration and Urbanization.* London: Cambridge University Press.

Kazgan, G. 1981. Labor Force Participation, Occupational Distribution, Educational Attainment and Socio-economic Status of Women in the Turkish Economy. Pp. 131–59 in N. Abadan-Unat, ed., *Women in Turkish Society.* Leiden: E. J. Brill.

Keddie, N., and L. Beck. 1978. Introduction. Pp. 1–34 in L. Beck and N. Keddie, eds., *Women in the Muslim World.* Cambridge, Mass.: Harvard University Press.

Kiray, M. B. 1974. Social Change in Çukurova: A Comparison of Four Villages. Pp. 179–204 in P. Benedict et al., eds., *Turkey: Geographic and Social Perspectives.* Leiden: E. J. Brill.

———. 1976a. The New Role of Mothers: Changing Intra-familial Relationships in a Small Town in Turkey. In J. G. Peristiany, ed., *Mediterranean Family Structures.* London: Cambridge University Press.

———. 1976b. The Family of the Immigrant Worker. Pp. 210–34 in N. Abadan-Unat, ed., *Turkish Workers in Europe, 1960–1975.* Leiden: E. J. Brill.

———. 1984. Büyük kent ve değişen aile. Pp. 69–79 in N. Erder et al., eds., *Türkiyede Ailenin Degisimi.* Ankara: Türk Sosyal Bilimler Derneği.

Kongar, E. 1976. A Survey of Familial Changes in Two Turkish Gecekondu Areas. In J. G.

Peristiany, ed., *Mediterranean Family Structures*. London: Cambridge University Press.

Levine, N. 1982. Social Change and Family Crisis: The Nature of Turkish Divorce. Pp. 323–49 in C. Kâğitçibaşi, ed., *Sex Roles, Family and Community in Turkey*. Indiana University Turkish Studies. Bloomington: Indiana University Press.

Lopata, H. Z. 1979. *Women as Widows: Support Systems*. New York: Elsevier.

Magnarella, P. J. 1974. *Tradition and Change in a Turkish Town*. New York: John Wiley and Sons.

————. 1979. *The Peasant Venture: Tradition, Migration and Change Among Georgian Peasants in Turkey*. Cambridge, Mass.: Schenkman.

Mansur, F. 1972. *Bodrum—A Town in the Aegean*. Leiden: E. J. Brill.

Olson, E. A. 1982. Duofocal Family Structure and an Alternative Model of Husband-Wife Relationships. Pp. 33–72 in C. Kâğitçibaşi, ed., *Sex Roles, Family and Community in Turkey*. Indiana University Turkish Studies. Bloomington: Indiana University Press.

Öncü, A. 1981. Turkish Women in the Professions: Why So Many? Pp. 181–93 in N. Abadan-Unat, ed., *Women in Turkish Society*. Leiden: E. J. Brill.

Özbay, F. 1981. The Impact of Education on Women in Rural and Urban Turkey. Pp. 160–80 in N. Abadan-Unat, ed., *Women in Turkish Society*. Leiden: E. J. Brill.

————. 1982. Women's Education in Rural Turkey. Pp. 131–48 in C. Kâğitçibaşi, ed., *Sex Roles, Family and Community in Turkey*. Indiana University Turkish Studies. Bloomington: Indiana University Press.

Şenyapili, T. 1981. A New Component in Metropolitan Areas: The Gecekondu Women. Pp. 194–219 in N. Abadan-Unat, ed., *Women in Turkish Society*. Leiden: E. J. Brill.

Sterling, P. 1965. *Turkish Village*. London: Weidenfeld and Nicolson.

Timur, S. 1974. Components of Growth. Pp. 27–58 in F. Karadayi et al., eds., *The Population of Turkey*. Ankara: Institute of Population Studies, Hacitepe University.

United Nations. 1984. *World Population Prospects: Estimates and Projections as Assessed in 1982*. New York: United Nations.

USDHHS. 1983. *Social Security Programs Throughout the World*. Washington, D.C.: U.S. Department of Health and Human Services.

White, E. H. 1978. Legal Reforms as an Indicator of Women's Status in Muslim Nations. Pp. 52–68 in L. Beck and N. Keddie, eds., *Women in the Muslim World*. Cambridge, Mass.: Harvard University Press.

Yenisey, L. 1976. Social Effects of Migrant Labor on the District Left Behind: Observations in Two Villages of Bogazliyan. Pp. 327–70 in N. Abadan-Unat et al., eds., *Migration and Development*. Ankara: Ajans-Turk Press.

Youssef, N. 1974. *Women and Work in Developing Countries*. Institute of International Studies. Berkeley: University of California Press.

6 The Widowed in Iran

1   For an extensive discussion of this subject, refer to "Sex Role Segregation and the Function of Women in the Economic System," in Helena Lopata's *Research in the Interweave of Social Roles: Women and Men* (Greenwich, Conn.: JAI Press).

References

Afghahi, Simin. 1977. *Problems of the Widow in Tehran City*. Institute for Social Studies and Research. Tehran: University of Tehran. (In Persian.)

Behnam, Djamshid. 1971. Nuclear Family and Kinship Groups in Iran. *Diogenes* 76 (Winter):115–31.

———. 1978. *Family Structures and Kinship in Iran*. 3d. ed. Tehran: Kharazmi. (In Persian.)

Chevan, A., and H. Korson. 1975. The Widowed Who Live Alone: An Examination of Social and Demographic Forces. *Social Forces* 51:45–53.

Goode, William J. 1963. *World Revolution and Family Patterns*. New York: Free Press.

Hemmasi, Mohammad. 1974. *Migration in Iran*. Shiraz: Pahlavi University Press.

Khazaneh, H. T. 1968. A Study on Endogomy and Distance Between Place of Birth of Spouses in Three Rural Areas of Iran and Tehran City. In *Some Demographic Aspects of Iran and Tehran City*, Mehdi Amani, (ed.). Institute for Social Studies and Research. Tehran: University of Tehran.

Litwak, Eugene. 1959–60. The Use of Extended Family Groups in the Achievement of Social Goals: Some Policy Implications. *Social Problems* 7:177–87.

Lopata, Helena Z. 1971. Support Systems Involving Widows in Non-Agricultural Areas: A Comparative Study. A research proposal to the Social Security Administration, Washington, D.C.

———. 1972. Role Changes in Widowhood: A World Perspective. In Donald Cowgill and Lowell Holmes, eds., *Aging and Modernization*. New York: Appleton-Century-Crofts.

———. 1977. Support Systems Involving Widows in a Metropolitan Area of the U.S. A report to the Social Security Administration, Washington, D.C.

———. 1979. *Women as Widows: Support Systems*. New York: Elsevier.

Maroufi, N. 1968. The Effect of Literacy and Employment on Age at First Marriage of Women in Various Parts of Tehran City. Tenth International Seminar on Family Research, Institute for Social Studies and Research. Tehran: University of Tehran.

Momeni, Djamshid. 1976a. Changing Patterns of the Iranian Family Structure. Paper presented at the Workshop on Family and Kinship, 27–30 November, Kuwait.

———. 1976b. Husband-Wife Age Differentials in Shiraz, Iran. *Social Biology* 23 (Winter):341–48.

Nagavi, Sayyed Ali Reza. 1971. *Family Laws of Iran*. Islamabad, Pakistan: Islamic Research Institute.

Nassehy, V., and J. R. Touba. 1980. A Comparison of Support Systems for Widows and Divorcees in a Metropolitan Area of a Developing Country, Tehran, Iran. Paper presented at the Fourth International Seminar on Family and Disaster, 16–18 June, Uppsala, Sweden.

Pilavar, Gamar. 1980. Age Gap in Marriage and Widowhood. Institute for Social Studies and Research, Comparative Family Section. Tehran: University of Tehran.

Rogal, K., and R. Moreau. 1983. The Youngest Martyrs. *Newsweek* March 21:51.

Shanas, E., and G. Streib, eds. 1965. *Social Structure of the Family: Generational Relations*. Englewood Cliffs, N.J.: Prentice-Hall.

Statistical Center of Iran. 1976. National Census of Population and Housing, Total Country, 1976—5% Sample. Tehran: Plan and Budget Organization of Iran.

Sussman, Marvin. 1965. Relationship of Adult Children and Their Parents in the U.S. In E. Shanas and G. Streib, eds. *Social Structure and the Family: Generational Relations*. Englewood Cliffs, N.J.: Prentice-Hall.

Touba, Jacquiline Rudolph. 1974. Decision-Making Patterns of Iranian Husbands and Wives Living in Urban and Rural Areas of a Region Undergoing Planned Industrialization in Iran. *International Journal of Sociology of the Family* 4 (Autumn):179–90.

———. 1975. Sex Role Differentiation in Iranian Families Living in Urban and Rural Areas of a Region Undergoing Planned Industrialization in Iran. *Journal of Marriage and the Family* 37 (May):437–45.

———. 1980. Sex Role Segregation and the Function of Women in the Economic System: Iran. Pp. 51–98 in H. Z. Lopata, ed., *Research in the Interweave of Social Roles, Volume 1: Women and Men*. Greenwich, Conn.: JAI Press.

———. In press. Effect of the Islamic Revolution on Women and the Family in Iran: Some Preliminary Observations. In *Women and the Family in Iran*. Ali Fathi, ed., Leiden: E. J. Brill.

Touba, J. R., and S. Afghahi. 1978. Widow Outcome in a Non-Western Society: Resources Affecting Widow Outcome in Tehran, Iran. Paper presented at the 11th International Congress of Gerontology, Tokyo, 20–25 August.

Vieille, Paul. 1965. *Origins des Ouvriers de Tehran: psychosociology du Travail Industriel en Iran*. Institute d'Etudes et de Recherches Sociales. Tehran, University of Tehran. (In French.)

Vieille, P., and M. Kotobi. 1966. Famille et Union de Familles en Iran. Communication au 6eme Congress Mondial de Sociologie, Comite de recherches sur la famille. (In French.)

7   Widowhood in Israel

1   This survey deals with the population of urban Jewish women, who constitute most of the female population of Israel. It covers the period from 1948, the year Israel became in independent state, to the beginning of the 1980s. It does not include the prestate period, non-Jewish Israeli women, or women living in agricultural settlements (kibbutzim and moshavim). For discussion on each of these categories, which have unique characteristics beyond the scope of this chapter, the interested reader is referred to the following sources: the situation of women before the establishment of the State—Bijaoui (1981), Bernstein (1983, 1985), Israeli (1981); women in Arab society—El-Haj (1983), Ginat (1975), Rosenfeld (1980), Shokeid (1980); women on the kibbutz—Tiger and Shepher (1975), Palgi et al. (1983), and Ben Rafael and Weitman (1984); women on the *moshav*—Padan-Eisenstark and Meir-Hacker (1975).

2   All the figures that have appeared thus far are based on Israel Central Bureau of Statistics, *Israel Statistical Yearbook—1980*. All figures dealing with life expectancy and causes of death are based on Israel Central Bureau of Statistics, 1978, *Causes of Death*.

3   There are two additional categories of single-parent families: single mothers and widows. Births to single mothers are rare in Israel; although this phenomenon has been increasing continuously over the years, births in this category still constitute only 1.1 percent annually of the total number of births (Israel Central Bureau of Statistics, *Vital Statistics*, 1980–81: Table 36). Widows will be discussed at length in the section on widows.

4   Levirate rites: In biblical times a widow who had no male offspring was obliged to marry her late husband's brother (and the brother was obliged to marry her) "to

build his (late) brother's house." If the brother refused to marry her, the widow could not marry someone else unless a levirate ceremony was performed. The widow had to remove her brother-in-law's shoe and spit in his direction to degrade him. The ceremony had to be performed in the presence of "the elders." At present, the Jewish religious practice does not approve of polygyny, thus the widow's marriage to her brother-in-law is not enforced. However, remarriage of a widow (who has no male child) is possible only after the abovementioned ceremony of levirate has been duly performed.

5   Since Israel declared independence in 1948, it has existed in a state of continuous conflict with its neighboring states, a situation that has produced six wars. Exact figures concerning death in military operations are classified.

6   In Hebrew, the term is Bituah Leumi, which translates as "National Insurance." This article will employ the American phrase, "Social Security," the meaning and implications of which may be more universally understood.

7   The civilian widows in the study were older, on the average, than the war widows, even though the latter were interviewed three years after their husbands had died. It appears to us, however, that these clear-cut findings can be attributed to additional background characteristics (besides age) that differentiate between the two kinds of widows—characteristics that were described in earlier sections.

References

Amir, Y., and A. Sharon. 1979. Factors in the Adjustment of Widows of the Israeli Defence Forces. *Megamot* 25:120–30 (Hebrew).

Atzmon, A. 1980. *Women's Rights According to the Laws of Israel: A Guide for the Israeli Woman*. Jerusalem: Publication Service of the Information Center, Ministry of Justice and Ministry of Labor and Social Welfare (Hebrew).

Ben-Porath, Y. 1983. *Trends in the Labor-Force Participation of Women in Israel 1955–1980*. Sussex: Conference on Trends in Women's Work, Education and Family Building.

Ben Rafael, E., and S. Weitman. 1984. The Reconstitution of the Family in the Kibbutz. *European Journal of Sociology* 25:1–25.

Bernstein, D. 1985. Women Urban Workers and Workers' Wives During the Twenties and Thirties. *Cathedra* 34:115–45 (Hebrew).

———. 1983. The Plough Woman Who Cried into the Pots: The Position of Women in the Labor Force in the Pre-state Israeli Society. *Jewish Social Studies* 45 1:43–47.

Bijaoui, S. 1981. *The Eyes of Eve: Woman in the Jewish Yishuv in Eretz Yisrael 1904–1948*. University of Paris, doctoral dissertation (summary in Hebrew).

El-Haj, M. A. 1983. *Family Life Styles among Groups and Sects in an Arab City in Israel*. Jerusalem: Hebrew University, Ph.D. dissertation (Hebrew).

Ginat, J. 1975. *A Rural Arab Community in Israel: Marriage Patterns and Women's Status*. University of Utah, Ph.D. dissertation.

Golan, N. 1981. *Passing Through Transitions*. New York: Free Press.

———. 1975. From Wife to Widow to Woman: A Process of Role Transition. *Social Work* 20:369–74.

Gordon, D. 1978. *Socio-Demographic Characteristics of Urban Widows Receiving Survivors' Pensions*. Jerusalem: Research and Planning Division, Social Security Institute, Survey 23 (Hebrew).

———. 1981. *Widows and Their Rehabilitation at the Social Security Institute*. Jerusalem:

Research and Planning Division, Social Security Institute, Survey 31 (Hebrew).

The Holy Scriptures. 1952. According to the Masoreth Text. Philadelphia: Jewish Publication Society.

Israel Central Bureau of Statistics. 1980–1984. *Yearbook*. Jerusalem.

————. 1978. *Causes of Death*. Jerusalem: Special Publications.

Israel Ministry of Defence. 1983. *Service for and Rights of Widows and Fatherless Children: Explanation and Information*. Jerusalem: Rehabilitation Division (Hebrew).

Israel Office of the Prime Minister. 1978. *Report of the Committee on the Status of Women*. Jerusalem: Government Printing Office (Hebrew). An English translation is available from WOMEN to WOMEN, 4 Sniffen Court, New York, N.Y.

Izraeli, D. 1981. The Zionist Women's Movement in Palestine, 1911–1927: A Sociological Analysis. *Signs* 7, 1 (Autumn):87–114.

Katz, R., and N. Pesach. 1985. Adjustment to Divorce in Israel: A Comparison Between Divorced Men and Women. *Journal of Marriage and the Family* 47, 1.

Leo, Y. M. 1978. *Judaism in Practice: Oral Tradition*. Tel Aviv: Massada (Hebrew).

Levy, T., and R. Mandola. 1979. The Organization of Widows: Planned Change Through Group Work. *Society and Welfare* (December):414–30 (Hebrew).

Lopata, H. Z. 1979. *Women as Widows: Support Systems*. New York: Elsevier.

Padan-Eisenstark, D., and H. Meir-Hacker. 1975. Women in a Moshav Shitufi in an Ideological Trap. *Megamot*: 423–37 (Hebrew).

Palgi, M., M. J. Blazi, M. Rosner, and M. Safir. 1983. *Sexual Equality: The Israeli Kibbutz Tests the Theories*. Norwood, Pa.: Norwood Editions.

Peres, Y., and R. Katz. 1981. Stability and Centrality: The Nuclear Family in Modern Israel. *Social Forces* 59, 3:687–704.

Rosenfeld, H. 1980. Men and Women in Arab Peasant to Proletariat Transformation. Pp. 195–210 in S. Diamond, ed., *Theory and Practice*. The Hague: Mouton.

Rotter, R., and H. Keren-Yaar. 1974. *Single-Parent Families in Israel*. Jerusalem: Research and Planning Division, Social Security Institute (Hebrew).

Shamgar-Handelman, L. 1983. The Social Status of War Widows. *International Journal of Mass Emergencies and Disasters* 1, 1.

————. 1982. The Concept of Remarriage Among Israel War Widows. *Journal of Comparative Family Studies* 13, 3:359–72.

————. 1981. Administering to War Widows in Israel: The Birth of a Social Category. *Social Analysis* 9:24–47.

————. 1979. *War Widows in Israeli Society: A Discussion of Selected Aspects of the Social Integration of Widows of the Six-Day War*. Jerusalem: Hebrew University, doctoral dissertation (Hebrew).

————. 1975. A System of Services for Single-Parent Families: Ministry of Defence Services for War Widows and Their Children. *Social Security* (March):106–114 (Hebrew).

Shokeid, M. 1980. Ethnic Identity and the Position of Women Among Arabs in an Israeli Town. *Ethnic and Social Studies* 3, 2:188–206.

Social Security Institute. 1984. *Statistical Quarterly*. Jerusalem: Research and Planning Division 14, 1–2 (November) (Hebrew).

————. 1981. *Survivors' Insurance*. Jerusalem (October) (Hebrew).

Tiger, L., and J. Shepher. 1975. *Women in the Kibbutz*. New York: Harcourt Brace Jovanovich.

8 Support Systems of Elderly Widows in the Philippines

1   The data for this chapter are taken from the author's dissertation, "Perceptions of Filial Responsibility by Elderly Filipino Widows and Their Primary Caregivers," 1985, department of family and child development, Kansas State University.
2   Rural–urban differences in the Philippines are defined as follows: urban communities are cities and municipalities having a population density of 1,000 or more persons per square kilometer; central districts of municipalities and cities having a population density of 500 or more persons per square kilometer; central districts regardless of population density having networks of streets, six or more commercial or recreational establishments, and some amenities of a city—e.g., town hall, church, public plaza, marketplace, school, hospital; *barangays* conforming to conditions listed above and having 1,000 or more inhabitants whose occupation is neither farming nor fishing. Rural communities are those that do not meet the above conditions (United Nations, 1980).
3   The 1982 exchange rate of 8.5 pesos to $1.00 is used. The current rate (1987) is approximately 20 pesos to $1.00.
4   A three-point scale is used for this purpose (1 = none or never; 2 = little, some, or occasionally, and 3 = much, frequently, or always).

References

Adams, B. N. 1968. The Middle-Class Adult and His Widowed or Still-Married Mother. *Social Problems* 16:50–59.
Almirol, E. B. 1982. Rights and Obligations in Filipino-American Families. *Journal of Comparative Family Studies* 13:291–306.
Bulatao, J. C. 1973. The Manileno's Mainspring. Pp. 93–108 in F. Lynch and A. de Guzman II, eds., *Four Readings on Philippine Values*. Quezon City: Ateneo de Manila University Press.
Castillo, G. T. 1976. *The Filipino Woman as Manpower: The Image and Empirical Reality*. Los Baños, Laguna: University of the Philippines at Los Baños.
———. 1977. *Beyond Manila: Philippine Rural Problems in Perspective*, vol. 2. Los Baños, Laguna: University of the Philippines at Los Baños.
Eggan, F. 1968. Philippine Social Structure. Pp. 1–48 in G. M. Guthrie, ed. *Six Perspectives on the Philippines*. Manila: The Bookmark.
Fox, R. 1963. Men and Women in the Philippines. Pp. 342–64 in B. E. Ward, ed., *Women in the New Asia*. Paris: UNESCO.
Gonzalez, A. M., and M. R. Hollnsteiner. 1976. *Filipino Women as Partners of Men in Progress and Development*. Quezon City: Institute of Philippine Culture, Ateneo de Manila University.
Hollnsteiner, M. R. 1973. Reciprocity in the Lowland Philippines. Pp. 69–91 in *Four Readings on Philippine Values*. F. Lynch and A. de Guzman II, eds., Quezon City: Ateneo de Manila University Press.
Illo, J. F. I. 1977. *Involvement by Choice: The Role of Women in Development*. Quezon City: Institute of Philippine Culture, Ateneo de Manila University.
Javillonar, G. V. 1979. The Filipino Family. Pp. 344–80 in M. S. Das and P. D. Bardis, eds., *The Family in Asia*. London: George Allen and Unwin.

Kâğitçibaşi, C. 1982. Old Age Security Value of Children and Development: Cross-national Evidence. *Journal of Comparative Family Study* 8:133–42.

Lightfoot, K. 1973. *The Philippines*. New York: Praeger.

Lopata, H. Z. 1973. *Widowhood in an American City*. Cambridge, Mass.: Schenkman.

———. 1979. *Women as Widows: Support Systems*. New York: Elsevier.

Mendez, P. P., and F. L. Jocano. 1974. *The Filipino Family in its Rural and Urban Orientation: Two Case Studies*. Manila: Centro Escolar University Research Development Center.

Montiel, C., and M. R. Hollnsteiner. 1976. *The Filipino Woman: Her Role and Status in Philippine Society*. Quezon City: Institute of Philippine Culture, Ateneo de Manila University.

Municipal Census Supervisor's Report. 1980. Los Baños, Laguna, Philippines.

New Philippines. 1974. The Filipino Family: Most Able Social Welfare Agency. Manila: National Media Production Center.

Porio, E., F. Lynch, and M. R. Hollnsteiner. 1975. *The Filipino Family, Community and Nation: The Same Yesterday, Today and Tomorrow?* Quezon City: Institute of Philippine Culture, Ateneo de Manila University.

Rojas-Aleta, I., T. L. Silva, and C. P. Eleazar, 1977. *A Profile of Filipino Women*. Manila: Philippine Business for Social Progress.

Shanas, E. 1962. *The Health of Older People: A Social Survey*. Cambridge, Mass.: Harvard University Press.

Shanas, E. 1979. The Family as a Social Support System in Old Age. *The Gerontologist* 15:408–11.

Steinberg, D. J. 1982. *The Philippines*. Boulder, Colo.: Westview Press.

Streib, G. 1958. Family Patterns in Retirement. *Journal of Social Issues* 14:46–60.

Szanton, M. C. B. 1982. Women and Men in Iloilo, Philippines: 1903–1970. Pp. 124–47 in P. V. Esterik, ed., *Women of Southeast Asia*. De Kalb: Center for Southeast Asian Studies, Northern Illinois University.

The Civil Code of the Philippines (Republic 386). Manila: National Book Store.

United Nations. 1980. *Demographic Yearbook 1979*. New York: United Nations.

———. 1983. *Demographic Yearbook 1983*. New York: United Nations.

9 Widowed Women in Melbourne, Australia

1   The research on which this chapter is based was carried out while Dr. Rosenman was at Latrobe University, Melbourne, and Dr. Shulman at the University of Melbourne. The research was supported by grants from the Ashworth Bequest, Affect Trust, Latrobe University, Institute of Family Studies, and the United States National Institute of Aging.

References

Clayton, P. J. 1976. The Clinical Morbidity of the First Year of Bereavement. *Comprehensive Psychiatry* 14 (March–April).

Kobatsiari, A. 1981. Greek Widows in Australia: How They Cope with Bereavement. Unpublished honors thesis, University of Melbourne.

McCaughey, J., S. Shaver, and H. Ferber. 1977. *Who Cares? Family Problems, Community Links and Helping Services*. Melbourne: Sun Books.

Maddison, D. C., and A. Viola. 1968. The Health of Widows in the Year Following Bereavement. *Journal of Psychosomatic Research* 12:2g.

Penman, R., L. Rosenman, and A. Shulman. 1981. Coping with Life Alone: Needs and Concerns of Widowed Women in Australia. In N. Grieve and P. Grimshaw, eds., *Australian Women: Feminist Perspectives*. Melbourne: Oxford University Press.

Raphael, B. 1975. The Presentation and Management of Bereavement. *Medical Journal of Australia* 2:909–11.

Rosen, A., A. Shulman, and R. Cartwright. 1981. Needs and Resources of Widowed Women in an Urban Community in the United States. Paper presented at the Gerontological Society meeting, November.

Rosenman, L. 1982. *Widowhood and Social Welfare Policy in Australia*. Sydney: University of New South Wales, Social Welfare Research Centre Reports and Proceedings, no. 16.

Rosenman, L., and M. Leeds. 1984. *Women and the Australian Retirement Age Income Security System*. Sydney: University of New South Wales, Social Welfare Research Centre Reports and Proceedings, no. 39.

Rosenman, L., A. Shulman, and R. Penman. 1981. Resource Networks of Widowed Women in Australia. *Australian Journal of Social Issues* 6, 1.

Rosenman, L., A. Shulman, and M. Levine. 1984. Widowed Families with Children: Personal Need and Societal Response. Occasional paper, Institute of Family Studies, Melbourne.

10 Wives and Widows in China

1   Information for this chapter has come from three sources: a review of American, European, and translated Chinese works; China's Third National Census (People's Republic of China, State Council and State Statistical Bureau, 1982); and direct interviews with women during a trip to China sponsored by the People to People Family and Institutional Care for the Aging Delegation, 1984.

2   The Constitution offers legal protection for senior citizens. The mandates are as follows:

Marriage Law. This statute governs marriage as well as family relations in China, including the rights of elder family members. The General Principles state: "The lawful rights and interests of . . . the ages are protected." "Within the family maltreatment and desertion are prohibited."

Article 15: "Children have the duty to support and assist their parents. . . . When children fail to perform the duty of supporting their parents, parents who have lost the ability to work or have difficulties in providing for themselves have the right to demand that their children pay for their support."

Article 18: "Parents and children have the right to inherit each other's property."

Article 22: "Grandchildren or maternal grandchildren who have the capacity to bear the relevant costs have the duty to support and assist their grandparents or maternal grandparents whose children are deceased."

Article 35: "In cases where the relevant part refuses to execute judgments or rulings regarding . . . costs of support, the people's court has the power to enforce the execution in accordance with the law."

Criminal Law. Chapter 7 (On Offences Against Marriage and the Family): "Whoever viley mistreats a member of his family shall be sentenced to imprisonment for not more than two years, or to detention, or to public surveillance....Whoever... causes grievous injury or death shall be sentenced to imprisonment for from two to seven years....Whoever, having responsibility for the support of an aged person, flagrantly refuses to support that person, shall be sentenced to imprisonment for not more than five years, or to detention, or to public surveillance." Detention is a sentence of fifteen days to six months in which the convicted is deprived of his freedom. Public surveillance is a sentence of three months or two years in which the guilty party is released and supervised by the masses of the unit where he works and in the neighborhood under the guidance of the public security organ. Such a person is expected to reform himself, and his freedom is partially restricted.

Article 50: "Working people have the right to material assistance in old age."

References

Beijing Review. 1981. *Growing Old in China*. Beijing, no. 43, October 26.

Bong-ho Mok. 1983. In the service of socialism: Social Welfare in China. *Social Work* July–August, pp. 269–72.

Buchanan, K. 1970. *The Transformation of the Chinese Earth*. London: G. Bell and Sons.

Chance, N. 1984. *China's Urban Villagers: Life in a Beijing Commune*. New York: Holt, Rinehart and Winston.

Chang, Kai. 1982. On China's Responsibility System in Agriculture. *October Review* 9 (July–August):65–69.

Ch'en Tung-Yuan. 1977. *History of the Life of Chinese Women*. Taipei, Taiwan: Commerce.

China Today. 1982. *From Youth to Retirement*. (Special Feature Series). Beijing: Beijing Review.

Croll, E. 1983. *Chinese Women Since Mao*. London: Zed Books.

Jin Mao. 1982. A Case of Remarriage. *Women of China*, August:34–35.

Lang, O. 1968. *Chinese Family and Society*. New York: Archon Books.

Lewis, M. 1982. Aging in the People's Republic of China. *International Journal of Aging and Human Development* 15 (2):79–105.

Li, Ch'ia-fu. 1978. *Lives of Ancient Chinese Women*. Taipei, Taiwan: Li Min.

Lopata, H. Z. 1979. *Women as Widows: Support Systems*. New York: Elsevier.

Nai Xin. 1982. Old but Not Lonely. *Women of China*, August, p. 35.

State Council and State Statistical Bureau. 1982. *The Third Population Census of China: Main Figures*. Hong Kong: Economic Information Agency.

Tung, Chia-tsun. 1937. The Statistics of Sacrificed Women. *Contemporary History III* 2.

Waltner, A. 1981. Widows and Remarriage in Ming and Early Qing China. In R. Guisso and S. Johannesen, eds., *Women in China*. Youngstown, N.Y.: Philo Press.

Yao, E. 1983. *Chinese Women: Past and Present*. Mesquite, Tex.: Ide House.

11 Widowhood and Social Change

References

Blumberg, Rae. 1985. Personal conversation.

Boserup, Ester. 1970. *Woman's Role in Economic Development*. New York: St. Martin's Press.

Brody, Elaine. 1985. The Changing Role of Women and Its Relevance to Aging. Paper presented at the twenty-fifth anniversary scientific meeting of the Boston Society for Gerontologic Psychiatry. Boston, 2 November.

Brown, Judith K. 1985. Introduction. Pp. 1–12 in J. K. Brown and V. Kerns, eds., *In Her Prime: A New View of Middle-Aged Women*. South Hadley, Mass.: Bergin and Garvey.

Cowgill, D. O., and L. D. Holmes, eds. 1972. *Aging and Modernization*. New York: Appleton-Century-Crofts.

Davidson, Nicol. 1982. Introduction. Pp. 1–12 in P. M. D'Onofrio-Flores and S. M. Pfafflin, eds., *Scientific-Technological Change and the Role of Women in Development*. Boulder, Colo.: Westview Press.

Giele, Janet. 1977. Introduction: Comparative Perspectives on Women. Pp. 1–31 in J. Z. Giele and A. C. Smock, eds., *Women: Roles and Status in Eight Countries*. New York: John Wiley and Sons.

Goode, William. 1963. *World Revolution and Family Patterns*. New York: Free Press.

———. 1976. Review of *Becoming Modern: Individual Changes in Six Developing Countries*, by A. Inkeles and D. H. Smith. *American Journal of Sociology* 82(2):443–48.

Gusfield, Joseph R. 1967. Tradition and Modernity: Misplaced Polarities in the Study of Social Change. *American Journal of Sociology* 72 (January):351–62.

Hareven, Tamara. 1976. Modernization and Family History: Perspectives on Social Change. *Signs* (2):190–206.

Higgins, Benjamin. 1977. Economic Development and Cultural Change: Seamless Web or Patchwork Quilt. Pp. 99–122 in Manning Nash, ed., *Essays on Economic Development and Cultural Change in Honor of Bert F. Hoselitz*. Chicago: University of Chicago Press.

Hochschild, Arlie R. 1973. *The Unexpected Community*. Englewood Cliffs, N.J.: Prentice-Hall.

Huntington, Samuel P. 1978. The Chance to Change. Pp. 30–69 in Norman Provizer, ed., *Analyzing The Third World*. Boston: G. K. Hall.

Inkeles, Alex. 1983. *Exploring Individual Modernity*. New York: Columbia University Press.

Inkeles, A., and D. H. Smith. 1974. *Becoming Modern: Individual Change in Six Developing Countries*. Cambridge, Mass.: Harvard University Press.

Koo, Jasoon. 1982. Korean Women in Widowhood. Ph.D. dissertation, University of Missouri—Columbia.

Lambek, Michael. 1985. Motherhood and Other Careers in Mayotte (Comoro Islands). Pp. 67–87 in J. K. Brown and V. Kerns, eds., *In Her Prime: A New View of Middle-Aged Women*. Hadley, Mass.: Bergin and Garvey.

Lee, Richard B. 1985. Sexuality and Aging Among Kung Women. Pp. 23–25 in J. K. Brown and V. Kerns, eds., *In Her Prime: A New View of Middle-Aged Women*. South Hadley, Mass.: Bergin and Garvey.

Lerner, Daniel. 1958. *The Passing of Traditional Society*. New York: Free Press of Glencoe.

Lopata, Helena Z. 1972. Role Changes in Widowhood: A World Perspective. Pp. 275–303 in Donald Cowgill and Lowell Holmes, eds., *Aging and Modernization*, New York: Appleton-Century-Crofts.

Lopata, H. Z., and H. P. Brehm. 1986. *Widows and Dependent Wives*. New York: Praeger.

Ogburn, William. 1922. *Social Change*. New York: Viking Press.

Papanek, Hanna. 1978. Comment on Gusfield's Review Essay on Becoming Modern. *American Journal of Sociology* 83 (6):1507–11.

Papanek, H., and G. Minault, eds. 1982. *Separate Worlds: Studies of Purdah in South Asia*. Delhi: Chanakya Publications.

Pelman, Anabel G. 1985. Personal correspondence.

Magdoff, Harry. 1982. Imperialism: A Historical Survey. Pp. 11–28 in H. Alavi and T. Shanin, eds., *Introduction to the Sociology of "Developing Societies."* New York: Monthly Review Press.

Nash, J., and M. P. Fernandez-Kelly, eds. 1983. *Women, Men and the International Division of Labor.* Albany: State University of New York Press.

Raybeck, Douglas. 1985. A Diminished Dichotomy: Kelantan Malay and Traditional Chinese Perspectives. Pp. 155–70 in J. K. Brown and V. Sterns, eds., *In Her Prime: A New View of Middle-Aged Women.* South Hadley, Mass.: Bergin and Garvey.

Rogers, Barbara. 1980. *The Domestication of Women: Discrimination in Developing Societies.* London: Tavistock.

Rohrlich-Leavitt, Ruby, ed. 1976. *Women Cross-Culturally: Change and Challenge.* The Hague: Mouton.

Smock, Audrey C. 1977. Conclusion: Determinants of Women's Roles and Status. Pp. 383–421 in J. Z. Giele and A. C. Smock, eds., *Women: Roles and Status in Eight Countries.* New York: John Wiley and Sons.

Tadasse, Zenebeworke. 1982. Pp. 77–111 in P. M. D'Onofrio-Flores and S. M. Pfafflin, eds., *Scientific-Technological Change and the Role of Women in Development.* Boulder, Colo.: Westview Press.

Touba, Jacquiline R. 1980. Sex Segregation and the Women's Roles in the Economic System: The Case of Iran. Pp. 51–98 in Helena Z. Lopata, ed., *Research in the Interweave of Social Roles: Women and Men.* Greenwich, Conn.: JAI Press.

Touba, J. R., and R. S. Afghani. 1978. Adjustment of the Widow in Tehran, Iran: Some Socio-Economic and Demographic Factors Related to Widow Adjustment in a Non-Western Society. Paper presented at the eleventh International Congress of Gerontology, Tokyo, 20–25 August.

Vatuk, Sylvia. 1985. South Asian Cultural Conception of Sexuality. Pp. 137–52 in J. K. Brown and V. Kerns, eds., *In Her Prime: A New View of Middle-Aged Women.* South Hadley, Mass.: Bergin and Garvey.

———. 1972. *Kinship and Urbanization: White Collar Migrants in North India.* Berkeley: University of California Press.

Ward, R. E., and D. A. Rustow, eds. 1964. *Political Modernization in Japan and Turkey.* Princeton, N.J.: Princeton University Press.

Weber, Max. 1904/1958. *The Protestant Ethic and the Spirit of Capitalism.* New York: Scribners.

Index

American widows: socializing patterns, 8–9. *See also* Chicago-area widows

Asian widows: in California, 3, 15. *See also* China, India, Korea, Philippines

Atatürk, 16, 82

Australia: children as support resource for widows, 188–89; comparison of Australian widows with American widows, 20, 191–93; demography, 170–71; economic conditions in research setting, 173; economic support systems of widows, 177–83; educational levels of widows, 182; employment-related problems of widows, 179–83; Greek widows in Australia, 175, 192; incidence of widowhood, 172; Income Security System, 179; marriage rates, 172; physicians as a resource of widows for counseling and support, 185–87; remarriage, 189–90; service support system of widows, 183–87; social support networks of widows, 187–90; social welfare policy, 19; women's changing roles, 19–20

brothers-in-law: in Indian levirate system, 51; in Israeli levirate system, 137, 138, 243–44 n.4; in polygynous marriages in Iran, 17, 113–14, 116, in Malo, Vanuatu, 29, in Turkey, 82, 88, 92

California: state-subsidized support programs for widows, 8

Chicago-area widows: comparison with Australian widows, 20, 191–93, Chinese widows, 199, 207, Filipino widows, 165, 167, Indian widows, 54, Iranian widows, 124, 131, Israeli widows, 146–47, Korean widows, 68, 69, 70, 74, Turkish widows, 96, 102–3; emotional support systems, 9–10; factors affecting widows' development of a support network, 3–4; need for service supports, 6, 7; patterns of socializing, 8

child marriage: in India, 13, 45; in Iran, 129; in Old China, 209

Child Marriage Restraint Act (Sarda Act) (India), 13–14, 46–47

child rearing: in Australia, 182; in India, 53; in Iran, 117; in Korea, 63–64, 73, 77; in the Philippines, 151, 152–53

children: cross-cultural economic importance of, 103, 220; problems associated with rural-urban migration of, 14, 15, 16, 17; role in widows' support networks in Australia, 20, 188–89, in China, 201, in India, 14, 48–50, in Iran, 17, in Korea, 15, 57–58, 67, 68, 70–71, in Malo, Vanuatu, 12, 32–33, in the Philippines, 7, 10, 19, 151–53, 157, 162, 167, in Turkey, 17, 19, 86, 92, 103

China: comparison of Chinese widows with Chicago widows, 207; contributions of widows to their families and communities, 204–5; divorce, 210; eco-